One Eye, One Ear – No Worries

One Eye, One Ear – No Worries

JOEL WHITWELL

Copyright © 2021 Joel Whitwell

All rights reserved. No part of this book may be reproduced or transmitted in any form or by any means, electronic or mechanical, including photocopying, recording, or by any information storage and retrieval system without the written permission of the author, except where permitted by law.

This book is a collection of memories. The personal stories and memories by individuals recorded here are their version of events and have been both provided and reproduced in good faith with no disrespect or defamation intended. Every effort has been made to ensure the researched information is correct. No liability for incorrect information or factual errors will be accepted by the author.

Publishing Details
Title: One Eye, One Ear – No Worries

First published 2021
Editing Fleur Chapman - www.fleurchapman.com.au.
Interior and cover layout Pickawoowoo Publishing Group - www.pickawoowoo.com

A catalogue record for this book is available from the National Library of Australia

ISBN 978-0-6450364-0-4 (paperback)
ISBN 978-0-6450364-1-1 (ebook)

This book is dedicated to my family who have never wavered in their support of me and to the memory of my friend P.J and all the other people I grew up with in the Harvey community who taught me the value of friendship during my formative years.

Table of Contents

One	The Beginning	1
Two	Kids Will Be Kids	4
Three	Teen Angst	11
Four	Adulthood Beckons	22
Five	Work To Live, Not Live To Work	28
Six	Experience Is The Greatest Teacher	34
Seven	Having A Ball	38
Eight	New Adventures Await	48
Nine	Facing A Sharp Reality	53
Ten	A New Century, A New Independence	58
Eleven	Not 18 Anymore	69
Twelve	The World Traveller Is Born	78
Thirteen	Oh, Canada…	88
Fourteen	Lend Me An Ear?	99
Fifteen	Moving Out Of The Fog And Into A New Year	103
Sixteen	The Next Big Adventure	106
Seventeen	Admiring Some Local Sights	123
Eighteen	Wedding Bells	132
Nineteen	Memories….Or Not	134
Twenty	Dreams Taking Flight	160
Twenty-One	Conquering The World	164
Twenty-Two	Lads On The Loose	185
Twenty-Three	Canada's Comforting Soil	191
Twenty-Four	Look Out, Sydney. Joel Is Back	202

Twenty-Five	Gather No Moss	207
Twenty-Six	World Trip #2	211
Twenty-Seven	New Opportunities	227
Twenty-Eight	When It All Comes Crashing Down	233
Twenty-Nine	Global Impacts	238
Thirty	World Trip #3	241
Thirty-One	Contiki #3	257
Thirty-Two	Bridge Over Troubled Waters	272
Thirty-Three	My Biggest Regret	279
Thirty Four	Moving Forward In Hard Times	282
Thirty-Five	Bitter Reflection	302
Thirty-Six	It's A Small World	306
Thirty-Seven	Speak From The Heart	317
Thirty-Eight	Lessons Learned	321

One

The Beginning

I've never been one to shy away from a grand entrance, and my birth was no exception. On January 14, 1979 at around 1.15 am, my parents Gordon and Peta Whitwell welcomed their second son into the family. All seemed to be going well, until they discovered something a little different about their child – he only had one ear and one eye.

The technical term for this condition is craniofacial deficiency. As a consequence, my first four weeks of life were spent in a Perth hospital before I was allowed to return home to start my life in Harvey – only to end up back in Perth for another three weeks. I had severe jaundice and required an emergency blood transfusion. This was just the start of many hospital stays over the next 25 years.

Mum and dad weren't concerned about how I looked, but they were worried there could be other issues, such as impaired brain function. Fortunately, those tests came back normal, but my parents realised they had a long road ahead of them. On one of those first few rushed trips to Perth, my poor dad fell asleep at some traffic lights along the way.

My brother Kelvin was only two when I was born and it was a difficult time of adjustment for him too. He couldn't understand why I had all of mum's attention. Eventually, things settled down and I was well enough to come home and stay there. The first thing mum did was take me down the main street of Harvey and show me off to the locals, just like she did with Kelvin. Even though I only had one eye and one ear, she never hid me from the world. I am forever grateful for that.

At around 12 months old I had my first operation to widen my mouth, which meant another week in hospital, then at four years old, I got my first prosthetic ear (which I later had a tumultuous relationship with!). My ear had to be glued on each morning, and occasionally that didn't quite go to plan. There were quite a few times I rushed mum to do the job as I was running late for the bus, which meant the glue job was a little haphazard! If my friends were ever surprised the days I turned up to school with my right ear either too high or too low, they were polite enough not to comment. Some days the glue didn't hold very well, so my ear was off by lunchtime. I would just pick it up and put in my school bag, then continue with whatever I was doing.

When I was about five, just before I started school, I received my first glass eye. This meant more trips to Perth to get the colour and the size right, but it also meant more fun and games. We live at the beach, so some days mum would be sitting chatting to her friends and watching Kelvin and I, when I would suddenly come running up, take my eye out and throw it to mum to look after. For the friends of mum's who didn't know it was glass, the looks on their faces were priceless.

Our family dog at the time also took a liking to my eye and grabbed it out of my hand one day. He swallowed it…then we had to wait for it to come out. To speed up the process, we fed the poor thing salt water, then after about three hours he threw it up. My dutiful mum cleaned it with disinfectant and I put it straight back in. Looking back on the incident now, I am kind of glad we made him spew it up instead of getting it out the other way!

Another time, we were up at the Logue Brook Dam with our family friends where I was sitting at the edge of this huge rock playing with my eye when suddenly it popped out and fell eight metres into the water. We spent the rest of the afternoon perfecting our diving skills, trying to find it, but it was like trying to find a needle in a haystack. No luck, so my parents had to endure more trips to Perth for a new one.

When I was five, mum had another baby, Andrew. Our happy family was complete. Around this time, I also started kindergarten, which was a daunting experience for me. Even though mum had a new baby to look after, I made her stay with me for the first few days. I was very clingy and nervous about meeting new people, as I wasn't sure how they would react to my different appearance. I needn't have worried though because the other kids seemed to really like me and wanted to include me in everything. They didn't seem to notice anything was wrong with my face. After a while, I had settled in so well, that mum didn't have to peel me off her as she attempted to leave anymore.

In 1985, at six years of age, I started year 1 at Harvey Primary School. Mum and dad wanted the best for me, so agreed with the school to put me in a special class for people with learning difficulties. As it turned out, that wasn't the right place for me and the teachers soon realised, so I went back to mainstream. Mum and dad were very happy with that, and I was excited to be back with my friends again, even though the school work was harder! I did have some trouble with my speech and was seeing a therapist in Perth, but this resulted in too much lost school time and a lot of travel for my parents. Fortunately for all of us, mum was able to have my therapy transferred to Bunbury. Year 1 passed without much incident, although if I remember correctly, I did get busted for pissing on the old school bell. I was generally a good kid, just slipped up from time to time!

Two

Kids Will Be Kids

By primary school we had moved from Harvey to Myalup, a smaller town about 20 minutes from Harvey, located on the coast.

My brothers and I, along with our growing group of friends, had a great time back then roaming Myalup and pretending to be *The Goonies* or playing army games. One time back in our bicentennial year of 1988, I went to a fair in Bunbury with my year 4 classmates. The fair had a map of the grounds, so when I got home later that day, I showed it to Andrew and said it was a treasure map. So, off we went to find the treasure! We set off deep into the bush, but before we knew it, we were lost. I didn't panic at first because we had the map that I thought could lead us home, but of course that was no good to us!

We ended up at the salt lake on the outskirts of Myalup where we waited until it got dark, but then Andrew started crying. I didn't know what else to do. I calmed him down and decided to wait it out at the lake. By 7 pm our parents had started to get pretty worried and came out looking for us. They finally found us about 8 pm. We all got grounded after that, but I didn't care. I honestly thought I was a Goonie back then!

Around this time, another family moved to Myalup and we became good friends with the three boys; Damien, Anthony and Jono. We often played in the bush across the road from their place. A favourite pastime was to dig trenches, put tin over the top and cover it with dirt to create 'the underground tunnels' - until someone discovered our hideout one night and trashed it. That was the end of that.

Unfortunately, Jono's family moved back to Harvey about a year later. I had become pretty close to Jono, but after they moved, we went our separate ways and didn't have much to do with each other for about nine years. Just after we finished school, we did manage to rekindle our friendship – a friendship that has since remained solid until this day.

I have fond memories of my school days with my friends, especially Douglas. He was my best friend from kindy until the end of year 4, then he left Harvey to move up to Bindoon. You never forget your first best friend you have in this world. We loved playing marbles at lunchtime, and I found my glass eye made a great addition! I used to carry it around in my marble bag and use it in the games. Looking back on it now, I'm kind of glad no one won it off me. I liked to gross the other kids out!

On the day of the sports carnival in year 1, I vividly remember Douglas and I being in the same race. I burst out of the blocks and was well in front, halfway down the track, when I looked behind me and saw Douglas was coming last. So, I stopped, waited for him, and encouraged him across the finish line while I ran beside him. He came second last, I came last. I was starting to grow a reputation for being a great kid with a good heart, and this was one example. When Douglas left in year 4, I learnt one of my first great lessons in life; friends come and go, but if you make the effort to keep in touch no matter how far away they are, you can always keep a great friendship going.

Luckily (somehow), my first 10 years of life were relatively injury-free, despite the antics I got up to with my mates. That was until I went wood chopping with dad and was climbing a huge stump and fell, landing on my wrist. I told dad, but since I wasn't crying, he didn't believe me and told me to wait in the car until he had finished. So, for the next hour, I waited patiently in the car, listening to music, with a broken wrist. When dad finally finished chopping the wood, he still didn't believe me that I was really hurt and took me home. Mum, on the other hand, took one look at my arm and drove me straight to the hospital, where they confirmed the break. Dad felt a bit sheepish, but I couldn't really blame him. You would think that a nine-year-old with a broken wrist would be crying and screaming, but I had endured so many operations already that I had begun to develop a high pain threshold. On the upside, my school friends got to sign my cast!

Another great childhood memory is the times we spent with our cousins Lauren, Shane and Lyndsay. Their parents, Terry and Lisa, owned a farm out the back of Wokalup and we used to go out there often as kids, and in turn, they would come out and spend time with us in Myalup. We had a great time out on the farm, playing in the shearing shed and the paddocks. The hay bales were fun too, but someone always ended up getting hurt from falling off. We even invented a game called 'run around the house'. It was just like hide and seek, but whoever was 'it' just had to run around the house instead of counting.

Nanna also lived on the farm and we spent a lot of time at her house eating pancakes and drinking Milo. We used to listen to Chad Morgan a lot, and every Christmas would put on a concert for our parents based a lot on Chad Morgan songs. We always included his hits like *Bobba Wobba Wedding* and *I'm My Own Grandpa*. We loved putting these concerts on, but for the parents, it was more about trying to look interested while gossiping with each other. The best one we ever did was in 1991. We put a lot of effort into this one – I still have the photos now. Even our parents were impressed that time.

Come the beginning of year 5, I was still trying to deal with Douglas leaving, but as I walked in on the first day, a kid I recognised but didn't really know came up and asked what class I was in. His name was Kim and it turned out we were both in Miss B's class. Kim and I were kindred spirits from the start, which unfortunately for Miss B meant we sometimes brought the worst out in each other! Instead of concentrating on our school work, we would muck around and get into trouble. Our antics started to disrupt the rest of the class, so one day the teacher decided she had separate us. To make it fair, she had half the class stand up the front while the remainder stayed seated. The seated kids had to draw a name out of the hat, and whoever they drew became their new class neighbour. As luck would have it, Kim drew my name out, but he was asked to draw another name instead. I ended up sitting next to Brett, who became another mate of mine.

At age 10, I also first found love (or, a kid version of!). Her name was Nicole, my primary school sweetheart. One day, Nicole and her friend Kelly snuck me into a shed on the school grounds to make out. Me with two girls – a dream come true! Looking back, I think I got more action with the girls as a kid than I ever have as an adult! The teachers weren't happy about the shed incident, though.

So, here I was, year 5 with a girlfriend and a few good mates. Life was good. Nicole, Kim, Brett and myself – our little circle was complete. Well, almost. Normie and his family moved to Harvey from Armadale in March of that year (1989). I was in music class the day he walked in. I didn't know it at the time, but he would also become one of my best friends, another friendship that is still going now as an adult. At first, Normie started hanging out with a different group, but we eventually persuaded him to join us after he saw we were having more fun.

My run of being hospital-free came to an end in September that year, as it was time for another operation on my face. With this procedure, they had to remove one of my ribs and place it in the side of my head to bring my face out a bit more. It was a huge operation, but I remember not being that nervous. I found we always seem to handle things better as kids than we do as adults. I remember the afternoon before the op, sitting with mum in the hospital play area reading a Sesame Street book. When it came time for my op, mum (as always) was by my side as they wheeled me into theatre. Of course, she couldn't come in, so once I was in there I was on my own. They used the gas mask to knock me out and I remember yelling for them to stop as they administered the anaesthetic, but no sound came out. Seconds later I was in la-la land and they began the complex procedure.

In the first few days after my op, I drank heaps of lemonade and threw up a lot. I was in intensive care and was pretty disoriented. I do remember the nurse coming in and taking the catheter out – that bloody hurt! When I was finally allowed to leave ICU, they wheeled me into a room that I was sharing with some other boys. I was a bit nervous at first as I was only used to making friends in my comfort zone – in my home town, at school – but I needn't have worried.

I got along with them all, but two I will never forget. Their names were Clinton and Simon. We had a great time, a friendship formed in A5 Ward of PMH. One night we were allowed to stay up and watch *He-Man and the Masters of the Universe* – for a time we could forget we were in hospital and were just a group of boys watching a favourite show together. I will always be grateful for that friendship, as it made my stay in hospital a lot easier than it could have been. Sadly, that friendship ended when it was time to go home, but I often think of those two and how their lives may have turned out.

One morning in A5 Ward, a nurse came in with a big bunch of get well cards and letters my school friends had sent me. To have that love and respect from people even way back then goes a long way to determining how my life is today. I still have those cards and letters!

When I was finally able to go home, it was bittersweet. I had recovered enough to return to my life in Myalup, but I was sad to say goodbye to Simon and Clinton. However, once I got there, I was glad to be home. My jaw had been wired together from the operation, so for a while mum had to put my food through a blender and I had to use a syringe to eat. Not a pleasant experience, as you could guess, but I was getting used to such things!

I couldn't go back to school straight away, but I heard everyone was missing me, so one day mum took me in for a visit. A great cheer went up as I walked into the classroom and I loved it, but for a minute was a bit overwhelmed by it all. Somehow I forgot I was only there for a visit, and sat at my old desk ready to start work. Mum quickly reminded me of our fleeting stay, so I had a quick chat to everyone and off we went. Before long, I was back at school anyway and the rest of the year passed without any major events.

That year my girlfriend Nicole had a Christmas party at her place. At first, I was the only boy there and felt a bit awkward, so we ended up going around and picking up Normie and Kim. We all had a great night and finished up sitting in the lounge room watching *Nightmare on Elm Street #5*.

The summer holidays came and went and before long we were all back at school. I was now starting in year 6, and later that year we went away for camp in Bridgetown. On the way, we stopped at an antique store and the old lady behind the counter was lovely. Unfortunately, just before we were about to leave, it was discovered that someone had stolen a bookmark from her. Kim got really worked up about it, he really felt for the lady. It was that day that I realised Kim, for all his rough edges, deep down had a good heart.

Heading into summer of that year, I began hanging around with another kid from my year, Brendon (Jacko). We both loved watching WWF, so we would meet up at the local pool after we finished swimming lessons and walk up to his place on the highway to watch the latest matches.

Jacko's place had a dam out the front with an island in the middle, and the only way to get across to the island was with a raft or canoe. One night we were camping on the island and telling stories, when at about 5 am the whole sky lit up like it was day time. We had never been so scared in our life and jumped up simultaneously. We boarded the canoe and headed for shore, but halfway back, the canoe sunk. It was the coldest swim I have ever done, but the warm shower after was bliss. It wasn't until much later that I found out it was my older brother Kelvin and his friend Procko throwing rocks at the power lines that caused the flash of light. Bloody good job, bro, got me wet for nothing!

It was also around this time that mum, dad and Kelvin went across to Melbourne to stay with a friend of dad's for a week and watch the footy. My brother Andrew (who had become known as 'Frog') and I went out to stay with our cousins on the farm. As a kid, bed-wetting was a bit of a problem for a while, but on our little holiday I was determined not to wet the bed. So, my solution was to wrap an elastic band around my penis before I fell asleep – which was (as you can imagine), not the brightest move. Not long after lights out, I woke in excruciating pain as the elastic was cutting off the circulation. I called out to Aunty Lisa, who then had to remove the band with a pair of tweezers. It was a pretty embarrassing moment, but I learned my lesson.

That summer, us Whitwell boys spent a bit of time with the holiday kids that came down from Perth to stay at their parent's beach houses. We spent the summer nights playing spin the bottle or spotlight. Spin the bottle was my favourite, especially if I got to kiss Belinda, as I had a huge crush on her at the time. Again, as summer does, the long days ended and it was time to go back to school. Now, year 7.

Three

Teen Angst

Normie and Jade had both left to complete the year at different schools, so it was just me, Kim and Nicole. I also became friends with a guy named Graham. That year was one to remember, but not for good reasons; year 7 was the first time I really experienced bullying. Until then, I had pretty much been treated like everyone else and maintained my overall popularity, despite my obvious facial deformity. I have read countless stories of young people being bullied and the dire consequences that had for them, so I am very aware of how differently my life could have turned out had I not grown up in such an inclusive, tight-knit, supportive community.

As it was, despite my popularity, there was always going to be someone at some point who would take it upon themselves to try to make my life a living hell. The boy who did this for me used to catch the same school bus. He would sit in front of me, then turn around and pull faces in an attempt to mimic the way I looked. He would also call me a few rude names. I was pretty shy and quiet on the bus so I tried to put up with it for as long as I could, but after a few weeks I decided enough was enough.

One day when he was leaning over the seat and really giving it to me, I snapped and grabbed the back of his head and rammed his face into the seat. His mouth hit a metal bar and split his lip, spilling enough blood to give him a scare. He spent the rest of that trip with his head between his legs, crying. I am not proud of that moment and can safely say I never again resorted to violence, but I felt I had to make a stand that day, somehow. While my method was far from ideal, it worked; he never even looked in my direction again after that.

Around this time, at age 12 or 13, something began to haunt me that stayed with me long into my 20s and 30s - the creeping in of depression. Up until then, I had always carried a positive frame of mind, but I began noticing moments of intense sadness. For example, I would be super excited to have friends come around and be really happy all week before, but as soon as they left, I felt really down and would spend the rest of the day moping. This wasn't just disappointment like most kids feel; this was real melancholy. I didn't know back then, but I realise now this was the early signs of depression, something that would almost bring me to my knees more than once in my adult life.

Year 7 ended with a fantastic graduation ceremony in the school undercroft and I started to look forward to the next chapter of my life, the daunting, but exciting chapter of high school, otherwise known as 'The Wonder Years'

The beginning of high school marked the end of my romance with Nicole, although we remained friends. Her family left Harvey for Rockingham, but I have managed to catch up with her a few times over the years since.

I still had the same group of friends; Normie, Kim, Graham and Jade. We met a popular guy named Ken too. Ken was big for his age, good at sports, popular and successful with the ladies, so he was a good mate to have! I was a little worried about how the other kids at the new school would react to my deformity, but as in primary school, I needn't have worried. For the most part, I was left alone, so bullying never became a big issue for me. For this, I am eternally grateful. Perhaps having Ken as a friend helped! My older brother Kelvin also kept watch for me and made sure no-one started up the teasing. He was always very protective of his little brother.

Year 9 brought a few unexpected, and unwanted, changes to my personality. Thankfully, it was only temporary, but it wasn't the best time in my young life. I started to shun my school uniform in favour of dressing in all black, trying to be more 'bogan' as I thought that was 'cool'. It didn't help that my brother Kelvin had also gone down that path and was probably the coolest bogan in school, but he could pull it off – I couldn't. I also lost interest in schoolwork and let my grades drop.

That wasn't all. I stupidly put my friendship with Jono in jeopardy too. After school one day, Normie confronted Jono and they got into a bit of a push and shove, and my name came up. Because of that incident, Jono never had any time for me during high school. It took a few years, but I was so grateful I was able to mend and rekindle that friendship later. Loyalty to my mates means everything to me.

During this rebellious phase, a few mates and I went camping up at Harvey weir and decided we were brave enough to try marijuana. Problem was, we didn't have any! Someone came up with the bright idea of breaking up a tea bag and smoking the leaves. It's safe to say we didn't get the effect we were hoping for! My older brother Kelvin heard about the story and stirred me up about it for years afterwards. Fair call.

That year, 1994, the world mourned Kurt Cobain – but my world centred around Harvey, Myalup and the boundaries of high school, and life was beginning to pick up again. My little bogan phase had passed and my friend Ryan from kindy had started back at Harvey High School after doing years 8 and 9 at a different school. It was great to see him back. Jacko was also still at school with us and I had also started to become closer to a few other guys I had grown up with, Calvin, Troy and Cory.

Joel Whitwell

The local production of *The Night of Stars* was a highlight that year, with local entertainer Tiny Holly as lead. I remember thinking back then as a starry-eyed kid that he was the biggest legend in town. We all loved getting together for these events; these were moments that strengthened the town as a community and brought people together in a positive way.

Unfortunately, that year the community had to come together for quite the opposite reason, to say goodbye to local football player Russell Flynn. He had played for the local club, the Harvey Bulls, and was well known in the local area. Many young boys (including myself) looked up to him as an inspiration both on and off the field. Sadly, Russell was involved in a car accident that Christmas and passed away. That was the first time I really felt the grief that death brought and had a tear in my eye as mum told me the news. Our family sent the Flynn's a sympathy card – a small gesture, but one from the heart.

As I was moving out of a downward phase, sadly, my brother Kelvin was struggling. He had hooked up with an older chick (she was 21, he was 17) and they moved into a house in Harvey together where they started to hit the drugs pretty hard. They would get high for a few days, then Kelvin would start flipping out, smashing stuff, and mum and dad would be called to calm him down. It was the start of the biggest challenge Kelvin would have to face in his life, and one of the biggest for our close family unit to work through together. It caused my brother and those closest to him a lot of pain over the years, the horror of drug addiction. Thankfully, he eventually pulled through, and we stayed by his side through thick and thin.

Kelvin was particularly close to Gran, even though all of us grandchildren had a great relationship with her. No matter what Kelvin did, Gran never held it against him and was always there when he needed someone to talk with.

One Eye, One Ear – No Worries

Grandad (dad's dad) passed away when us boys were very little and we never had a chance to get to know him, so having Gran there for us meant a lot. I'm sure Gran never got the chance to get lonely though, as she as so many grandchildren and always random visitors stopping by. I remember going around to Gran's place for tea every Christmas day and getting out on the spare block and playing cricket. Gran's curry and rice was to die for and was always the highlight of the visit for me.

I was now starting a new year and a new chapter in my life – upper school. Some students had left, but I pretty much had the same group of friends, Normie, Kim (who went by the nickname 'Bomber'), Troy, Calvin, Jacko and a new kid from the Philippines, Emmanuel. This was not a very academic year for me; my mates and I were more interested in being the class clowns than actually learning. Not wise! I remember one time in science class doing work with Bunsen burners on the side bench near the windows. I was sitting next to one of my friends and when he wasn't looking, I pushed the Bunsen burner up against the curtain, which caught alight. We caused a bit of a scene, and our science teacher wasn't too happy.

The school organised a police officer to visit to deliver a speech to us all about behaving responsibly when we finished school and started out in the real world. Just before he arrived and when no one was looking, Normie stuck a plug in one of the sinks and I turned on the tap just enough so you couldn't notice unless someone pointed it out. Halfway through the police officer's speech, we were interrupted by the sound of water overflowing, which had then begun creeping into the room. Job done. The officer cut his speech short, and to this day I'm not sure he left with any confidence about how we were all going to turn out!

Another time I attempted to get the math's teacher's attention by poking him in the stomach with a ruler instead of putting my hand up. That got me sent outside. Maths was also the class I decided, out of boredom, to throw my file at the ceiling fan. Again, I was sent outside, this time asking Normie as I passed his desk, "you coming, mate?" Normie didn't say a word, but picked up his file and threw it at the fan as well. I guess that was his way of saying, "yeh, I'm coming with you."

My antics only worsened as the year progressed. At the start of each day, we all had to attend form to have our names ticked off the attendance sheet and prepare for the day ahead. We had four forms in year 11, with different students allocated in each – Wellington, Mitchell, Hayward and Forrest. I was in Wellington. Halfway through the year, we had photos taken of each form for the end of school yearbook. I did the right thing and got my photo taken with Wellington, but then when no one was looking, I managed to jump in with Mitchell as well. I thought I was done for, but somehow the teachers didn't seem to notice. At the end of the year I grabbed my copy and hastily checked the photos. Sure enough, there I was in both, with my name even written underneath. Twins with the same name and only one eye and one ear?! Not sure how I was never pulled up on that one.

One of the poor relief teachers that year got a shock courtesy of my glass eye. Normie wanted to play a joke on him and told me to take my eye out. He then went running up to the teacher with my eye in his hand, screaming, "look, sir, I lost my eye!" Funny…but maybe not for the poor relief teacher!

Halfway through the year, Normie left school to work at a local bakery as an apprentice, so I lost my sidekick (probably to the relief of the school!). Bomber had also left a few months earlier to get a job at EG Greens (now Harvey Beef). Our group at school was dwindling, but we still managed to catch up regularly outside of bell times.

To this day, I still don't know how I managed to graduate in year 12 given my antics the previous year. To be honest, I was lucky not to have been kicked out of school. What probably helped was my stint playing football with the Harvey Police boys. I didn't play much sport, but that was my best year of footy. Malcolm Cooke was our coach that year. We played Bunbury in the first round and I came on in the last quarter in a close game, got a few kicks in and ended up scoring the winning goal. Not a bad start to the season! The next week was even better. We won by 20 goals and I ended up kicking five of those. I was the talk of the town; the boy with only one ear and one eye kicking goals on the footy field.

Sadly, my form dropped off a bit after that, but I still had a pretty decent year and won the coaches award. I would have loved to have played the grand final with that top group of blokes, but unfortunately we were knocked out in the first semi. Even though I was named in the Harvey Reporter as one of the best players on the ground, I would have traded those accolades for a flag any day.

Near the end of year 11 my friends and I also decided to put together a team for the B-grade men's basketball competition, and what a team! Normie and his older brother Danny, Emmanual, Troy, Bomber, myself and our other friends Riad and Graeme rounded out the line-up. That was the start of two years not winning a game, but we had a lot of fun together trying.

Year 11 ended with me needing to do a bit of thinking about my future. What had I achieved this year? To put it bluntly, not a lot. I found I could make people laugh by being the class clown to pass the time, but at the end of the day, my report card showed my grades were the lowest they had ever been. That is not really how I wanted to end my school years. I decided I was going to return to school and complete year 12 and put in much more effort so I could graduate and finish school on a high.

It was also around this time that I started to think deeply about my life and what I had overcome. I realised back then that I could inspire a lot of people if I try to stay positive and give life my best shot, and doing well at school was the first step. While looking through some things at home, I came across an old copy of the Harvey Reporter (the local paper) that mum and dad had kept. It featured me on the front page when I had my first big operation back in 1989.

South Fremantle footy player Ned, originally from Harvey, was kind enough to pay a young Harvey boy a hospital visit. He even gave me a football signed by all of the South Freo players and we had a photo taken together, which was the one that made the Reporter. That visit meant a lot to me that day, but even more so that summer after year 11 when I was able to look back on my life and see how much I meant to the people of Harvey. I still have the football and that copy of the Reporter with me.

Despite my newfound positive outlook on life, as I got older, the staring from strangers began to bother me much more. It wasn't so bad in school, that was within my comfort zone, but whenever I ventured out into public, such as when I had to go to Perth with mum for a check-up, I could feel all eyes on me. Mum, bless her, tried her best to reassure me that they were only staring because of how good looking I was. As a very young child, I believed that, but as the years went on, I knew that wasn't the case.

Unfortunately, that summer leading into year 12 was the year I discovered I really liked drinking. Over the coming years, I developed a reputation as a big drinker who, after a few bevvies, would come out of his shell and make people laugh. I was the life of the party.

This started around Christmas that year when the junior fire brigade had a windup at the fire station. Everyone was drinking beer, so at age 16 I decided it was time to try it. I had one, then one thing lead to another, and by the end of the night I was out the front throwing up on the lawn. My legacy had begun! Another time, I filled in for someone in the senior fire brigade team and straight after the demo the kegs came out and the beer started flowing. I had a few there, then on the way home dad stopped at every pub. So, by the time we got home, I crawled straight into bed without taking my clothes or shoes off. I forgot I had to start year 12 the next day…

My first day of year 12 went pretty well, despite my massive hangover! Only 28 of us decided to return. Troy and Calvin had left at the end of year 11, but Aggie was still there and I also became good friends with some others, including Tony, Scott, Daniel, Riad, Coralee, Cass (who, more than anyone, encouraged me to write this book) and an exchange student from Argentina, Julian. After my first day I was relaxed and confident that I had made the right choice by returning to finish my final year of school, even though I knew I had a bit of work to do to improve my grades enough to graduate.

After a week or two I had another hurdle to overcome, which I was starting to get used to, but it meant a missing another week of school. It was time for another operation. The rib they had put in to bring my face out had grown and was pushing up against my skull, which forced my jaw to lock up and made opening my mouth difficult. To fix it, they needed to remove some of the rib. It was only a small procedure, compared to the others, but operations are never a pleasant experience. I was given some schoolwork to do while in hospital so I wouldn't fall behind so early in the year.

A few of the kids in year 11 and 12 wanted to come up to see me, including Jono who I had caused a problem with a few years earlier. We were still a way off properly rekindling our friendship, but I was heartened by the fact that he wasn't holding a grudge. As I was only in hospital for about a week, they never made it in to see me, but the thought meant a lot. Before we knew it, I was back in class and doing well.

Joel Whitwell

In English class that year we had to write an essay on the movie *Dead Poets Society*, and I aced it. Now, in my early 30s and looking back on my life, I realise I have tried to grab every opportunity that has come my way, and I guess that is what the saying 'carpe diem', or 'seize the day', means.

Country Week came halfway through that year and I had made the volleyball team. Country Week is an annual sporting competition between the local country schools that is held up in the big smoke (Perth) and covers a variety of sports, including football, netball and basketball. I shared a room with Tony and another two blokes from the Ag school, which is another school in Harvey. Nothing too exciting happened on that trip, but I do remember trying a cigarette for the first time (ironic…at a sporting event…). Fortunately, all I got out of that was a bad head spin, so I didn't really enjoy it, although I did revisit smoking as a social habit later on.

By the end of year 12, I had risen to the challenge I set for myself and graduated high school. This marked the time for another challenge – getting my drivers' licence. I thought only having one eye might have been a problem, but the instructor didn't make much of a fuss about it. As long as I could prove to him that I could drive safely and correctly, then I guess that is all that mattered! I hadn't had much experience driving and wasn't very confident, so I was still taking lessons when I graduated from school, but I did get there in the end.

Leading up to graduation was a local tradition known as 'muck up night', where the year 12's got to sleep overnight at the school and have a bit of a celebration. I didn't know it at the time, but nights like this were widely known as stepping stones to building up my reputation as an A-grade drinker that would reach legendary status by the time I reached my 20s. One of our classmates had repeated the year, so he was older and able to supply the booze, and before long we were sitting in the gym and common room, reminiscing about school days, getting drunk and having a good time.

By around 10 pm, the night started getting blurry and all I can remember was writing on the gym walls, helping Tina blow up water balloons and sitting on the school oval with Julian and talking some drunken ramble for what seemed like hours. Then, the sun was up, and the lower grades were starting to arrive at school. I vaguely remember standing in the gym, looking around at all the mess, thinking "what a fucking awesome night that was!" The rest of the morning was even more of a blur. We went back to Aggie's place around lunchtime to keep drinking, then by around 2 pm, Aggie passed out and I decided I finally needed some sleep too.

For some reason, I opted to go back to school to sleep it off in the common room. I walked into the gym, and the whole school turned to look at me! They were having an assembly, and I wandered straight into it! I was pissed as a fart, but remember seeing the wall above the headmistress had written in massive letters JOEL WHITTY (thankfully, only in chalk!) I made it to the common room and passed out, then ended up at home later for a quiet weekend.

Graduation day rolled around the following Monday and I was excited; it was a big day for me. Considering where I was at in year 11, it was a great achievement to be able to walk up on stage for that certificate with my classmates. The ceremony was held in the new gym in front of the whole school, and it was well put together. I was the last one called up to get my diploma and received a standing ovation. It was a proud moment. Mum and nana were there, which meant a lot. After the ceremony, we had afternoon tea in the old gym where we got to mingle and take photos. I got one with Coralee, who was the school captain, and to this day it is still one of my most treasured photos.

Tony and I went back to Aggie's afterwards to have a beer and celebrate our achievement. I had known Aggie since kindergarten and we had been through a bit together, so to spend the day with him and Tony meant a lot. We knew we were about to head out into the real world, and we would eventually go our own way in life, but at that moment the three of us were able to share a beer and just 'be'. I had a few drinks with them (as you do) and went home to think about the future and what the next step would be, but deep down, I guess I already knew what was coming.

Four

Adulthood Beckons

Dad had worked at EG Greens (the local meatworks) for roughly 25 years and worked his way up to supervisor, so had no trouble scoring me a job in the boning room. I got straight into it, due to start the Friday after graduation. As of the time of writing I am now 40 and have secured a job as an Inspector working for the Government.

For a few years after I started, my attitude and reliability were nowhere where they should have been. Whenever the business was quiet and they had to lay people off, a lot of good workers lost their jobs and I really should have been one of them. Looking back, I do believe I was looked after because of my father's loyalty to the company. It is hard for me to admit this now, but it was a part of my life I need to accept and own, and thankfully I was able to turn things around before it was too late.

I worked hard to get my record up from one of the worst to one of the best, and earn the respect I hold today. I like to think this hard work was my way of giving back to the company after the faith they showed me in my younger years.

After I finished school, I'd finally had enough driving lessons for the instructor to be confident in my abilities to book me in for the test – which happened to fall on that first day at EG Greens! Not bad hey, the first day of work and I already had to take time off! Luckily, I passed the test, so it was a great day; the first day in paid employment and a driver's licence to match my newfound freedom (although I was yet to get a car).

Work began ok, despite my attitude, and I was happy just cruising along on the basic jobs like pushing fat tubs and packing fat instead of trying to improve my skills. Now away from the comfort zone of school, I did encounter some staring and the occasional snide remark. However, Harvey was still my home town and most people generally left me alone and didn't give me a hard time because of my face. I was grateful for this, as I had also been grateful to escape the torments of bullying in school.

My 18th year was coming up, which meant one thing – my childhood was coming to a close. At this stage, I started reflecting on my childhood and what I had overcome, and the events that shaped my life over the past 18 years. Like the visit from Ned, there was one other event that probably meant more to me later in life when I looked back than it did at the time. This was my first interstate trip.

I was off to Melbourne with nanna and my cousin Lauren. Nanna had tickets for us to go and see *The Phantom of the Opera,* so we went for three days to make the most of it. The top floor of our hotel had a pool and a spa, so Lauren and I spent quite a bit of time up there. By then, I was a mad AFL fan, so it was also a great opportunity to check out a few of the footy ovals I had seen on TV. We visited Princess Park, Waverly and the MCG, where I was blown away by the size and hoped one day I would make it back there for a grand final.

Another great memory from that trip was going for a ride on the trams and I remember thinking, "shit, we don't have these back home in Perth!" *The Phantom of the Opera* was spectacular and as a youngster I was impressed by the ability of the performers to put on a show like that.

The trip was amazing and without incident – until we got back to Tullamarine (Melbourne) airport waiting to catch our flight home. Lauren had to go to the toilet and, being young and naive, she left her camera on the bench while she went in. In those few minutes she was gone, someone came along and pinched it. I had never seen Lauren so upset, as all her photos from the trip disappeared just like that.

I sat with her in the airport thinking there may be a lot of good people in this world, but there are also a lot of heartless and cruel bastards. That truth really hit home, so I guess I had always been a bit naive too. Even for someone who had to put up with staring and a few snide remarks because of my face, I still always look for the best in people. Despite the camera incident, I still look back on that trip for what it was – an awesome and memorable experience, and I won't let one bastard ruin that.

Around this time, Marcus and Emma moved to Myalup with their parents and I became good mates with Marcus. As a close-knit group of local teens, Frog also developed a close bond with Marcus and would often just hang around town doing crazy shit. That is how the town was, everyone looked after each other and we all felt safe to go out and be kids in our neighbourhood.

By the time I was due to celebrate my 18th birthday, I had well and truly discovered alcohol and parties (as mentioned!), so mum and dad agreed to let me have a party at our place in Myalup. The build-up was exciting. My friend Normie had started a band with his brothers and cousins, so I organised for them to play on our spare block where the party was being held.

The day finally arrived, people started turning up by around mid-afternoon. My old friend Douglas made it, even though we hadn't seen much of each other since he left Harvey at the end of year 4. It was a nice surprise to see him again! He ended up only staying an hour or so as he wasn't drinking and we were all quickly getting messy. I later found out that Douglas had leukemia and he passed away not long after my birthday, so that hour was special – it was the last time I ever saw him.

By nightfall, the party was in full swing. Everyone was getting drunk and having a great time, and I was right amongst it, I felt like a star. We ended up down at the beach for a time and Tony went for a drunken swim, while back at the house, Aggie started dancing on one of nannas chairs and broke it. It was safe to say my mates and I were living it up for the night! I vaguely remember dad putting me to bed in the top bunk, only to hang my head over the side and throw up on poor Julian sleeping on the floor underneath.

Thankfully, the fallout the next morning wasn't too bad. A few sore heads and hangovers were floating around, but you expect that! Aggie took it upon himself to go waltzing into mum and dad's room to wake them and see if they wanted the newspaper while he was at the shop. Everyone thought this was pretty funny, but that's just the type of character Aggie is. He didn't give a fuck, and everyone loved him for it.

The night had turned out pretty epic, but sadly I don't have any photos to prove it! There was someone taking photos, but I'm not sure what happened to that camera and no photos have ever turned up. Remember, this is in the days before smartphones were commonplace!

Not long after my 18th birthday, I decided it was time to buy my first car. I saw one for sale just down the road, and it was perfect. It was a red Mazda, quickly dubbed 'The Merk'. Everyone loved that car, and it became almost as well-known as its owner! Jacko had the honour of being the first in the passenger seat. It felt so good to have my own wheels.

As for work, I had already been at EG Greens for almost two months, but for some reason my heart just wasn't in it. All the kids were almost ready to go back to school and I realised how much I missed that life. I'd graduated in non-TEE (which stood for Tertiary Entrance Examinations; I graduated but without the option to go straight to university) so I decided to go back and give TEE a go to broaden my options. However I'm not really sure why! Looking back I put it down to just not being ready for the real world. Mum and dad weren't happy with me returning to high school to do my TEE, but they respected my decision.

Just before I was to start school again, Julian was due to leave Australia and go back to Argentina, so Riad and I went to catch up with him at Binningup beach to take some photos and say goodbye. I promised him that one day I would visit him in his home country, and it is a promise I always intend to keep.

I finished up in the boning room at work and went back to school, but as soon as I started, I realised I had made the wrong choice. It just didn't feel right; it felt strange that everyone I graduated with the year before was out there having a go in the real world. Funnily enough, though faded, you could still clearly see my name up on the gym wall from muck up night the previous November – I was quietly pleased with that.

I stuck it out and was fuelled by the prospect that I could actually hold my own in the harder subjects. My classmate Emma and I teamed up for an assignment and we aced it, proving to myself that I could do this. I also made a few new friends, including Daniel, who had moved from Geraldton. That year, I also met someone who would eventually play a big part in my life and help shape the person I am today – Paul (PJ). While we didn't connect instantly at school, it was only a matter of time before we formed a very close bond.

Despite the positives, my stint back at school was short. I left again (for good) a few weeks after the start of the year. I couldn't get my job back in the boning room straight away, so I got a job picking tomatoes. Talk about a shit job…sitting on a cart going up and down lanes all day picking fruit wasn't my cup of tea, but if I wanted to live peacefully under the same roof as dad, I had to have some sort of job.

While my working life sucked, my social life was starting to pick up pace. My friend Scott would come out to our house most weekends while him, Frog, Marcus and I would get pissed, run amok and do crazy stuff in the Merk. Whenever we would rock up at parties, the car would be so full of smoke, people wouldn't know who I was with until they all piled out (and our eyes were as red as the Mazda)!

Easter weekend that year I had the opportunity to reconnect with an old mate, Jono. We were drinking down at the beach one night when I bumped into some people I knew from school, Jono being one of them. We were both drunk and ended up having a bit of a laugh together, especially when Jono told me that earlier on in the night he had gone to sit on the wall, missed it by a mile and landed on a rock. Ouch. That may not seem all that funny now, but as a drunken teenager, it was hilarious. This was the first time the two of us had spoken in years, and even though we didn't dig up the past, it was great to spend some time together. I knew in my heart that we were back on track to repairing our once-strong friendship.

Five

Work To Live, Not Live To Work

My career as a tomato picker came to an abrupt end when, after a camping trip with Riad and Scott, I didn't make it to work when expected on a Saturday. When I turned up the following Monday, they told me my services were no longer required – in other words, I was sacked. Dammit. I was really looking forward to a long and exciting career in the field…!

Thankfully, I wasn't out of work for long. I scored a part-time job out at an emu farm not far from our place. The pay wasn't terrific, but back then I really only needed money for fuel and drinks on the weekend. The man I worked for, Arthur, seemed to like me and always had a story to tell, so I enjoyed my time there. I had tasks such as repairing fences and collecting emu eggs.

So, this was where I was at during this point in my life. Working at the emu farm during the week, then Friday would roll around, Scott would come to pick me up, we would get drunk and end up at the disco in town (if it was on) then head out to the Wokalup Tavern. My mate PJ's parents had bought the tavern (the Woky) the year before, so he would often come down to the bar and have a chat, where we started to form a pretty tight friendship.

It was also around this time my friend Troy had his 18th birthday. He was living with Aggie out at Cookernup in what was soon to be known as a bit of a party house. The Friday night of his 18th, I got a lift out there and pretty soon was right into the swing of things. The next thing I remember is waking up in the morning on the pool table with a massive hangover. This further cemented my growing reputation.

I told Arthur about it at work on Monday and he told me that if I kept it up, I would have just as many stories as him by the time I was his age, providing I survived.

Basketball was still going strong, although we were yet to win a game after two seasons. One game we extended a massive lead at half time, got carried away and rung the pub to order a celebratory carton, then ended up losing again. We didn't pick up that carton.

Next, I decided it was time to try a different sport and put a mixed netball team in the local competition. We were aptly called The Delinquents and included a mix of people I knew from school and around the area. Our first game was not exactly how I planned…On our way to Harvey for the match, one of the other guys and I decided to smoke a few cones. When we rocked up at the Rec Centre, the Merk was filled with smoke (as usual) and we were pretty stoned. I found out it is not good to try to play netball in that state; I didn't do that again…however, I may have played after a few drinks on the odd occasion! That kept things interesting.

The team had a pretty good year, winning more than we lost. We made the preliminary final but got knocked out of the competition there.

Around August of that year (1997) I got my old job in the boning room back, so I had to leave the emu farm. I was going to miss Arthur and his stories, but I had to move on. Sad to say, my work ethic had not improved much, so I was happy to be just plodding along doing the basic, easy jobs.

Around late August I made a decision, that although it didn't change my life too much, it would bring a whole new group of people into focus and I was able to form some of the best friendships I will ever have in this world. On a Thursday night, I drove out to the Woky to have a beer with Aggie and Jacko. They were going down south for the weekend and wanted me to go. I was tempted, but there was meant to be a disco on in Harvey the following night and there was a good chance the girl I had a crush on would be there, so I would 'bump into her'.

Jacko and Aggie tried to talk me into coming down south, but I had made my mind up. So the next night I jumped in the Merk and drove into Harvey, only to discover I had gotten the dates wrong and the disco wasn't even on! Instead of getting too upset, I decided to cruise around town and see what else was happening.

I came across a mate of my brother's, Matty, who told me there was a piss up at Choco's place. I knew Choco from school, he was a year younger than me. So, Matty and I decided we would drop around and check it out. I didn't know how they would react to us, rocking up uninvited, but I needn't have worried. They all boosted up when I knocked at the door and before long I was sitting at the kitchen table sculling beer and getting right amongst it. One of the guys, Matt, was saying to me "I got a lot of time for you, Joel Whitty". Well, he has proven to be a man of his word as that night was the start of a great friendship.

Needless to say, we all got a bit drunk that night. At one stage, a few of us jumped in the Merk, Riad driving with Matt and myself in the back with our legs hanging out the window. We headed out to the Woky to get more booze. The rest of the night became a bit of a blur until I woke up the next morning in my car. It was a great night.

The following Saturday I worked in the morning then not long after I got home, Choco rang. He said a few of the crew were going camping and asked if I wanted to come. I must have made a pretty good impression at the party then! I agreed and headed down to meet them at Myalup beach. We all stayed at the beach for a while, then it got too windy so we decided to head into town to camp at the Harvey Weir instead.

On our way through Harvey, we stopped at the local café downtown where one of the guys from school, Shawn, was working. Matt went in and told him we were going camping, and Shawn agreed to meet us up there when he finished work. We got up to our spot, lit a fire and sat around drinking beer and getting rowdy. We all grew up in the same area, but before the previous weekend, I hadn't had much to do with them. That night at the weir I was totally at ease and it felt like we had known each other forever. I guess that's how life works sometimes.

Shawn finally rocked up and I got to know him a bit better too. At 17, he already had a beard like Jesus, drunk like a fish and smoked like a chimney. We had a great night but woke up a little dusty in the morning, so decided to head into Bunbury to get some pizza. There were a few of us, so we took two cars. The feast became a competition to see who could eat the most pizza, and I was one of the winners! I finally made it home at the end of the weekend, happy in the knowledge that I had made some great new friends and had plenty of good times to look forward to.

The following weekend was Aggie's 18th out at the party house in Cookernup. I drove the Merk into Harvey and for some reason I went by the Rec Centre first. PJ was just coming out of the Centre, and as we had started to become good friends, I asked him if he wanted to come, which he did. When we got to the house, the only park I could find was next to a ditch, but I went too close and the Merk ended up tipped over a little (we were very lucky it didn't end up on its roof!). As usual, my entrance received cheers, then another cheer as PJ climbed out of the Merk via the driver's side as his door was jammed shut by the ditch! Another good night was had, where I ended up back in the Merk by morning, covered in spew.

By this stage, Jono had moved back to Harvey after a few years in Mandurah and was staying with Cory and Janelle (cousins) out the back of their dad's place in the games room. I often visited with my new group of friends, drinking piss and boosting up.

November that year, the next lot of year 12s graduated, which included a lot of my new friends – so, of course, there was a party to celebrate. Jono had started work at Greens as well and we were both on nightshift, so after work Jono, Cory and I went back to the games room, had a few drinks, then around midnight started to walk out to the party. It was on that walk that Jono and I brought up the incident in high school that caused us to have a falling out, but we were both confident that our friendship was back on track, so nothing much more was said.

By the time we got out to the party, the celebration was in full swing. We joined right in and kicked on until the sun came up. Cory (Cozzo, as he was soon to be known) and I decided to go for a walk in the paddocks. I was busting for a piss, so decided to do it on the electric fence. All was ok until I then tripped and landed on the wires!

As it turned out, it was me, Jono and Cozzo that did the bulk of the celebrating that night, even though we weren't graduating!

A few weeks later, there was another graduation party at someone else's house, so Jono, Cozzo and I decided to turn up and celebrate again with them. Jono was well behaved this time, but Cozzo and I overstepped the mark and took the celebrations a bit too far. At one stage, we snuck into the shed and poured cement and milk all over the floor (not sure what we were trying to achieve there), then I pulled a chainsaw off the shelf and tried to convince Cozzo it was the Texas Chainsaw Massacre. It wasn't long before we were told to leave and started the long walk back into Harvey. We made it as far as the highway, where as luck would have it, Riad was driving past on his way back from the nightclubbing in Bunbury. We jumped in the back of the ute with Shawn (by then known as Boo Boo), who had already passed out. We went back to the games room and did the same. I apologised to the party host not long after that night.

Not long after that night, it is sad to say, the life of the Merk came to a tragic end. The day of the Merk's demise started like any other day. We were kicking back at the games room when Jono suggested we take the Merk out for a drive to Myalup beach and I thought it was a good idea, so off we went. On the way to Myalup there is a gravel road you can turn onto that is a bit of a shortcut. We were going down this road at a steady pace, when suddenly we came up to a corner a bit too quick. I slammed on the brakes, we lost control and ended up going head-on into a ditch. Luckily, we weren't hurt, but the Merk wasn't in good shape.

We finally got someone to pull it out, but the front end was all dented in. We managed to drive it the rest of the way to my place in Myalup and check the damage to see if it could survive or not. Jono thought it didn't need much repair work, but I decided it had already been through enough in one lifetime and it was time to let it die a peaceful death. I won the argument as it was my car, so for a little while, I had to rely on mum and dad or friends to get around.

New Year's came around and a big group of us went to Mandurah to watch the Screaming Jets play at the foreshore. I remember sitting in the back of Shawn's car drinking on the way to Mandurah, so I was in fine form by the time the band started playing. It was a great night and we all got pretty drunk, and I woke up the next day at a friend's in Harvey, and wasn't sure how we got back there!

Heading into 1998 was a great time for me and my group of friends. We were young and experiencing life to the fullest. Around this time, Jono moved out of the games room and in with an older bloke who we knew as Butch, who's daughter was dating a friend of ours. Another guy, James, also moved in with them. They had a place on Merriedale Crescent and I started to become a regular visitor at the weekends.

Six

Experience Is The Greatest Teacher

A few weeks after New Year's I turned 19 and decided to celebrate by throwing a massive beach party in the car park at Myalup beach. I was starting to become pretty well-known, so I was confident word would get around and I would have a decent turnout. A few of us turned up early to set up then waited for everyone to arrive. Around 9 o'clock I started to get a bit down as there was only about eight of us and I thought no one else was going to show, so Marcus and I grabbed a few beers, went to the top of a sand dune overlooking the carpark and started drinking. Not long after we got up there, we saw a few cars come over the hill, followed by a few more.

Over the hour we spent up the dune, we watched our group of eight expand to well over eighty, all boosting up in the carpark – we were loving it. After a while, seeing as it was my party, we decided we better go down and mingle. All was going well, until things got a bit out of hand later in the night. A bloke I knew from work, Mark, got into a fight with a local, Brad. Unfortunately for Mark, Brad was well-known to the crowd and the whole party ended up turning on the newcomer and chased him into the sand dunes, apparently trying to bury him. Needless to say, he didn't come back to the party. I did bump into him a few days later at work and he was pretty good about it, considering. I was one of the few people who didn't try to bury him, but still, it was my party and if I had 80 people try to bury me, I would be pretty pissed off.

Not long after the famous (or infamous) party, I decided it was time to get myself another car as I couldn't grieve over the Merk forever; time to move on. I got a loan and bought myself a blue VP Commodore '93 model. It was pretty flash and a big step up from the Merk. I must have worn the tyres out pretty quick doing laps around town, but I was young thought I was pretty cool to be driving a car like that!

One night, Matt, Cozzo and I took a trip into Bunbury. To get to town you had to go around a massive roundabout and we remembered one of the other boys bragging that he had gone around it 20 times before exiting. We thought it was a good idea to try to break that record – which we did, then went around a few more times for good measure. If I remember correctly, we ended up going around it 120 times all up. Matt was so impressed, that as soon as we got into Bunbury he rang up the rest of the crew to let them know.

1998 brought another turning point in my life when I realised, no matter how good things seem to be, life can always throw a curveball. I had recently become friends with a bloke we called TC, who's older brother was best mates with my brother Kelvin. TC was a bit of a character who always seemed to be happy and high on life. To this day, I don't know how he did it.

One night, TC, Bomber and I were driving around in the VP when we decided to visit my older brother Kelvin, who had recently moved into a house out on the highway near Wokalup with a few of his mates. This night, he wasn't there, but there were two older blokes sitting outside so we decided to join them.

One of the blokes, who was pretty big, took one look at my face and I will never forget what came out of his mouth; "You must be the ugliest c#&t

I have ever seen. You should be put down. If I looked like that, I would kill myself". Bomber, TC and I looked at each other in utter disgust, shocked by what we had just heard. I handled it the best way I could; I got up and left, and my two friends followed me.

To their credit, they also handled it very well, as we were all teenagers still and no one expected that to happen. On the way back into Harvey, they tried to comfort me, as friends do, but the tears were already starting to form and I didn't want to cry in front of my mates, so I told them I wanted to be alone. I dropped them off, found a quiet place to park and cried my eyes out.

Those words coming from a complete stranger could have destroyed me that night, but in fact, it did the opposite. After all my tears ran out, those words of hatred made me stronger, as I knew in my heart something like that was going to happen sooner or later. If I was going to make a name for myself in this world with a facial deformity, I needed to develop a thick skin to handle comments like that. I finally made it home and the next morning decided not to tell mum and dad about it, as I didn't want them to worry.

However, Harvey is a small town…I'm not sure what became of that gentleman as he ended up leaving town not long after that night (wink, wink). But in saying that, even though what he said haunted me a bit from time to time, if I was to ever run into him again and he was remorseful and sorry, I would find it in my heart to forgive him. Life is too short to hold onto grudges, and holding onto anger only really hurts yourself in the long run.

A little while after that in early March, night shift at EG Greens finished up and a lot of us were about to get laid off. So, to celebrate, Matt and I decided to head to the Harvey pub to get on the booze (what else?!). It wasn't open yet, so we went to the local bottle shop, got some takeaway drinks and sat on a bench down the main street of Harvey. You probably couldn't get away with that these days, but back in 1998 we were still young and could push the limits right to the brink. While we were there, we got talking and laughing with an old local, who informed us that he had just been told he only had one testicle. We all thought that was pretty funny at the time.

The pub finally opened, and Matt and I went down there to continue the festivities. The day got pretty out of hand, and at one stage we asked someone to drive us to the school, as the ball was coming up and we both wanted to go and therefore had to find a partner. After about 10 minutes though, we came to our senses and realised that we probably wouldn't find dates in our current condition. How we didn't get caught being drunk on school grounds, I will never know.

We headed back to the pub and Matt looked at his watch, mumbling something about work. I didn't catch what he said, but then it hit me. Shit, we still had one more nightshift to go. So, we finished our drinks, jumped in the VP and pulled out of the carpark. I'm not sure how I managed to drive that day…we even passed a cop on the way who looked straight at us. Luck must have been on my side, as he kept going instead of pulling us over.

Halfway down the main street, Matt decided he was way too drunk to work, so I dropped him off at the local café in town and watched as fumbled with the car door before finally getting inside the cafe. I went on my merry way to work. I don't remember much from that last nightshift, except that I didn't actually do much work. Instead, I just wandered around chatting everyone's ear off while they tried to be productive. The boss must have known I was drunk, as I was very quickly put on the list of people who were about to lose their job. Sorry dad…again.

Fortunately, I wasn't out of work for long, as I quickly found a job at Sumich Market Gardens picking celery. It was handy, as it was close to home, but with winter just around the corner the idea of picking celery all day in the rain didn't really rate as my dream job. But, it meant a pay check coming in every week, so I stuck at it, at least until something better came up or I could get back into EG Greens.

Seven

HAVING A BALL

By this stage, Matt had found himself a date for the ball. He was going with a girl named Julie, which made me more determined to find someone to go with too (and not being at school anymore, I could not go on my own). My cousin Lauren had a good friend in her year named Diana, who I thought was pretty. So, I asked her if she wanted to go to the ball and to my surprise, she said yes! I was rapt. I found out that on weekends she worked part-time at Foodland, which was located on the main street of Harvey. One Saturday, I decided to try to impress her to prove she made the right choice by going with me. I went around to Butch and Jono's place, picked up a couple of friends and drove towards the main street of Harvey with one thing on my mind – to impress Diana in my cool VP.

As we drove past Foodland, we saw Diana working the checkout so I tooted the horn and we all started waving. We looked pretty cool, until I rammed into the car in front of us and smashed the front end of my VP. That part was definitely not cool, but the look on her face was priceless. The driver of the car I'd hit pulled over, but I just wanted to get the fuck out of there so I quickly drove back to Jono's place.

The first thought that went through my mind when I parked up was, "shit, I certainly fucked that up!" On top of the damage to my car, I soon received a bill in the mail to pay for the damage to the other car, so I was out of pocket a bit. But, believe it or not, there is good news from this story – Diana was still happy to go to the ball with me, what an awesome chick!

The lead-up to the ball was pretty exciting, though as much as I tried otherwise, I kept finding ways to almost stuff it up. A few weeks before the ball, I attended a party that Diana was at and, as I tended to do back then, I got pretty drunk. At some point during the night, Diana was standing with a group of people trying to work out seating arrangements for the ball. She called me over to fill me in on their plan, but as I was walking towards the group, I stacked it and ended arse-up in front of everyone. Diana, God bless her, always saw the funny side to all of my fuckups and still seemed happy to be taking me to the ball.

A week later, the weekend before the ball, Tiger decided he wanted a night out in Bunbury to go nightclubbing. Since I was a year older and Tiger was born in December that year, we were the only two from the crew who were of legal drinking age. So, Friday after work I picked him up in the VP and we headed down to Bunbury. By this stage, our friend Caliopi was living in Bunbury, so she said I could leave my car there and stay the night if need be.

Anyway, we got there, had a few drinks, then Tiger and I headed into town.

As the night wore on and we got more and more drunk, we somehow bumped into Choco and Aggie. Choco wanted a lift back to Harvey and Aggie needed a lift to Myalup and since I wasn't shy about drink driving back then, I decided to get the VP and give them a lift. It was a pretty crazy drive. We dropped them off and since it was only 1 am and the clubs were open until 6 am, we decided to head back to Bunbury to continue our adventures.

I don't think we even made it past Wokalup before we both blacked out. The next thing I remember was waking up in the driver's seat (as I tended to do a bit back then) and my first thought was "what the hell happened last night?" My windscreen was fogged up, so I turned my demister on and soon realised we had parked on someone's front lawn. Tiger was asleep in the passenger seat, so I woke him up. He had no recollection of the night after we left Harvey, so we weren't sure if we made it back to the clubs or not.

But, that was the least of our worries – we were alive, but were still parked on someone's front lawn and it wouldn't be too long before they noticed. I turned the key and started driving. It took us a few streets to realise we were in Australind, a coastal town about 10 minutes north of Bunbury. We eventually got home and after I dropped Tiger off, I jumped in a nice warm bath to recover.

I wish I could say I laid in the water that day thinking about how my life was getting out of control, but unfortunately, my mind was operating on quite the contrary. I was living and loving that lifestyle and the only thought at that point in time was that the ball was coming up and I couldn't wait to go.

The following Saturday, the big night had arrived. I was all suited and booted by the afternoon, talk about eager! Tarin was living at her mum's by then, so we all met there for pre-ball photos. There were four couples; Diana and me, Matt and Julie, Tiger and Tarin, and Choco and Tania (Diana's sister). Diana looked gorgeous in her ball dress and I felt so lucky to be her date for the night. The ball was held at the Lord Forrest Hotel in Bunbury, and as I walked in, arm in arm with Diana, I had the biggest smile on my face.

I am proud to say, that unlike previous weekends, I was on best behaviour that night (although Matt and I did sneak out to the VP a few times to have a few lemon Ruskies we had stashed!). I remember having a slow dance with Diana to the song *My Heart Will Go On* and all in all it was a fun and very memorable night.

After the ball, we went back to the after-ball party, got drunk (as you do) and I woke up the next day on the couch at Tarin's mum's place with a mild hangover.

While my social life was on track, I was hating my job at the market gardens. In a stroke of luck, my old buddies from school, Normie and Bomber, also got a job there. It was great to be hanging out with them again like we were back in school. Nothing much had changed and we were still mucking around and being clowns, just this time we were getting paid for it!

We also became friends with another young bloke working at the gardens, named Nathan. He had recently moved to WA from New Zealand after his dad landed a job at EG Greens. Nathan had recently joined up colts footy at the Harvey Bulls footy club, so played alongside Jono, Matt and a few of my other good friends.

After training with the club the night of the ball, Nathan had gone out with Jono for a few drinks and met up with me later on. Like everyone who meets me for the first time, he had sympathy in his eyes when he saw my face. To his credit, he quickly dismissed any apprehension and just treated me like anyone else and we became friends in no time.

The first weekend we hung out together, we decided to sit in my VP down the main street of Harvey all afternoon drinking lemon Ruskies. Not sure why we sat in the car when we could have pulled up a stool at the pub, but I guess I just like to sit and watch the world go by from the comfort of my own space. Before long, Cozzo and PJ came along and stopped for a chat and when they saw the empty bottles at our feet, they thought we were mad. As with many other days before it, the drinking continued and I'm not quite sure how I got to bed.

The next day, we were all back at work picking celery. As much as I hated my job, there still were some pretty good times in my life. I worked all week, then on Friday night I would usually head around to Jono and Butch's place to get drunk and play cards. Sometimes, Nathan would come with me. We would all get pretty drunk, but it was always a great night.

In July, the year 11's and 12's from the local high school went to Perth for Country Week. I came up with the bright idea of heading up for a few days to support our local community, but really it was just another excuse to try to impress Diana (as you can probably tell by now, apart from the ball when I was on my best behaviour, I hadn't otherwise done a very good job at impressing her so far!). After work on the Wednesday, Bomber, Nathan and I jumped in the car and headed up to the big smoke, listening to Cat Stevens' classic *Father and Son*. We headed over to where the sports were at Perry Lakes Stadium, and I remember watching the netball, which brought back fond memories of playing the year before.

After the competition finished for the day, the school went back to their hotel, got ready and went out for tea. We didn't have a place to stay that night, so my mate PJ (who was in year 12 at the time) somehow got a key to a spare room at the hotel. As soon as the bus left to take the students out for tea, we drove into the hotel car park, snuck up to the spare room with a carton of beer, and started drinking.

Before long, we were drunk, which meant we weren't being as sneaky as we could have been, plus Bomber broke the light switch. The bus arrived back later and the teachers saw Nathan's car and knew something was up. We tried to hide, but we didn't have time to clean up the empty beer bottles and my legs were sticking out from under the bed, so we were pretty much done for. The teachers came in with a few of the student leaders and started going mad, The three of us were pretty drunk, and it quickly turned into a pretty embarrassing scene. We were told to leave in front of the whole

Country Week team and had to do the walk of shame to the car. Nathan and I got to the car quickly and hid under some blankets, but Bomber wasn't so fast and was told to go back and clean up the mess we left. Once he had removed the empty beer bottles and had his humiliation extended way too long, he made it back to the car with us still hiding. We drove off – with everyone still watching the comedy unfold. We made it back to Harvey, the shame of our antics hanging over our heads for quite a while afterwards.

It wasn't long before the four of us either quit or got sacked from the market gardens. I hate to admit it, but I was one of the ones who got fired. They were making us work Saturdays and I remember thinking "stuff that, weekends are my time!". So, I didn't turn up one too many Saturday mornings in a row and they got rid of me.

As luck would have it, a job opened up for me back at EG Green's as a labourer on the slaughter floor. I'm not sure why they gave me another chance, as my work ethic was still questionable, but perhaps they saw some hope for what I could become (or, my dad pulled a few more strings!). It was good to be back there and I believed my future was a lot brighter than it would have been as a celery picker.

At that time of my life, my goals were pretty simple – I lived for the next party. Jono was turning 18 in August, so that was firmly on my radar. The party was to be a combination celebration for Jono and two others, Janelle and Terrance, who's birthdays were also around the same time.

The party was at the old golf club (Scout Hall), which was just off the highway leading out of Harvey heading towards Perth. Back in the day, it was a great location for a party and we had plenty of memorable (or unmemorable, depending on how much was drunk!) nights there.

The night before the party, I went around to Jono's place to see how the build up was coming along. Back then, Jono was big on a game called fireball soccer, where you take a roll of toilet paper, light it on fire, and run around throwing it at each other. Jono had the kerosene and toilet rolls all ready to go when I visited him Thursday, the night before the party.

Another thing I was looking forward to was that a few of us had decided to try acid for the first time. Jono wasn't involved, but several others and I thought what better way to celebrate his coming of age than to trip out on acid? When the big night finally arrived, my friends popped their acid straight away, but I held back. I didn't want to be tripping out too early in case I made a fool of myself. By about 8.30 pm I felt relaxed enough to give it a go.

Not long after, one of the boys had climbed a pole in the middle of the hall and started acting like a monkey. Someone took him back to the games room and I remember thinking, "shit, I hope this is a good idea!". Suddenly, as if it was winter, a storm hit and everyone quickly moved inside the hall for shelter. However, since my trip had begun, I didn't realise it was pouring with rain and stood out there on my own watching the lightning in the distance, thinking about how cool it looked. Finally, Brad tapped me on the shoulder and encouraged me to come inside with everyone else.

I was in my own little world. People were talking to me, but their lips were moving that quick that I couldn't work out what they were saying. I made eye contact with Cozzo over the other side of the room, but realised he was in the same world as me! That made me feel a little better and I stopped freaking out quite so much.

The storm died down and soon after so did the party, until there was only myself, Cozzo, Terrance, Boo Boo and Nathan. We were all in a right state, with some of us now getting into smoking buckets between beers. We heard a loud bang in the hall sometime later and when we went to investigate, we found one of the guys laying on the floor. He had tried to jump a bin but landed flat on his back instead. We couldn't help him up as we were too busy laughing!

About 4 am, Nathan remembered he had to work in a few hours and needed to go home and get ready, so he and I decided to drive back to his parent's place in Binningup in the VP. Since I was not capable of driving at all, Nathan got behind the wheel. I was still tripping pretty hard, so it felt like the main street of Harvey stretched on forever. I remember watching house after house swish by, wondering if the trip would ever wear off. We finally got back to Nathan's house, where I fell asleep in the passenger seat while he went inside, got ready for work and drove away in his own car – leaving me asleep in mine.

Nathan's dad later came out to the car and woke me up, asking if I wanted to come inside, but his lips were moving so fast to me I couldn't work out what he was saying. Instead, I hopped over to the driver's seat and drove myself home, where I crawled into bed and stayed there all day. It took me a long time to recover from that night!

Due to popular demand, I decided to host another beach party at Myalup. This time, no one got belted up and chased through the sand dunes! A few locals did complain about the noise though – enough for the Harvey Reporter to take notice and do an article on Myalup no longer being a sleepy hollow due to the beach parties. I thought that was a bit of an exaggeration but nevertheless decided to halt the beach gatherings for a while.

A strange realisation happened a little while later, courtesy of a local drunk who was well known in town. I was out having a few beers one night at the Woky, and on the way back I bumped into him and he hit me up for a chat. He was a lot older than me and I didn't know him that well, but I was happy to stop and listen to him for a bit. While we were talking, he pointed to my friends and said that one day they were all going to go off and get married, then who would I drink with? He wasn't trying to be mean, just drunk chit chat, but to be honest it made me realise how simple-minded small towns can be.

I was only 19, and marriage was the last thing on my mind, but who was he to predict I was going to have a lonely life because of my face? Who was to say I wouldn't end up married like my friends?

I did get over that comment pretty quick, as I knew there was no malice to it, but I never forgot that night and the wake-up call of prejudice and assumptions that still ran through my everyday connections.

My pride and joy, my poor VP, nearly met its early demise one night when I was out and about with my mate PJ. We had been driving around Harvey and drinking, when he decided to go to a party of a fellow year 12 student. I dropped him off, then drove out to the Woky to see what was happening there. I was quite intoxicated by this stage, and by the time I got there, the tavern was closed and patrons were just standing around in the car park.

There were a few mates there, so I decided to take them into Bunbury to the clubs. They climbed in the VP and I put my foot down to make a big exit out of the car park, but instead I slammed straight into a pole and smashed in the front end. Unfortunately, the crowd loved it, but the VP didn't! I ended up staying at Jono and Butch's place that night and it would be another month before I got the car back on the road. More money down the drain!

After graduating from high school, PJ joined us out at EG Green's for work. By that stage, we were already good friends, but getting the chance to work together further fuelled our respect for each other. Heading into the busy season, EG Greens had two shifts going, night shift and day shift. Cozzo, Matt and a few of the other boys I knew ended up on nights, while PJ and I were on days. This meant we spent a lot of time together and that summer we formed one of the closest friendships I have ever had in this life. We did everything as a team.

As neither of us had a car at that stage, I was staying out at Normie's place during the week and borrowed his push bike to get around. After work, PJ and I would ride around Harvey on our bikes without a care in the world. We did get done by the cops a few times for not wearing a helmet, but we really didn't care back then. When it was hot, we would ride down to the local pool, shoot some hoops and go for a swim. We had our whole lives in front of us, but we weren't thinking too much about the future. Back then, it was all about the now.

In December that year, PJ turned 17 and had a party out the back of the Woky to celebrate. It was another great night. The following evening, another friend Michelle had a belated graduation party at her parent's house just out of Harvey. I don't remember a lot from that night, but as it turns out, Michelle took a great photo of PJ and I. This photo resurfaced five years later when PJs life was tragically cut short. Michelle sent a copy to PJ's mum, Leigh, who passed on a copy to me. That photo still hangs up in my house, a reminder of a beautiful friend who I miss very much.

By the end of the year, the VP was finally drivable again. PJ and I didn't need to ride our bikes anymore, although looking back now, that was kind of a shame. However, at that age, we were all for the easy option!

Just before Christmas, Two of the boys, Darren and Paul, had a joint party out at the Cookernup town hall to celebrate their 18th and 19th birthdays. As always, I rocked up with PJ in the passenger seat. I ended up blind drunk, falling onto the gravel and cutting my face open. Not a proud moment.

Eight

New Adventures Await

Heading into the new year, now 1999, I decided it was time to move out of home and live with Jono and Butch. They now had a place on Pinner Street and I was looking forward to the challenge of living away from mum and dad. I had relied on them a lot in my younger years, especially mum, but it was time to stand on my own two feet. I settled in quite well and the rest of the summer pretty much entailed getting drunk with my housemates and PJ.

A new mate also joined the crew at that time – Scotty. When he got going after a few beers, he was one of the loudest people I have ever known, but I loved that. He was always full of life and keen to have a good time. He joined our group of friends after he started dating Janelle.

Our school friend John had left to join the army, but he had come home to visit family so I took the opportunity to catch up with him at the pub one afternoon. While we were sitting enjoying our bevvies, another local guy joined us. He was drinking beer and Stone's(Whiskey) and egged us on to try it, so we thought, why not? Well, I don't even remember finishing the first one. The next thing I remember is waking up on Jono and Butch's front lawn. By this stage, about four hours had elapsed since I was drinking with John and it was about 5 pm. I picked myself up and headed for my new room to sleep it off. I heard John ended up in worse shape than I did, but I didn't get the chance to see him again before he left.

The summer ended with one of the best days of my life with my good friend, PJ. I had heard about these things called mystery flights, where you buy a cheap ticket (around $150) and they fly you to any city in Australia, spend the day there, then fly home that night. I thought this sounded like a great adventure and PJ agreed, so we jumped on board. We were so excited, especially after the travel agent rung a few days later to let us know our mystery destination was Sydney. I rang PJ straight away and told him we were off to the harbour city. We booked a couple of days off work and couldn't wait for the day to arrive.

Our trip was booked for a Tuesday, so when we finished work on the Monday we decided a beer was in order. We told everyone who came into the pub we were going to Sydney – they didn't seem to care, but we were excited! After our drink, we did a few laps of Harvey with the window down, waving to everyone and saying, "see you all when we get back from Sydney"! It was all innocent fun, and I miss it more than anything. After a few laps, I finally turned to PJ and said, "let's go to Sydney, mate!" and he replied, "let's go to Sydney, Whitty!".

We headed up to Perth and found PJ's nanna and pop's place. They were great people, very welcoming and more than happy for us to stay a night either side of our day trip. We decided to have an early night, as we knew we were in for an early start, and headed to the spare room at a decent hour. Before I knew it, we were up and getting ready as our flight was due to leave Perth at 6.30 am. PJ's uncle was living there as well and was charged with the job of driving us to the airport in my VP.

At age 20 and having never experienced much outside of the south-west and Perth, the flight itself was almost as exciting as getting to Sydney. PJ was a few years younger than I, so I could imagine how excited he was too!

Joel Whitwell

We finally arrived at our destination at 1 pm Sydney time and got a taxi to the city. We got dropped off at William Street and walked towards the harbour. We came to an intersection where a motorbike had been cleaned up by a car, but luckily no-one was hurt. I remember thinking, "shit, you don't see that in Harvey". Back then, digital cameras weren't around, so we had taken an old disposable camera. Just before we got to the harbour, we spotted a Porsche, so had to each take a picture posing with it. What a great start to our time in Sydney!

We made it to the harbour and I thought, "oh, so this is what all the fuss is about!". It was beautiful. We took a few photos of each other on the steps of the Opera House, then PJ went to find a phone booth (this was also pre-mobile phone days!) to ring his Uncle Mick, who lived in Sydney and was going to try to meet up with us for a beer.

We had a few hours to kill, so we climbed up to the lookout on the Harbour Bridge to take more photos. It was a magical day and a memory I will have for the rest of my life. This was before the days of the bridge climb, so we didn't get a chance to walk all the way up, but planned to one day.

The time came to find Mick for that beer, so we headed to a local area not far from the harbour known as 'The Rocks', filled with old-style pubs. We met at a place called The Orient. Mick was a great guy and I hit it off with him straight away. He knew a lot about the city and had lots of fantastic stories to tell.

I'm not sure if Mick or PJ noticed, but there was a bloke sitting at the bar on his own who kept looking at my face. I was a bit unnerved, but I was having such a great day that this became one of the first times I handled people staring at me and didn't get upset. I have such wonderful memories of this trip for the adventure it was with PJ, but also that it gave me the opportunity to overcome something I was going to have to live with for the rest of my life. If I wanted to travel, to work and to live my best life, then I was going to have to learn to deal with the staring. That afternoon at the pub with Mick taught me that I could do this. There are some days you look back on and realise were life-changing – and this was one of them.

Before long, darkness came and it was time to head back to WA. The flight was due to leave at 8.30 pm, so we finished our beers and Mick took us over to the airport. I suggested we miss the flight on purpose so we could stay longer, but we thought we had better not. On the way to the airport, Mick took us on a detour through the infamous Kings Cross. Seeing all the hookers and drug dealers scattered all over the place was a real eye-opener for me and was an unforgettable part of the trip – and what a way to finish up our experience in Sydney! We said goodbye to Mick, got on our flight and flew back to Perth knowing we had just enjoyed a day we would never forget. PJ's uncle picked us up from the airport and drove us back to his grandparent's place where we stayed the night.

The next day, we got up, had breakfast and drove back to Harvey feeling on top of the world. I dropped PJ off at the Woky, then drove out to Myalup to visit mum and dad to tell them all about our day in Sydney.

The next day, we were back at work and getting on with life, but we were both happy knowing we had done something worthwhile and could look back on with great memories. We talked about going on another mystery flight in the next year or so, but sadly, it never happened.

The next few months passed by without anything too eventful happening, but in May that year the school ball was on again. I decided I wanted to go once more while I had the chance. I knew a girl in year 12 named Adelle who I thought was a pretty cool chick, so I asked Lauren to hit her up and see if I could be her date – and she said yes! Lauren ended up going with a friend of mine as well.

My mate Matt's younger brother Adam also went to the ball as part of our posse. I already knew him through the family, but that year (1999) he was starting to have a bigger impact in my life and I had grown just as close to him as I was with his big brother. We all decided to head to the ball in style, so hired a Limousine for the evening. The ball was held at the Lord

Forrest Hotel in Bunbury again, so we asked the Limo driver to pick us all up from one house and drive together to the event, drinking lemon Ruskies all the way.

The ball was another memorable night, and the group of us headed back to Adelle's parent's place for the after-party. I met up with some of my other friends there, including Jono and Scotty, and proceeded to get a little loose (as we always did!). By about 5.30 am, I decided to pack it in and find somewhere to get some sleep. So, I went inside, found a bed and crawled in. Little did I know I had walked into Adelle's parent's room and was now lying in bed with them! They woke with a fright, understandably, but when they realised it was their daughter's ball partner, they took me into the kitchen for some coffee. Such lovely, understanding people! I was lucky to get away with that slip-up! However, the story soon got around Harvey and my reputation as a larrikin was growing further.

Nine

FACING A SHARP REALITY

About a week after the ball I received a letter in the mail informing me I was booked into Royal Perth Hospital at the start of June for another operation on my face. I was now aged in my 20's, so had moved on from the children's hospital. I knew I was due for another stint in the ward, but it all happened quite quickly – but thankfully that meant less time to get too nervous.

In this procedure, they were going to take some muscle out of the back of my shoulder and put it in my face to bring it out a bit more. It was a pretty big job. Jono and Butch could see I was freaking out a little, so being the good friends they are, they helped keep my spirits up and to stay positive. I had to book a few months off work, but EG Greens knew my history so it was no problem.

I also worked out with Jono and Butch that I would go back home to mum and dad's after the operation to recover. Little did I know then that I became so settled back at home, that it was a bloody long time before I moved out again!

The day before I went to hospital, I packed up my stuff, headed home then mum and I drove to Perth – something we had done together so many times already. I booked into the hospital, found my room and as usual I had to fast overnight, which meant no food or drink other than some water. This was common practice before any surgery, so I was quite used to it all.

The anaesthetist came in to visit that night to introduce himself and go over the process for the next morning. It was going to be a pretty big operation, so I was going to have to spend a few days in intensive care afterwards to start the recovery and ensure there weren't any major complications. Basically, I was going to feel like I had been hit by a truck, but I had come to expect that. The anaesthetist finished by reassuring me that I was in safe hands, then he left me to get some rest before it all began the next day.

I was awake early on operation morning and was feeling pretty nervous, but I just wanted it over and done with. Mum had booked into another room, but true to form she was back by my side early that morning to be there for me as she knew how I would be feeling.

Around 9 am the nurses came in to wheel me down to the operating theatre. Mum stayed by my side until she wasn't allowed any further, gave me a kiss (as she always does) and promised she would be there when I woke up. They wheeled me into the theatre where I met the doctors and nursing staff. I was scared as hell, even though I knew it wasn't anything I hadn't been through before. Soon enough, it was lights out and the operation was underway.

Many hours later I woke up in intensive care, but the next few days were a blur and it took me a while to get my bearings. I knew mum was always there though, and that is all I really needed. After a few days, she had to go home to take care of a few things and it broke her heart. I tried to be strong but couldn't help a few tears as she left. Mum rang Gran on the way home to tell her I was a bit upset and she even broke down – and she was meant to be the strong one in the family! Mum reckons all Gran could say was, "poor kid, he has been through so much".

After a few days, I was able to leave intensive care and go to my own room on the wards and Mum was back from her errands at home. I was so happy to have my own space to recover. As much as I enjoyed meeting new people, my face was really swollen and I was still wary of how people would react to me. Mum stayed with me 24/7 and I found in those quiet times laying in the hospital bed gave me the opportunity to reflect on my life and the people I had known.

I thought about my friend Douglas who had sadly passed away, and even though we had grown apart since being friends in childhood, it shook me knowing someone I had been so close to was gone. I thought about my friends back in Harvey and the adventure we had been on, longing to be out there on the beach with a beer in my hand again. Soon…

About a week later I received some get-well cards from my mates back home, which went a long way to lift my spirits. Even though I looked like the elephant man after this latest surgery, I knew my friends could see past my face and would always be there for me, no matter what. They reaffirmed that, in this superficial world, if I could just keep my positive attitude then I would be alright.

After three weeks in hospital, my mate Bomber celebrated his 21st birthday. He was one of my oldest friends, so I had to try to make it. The only problem was that I was due to stay in hospital for another week, but I pleaded with my doctor to discharge me early, and to my surprise – he did! But, there was one condition; I was not allowed to touch alcohol. So, I left the hospital Friday morning and by that night I was at Bomber's party and, true to form, was getting drunk. I kept a hood over my head to protect the side of my face and to try not to freak anyone out, because I was still looking like the elephant man. I was on antibiotics, so got drunk pretty quick and it ended up being a great night. I'm sure Bomber will always remember the great lengths I went to in order to make an appearance.

I was back living at mum and dad's and still had a few months off work, so it was a pretty boring time. Most weekends I would sit at home and wonder what everyone was up to. I didn't like to miss out on much, but knew I had to rest for my own good.

Sometime during those months I went to the local hospital to get the dressing changed that protected the spot where they took the muscle from my back. The doctor who saw me was only new to town and one of the first things he asked was what had happened to my face. I told him I was born like that and I will never forget the sympathy in his voice as he said, "oh, I'm sorry to hear that. It must be hard for you. People can be so cruel. It must really affect your social life." I was too tired to fill him in on my history, so I didn't say much but remember thinking, "if only he knew!"

The boredom continued for a little longer, the highlight of my days being waking up before 11am to watch *Home and Away* (the early years). After what felt like an eternity sitting at home, I decided to take a trip into Harvey one Friday afternoon to catch up with Jono and Butch. We played cards and had a few beers while they filled me in on what had been going on.

They told me that one of our friends was having a hard time and drinking a lot every night. He would work a few hours, grab a bottle of spirits, go around to another mate's place and polish off the bottle, then go home and pass out until rising some time the next afternoon to do it all again – all without skipping a beat. He was stuck in this same cycle day after day and I was shocked at how dark his life had become. Looking back, as his mates, we should have done more to help him through this stage, but we were young and didn't realise how serious it could have become for him.

My friends and I hosted an AFL Grand Final party in September that year. One of the guys organised a keg and we were all to chip in $30 each. Since I was still not back at work, I looked forward to social gatherings like this as it broke up the boredom and kept a bit of excitement in my life. The game started at 12.30 pm and, as expected, by quarter time we were all drunk. It was great being with my friends again after my stint in the hospital and then stuck at home, and even though my face was still pretty raw and swollen, my friends didn't treat me any differently to usual. That is a lesson I learned early on in life – there is no greater gift than friendship and, of course, family.

The day ended up being another blow-out and at some point later on, Normie, Nathan, my cousin Lauren and her friend Kristie picked me up from the party and we went camping up at the Harvey weir where I continued drinking until 6 am. It was a big weekend, and my legacy as a big drinker was further cemented, despite my recent surgery. I heard people over the coming weeks commenting, "how much can Joel Whitty drink?!"

By October, it was time to go back to work and I was actually pretty relieved of that. I was bored out of my skull, it was time to get back to my usual routine. The team was happy to see me back and treated me with respect, as by now they all knew about my face and what I had been through. Unfortunately, even after time off, my work ethic was still not what you would call optimal. I was just going through the motions, expecting to get paid good money for doing very little. I was still a few years away from improving in that area, but I am grateful EG Green's stuck by me!

It was also around this time that Adam was starting to play a bigger part in my life, especially after our fun at the ball earlier in the year. I had always known him as Matt's quieter younger brother – we had always got along – but he was now becoming a trusted mate as well. On New Year's Eve that year, Adam rang me to see if I wanted to go to Perth to celebrate. I was up for anything, so off we went – and only made it as far as Harvey pub! We had stopped in for a couple of drinks before continuing, but ended up so drunk so fast, that we decided to just stay there.

Ten

A New Century, A New Independence

The start of the year 2000 was an exciting time in my life, as my 21st birthday was coming up. True to form, I organised invitations to the celebration for half of Harvey. My birthday is the 14th January, but dad was coach of the Harvey fire Brigade and they had a demo on that weekend, so we planned the party for the weekend after.

The weekend before my party, another friend had a keg at his place and I turned up after having next to no sleep from partying with Scotty the night before. I quickly downed a bucket bong and that, combined with lack of sleep, just made everything extremely funny. Cozzo was there that night and he and I always seemed to gravitate to each other whenever we are in that state of mind. At one stage when everyone was just sitting around chatting, one of the guys, Luke, walked in and went to sit down but missed the chair and landed on his bottom. Cozzo and I laughed so hard, we almost fell off our own chairs! It was another epic night and I couldn't have asked for a better build-up to my 21st.

The big day finally arrived and as much as I would have loved him there, my older brother Kelvin couldn't make it as he had recently moved to New Zealand with his girlfriend to make a better life for himself. Around that time, they welcomed a baby girl into the family, named Alanah. This was a very exciting announcement and the first grandchild for my parents, who absolutely adore her.

On the day of the party, a few close friends turned up early for a few pre-celebration drinks. Before long, the others started arriving, including a surprise visit from my old friend Aggie. As far as we all knew, he was travelling around Australia, but had made it back without anyone finding out! He was good at doing things like that, turning up unexpectedly just at the right times – and my 21st was a great time! A massive cheer went up when he made his entrance.

Over 100 people ended up attending my party and it was fantastic to catch up with a heap of school friends I didn't see much anymore. Amongst the revellers were Scotty, Ken, Normie, Calvin, Troy, Tony, Brendon, and Marcus, as well as my younger brother, Frog. PJ and Cozzo were also of course there, as well as all the usual crew I had been hanging out with. The attendance list pretty well included all of the great friends who had come into my life over the 21 years and I was thrilled to be able to celebrate this milestone with them.

I ended up drinking until sunrise, then followed Calvin down to the beach where I almost drowned, so I decided a better idea would be to go back to the house and get some sleep. Just as I was drifting off, I felt someone tapping a beer on my nose. It was Scotty and he was ready to get going again! It was my 21st and I couldn't let him down…so we went back outside and continued drinking into the day.

As we were sitting there, we saw someone stumbling across the lawn – it was our friend Matt who had fallen asleep on the neighbour's trampoline! He sat down, grabbed a leftover can of Beam from the esky and got stuck into it. The day became pretty messy. At one stage, Scotty's girlfriend Jodie drove us in the VP to Bunbury for pizza, as she was the only sensible one not drinking. Back home, we all became pretty loud and the neighbours were starting to complain, so I was a little relieved when everyone finally called it quits. Thank fuck for that, I could finally get some sleep!

Compared to other years, this one was pretty uneventful. I continued working at EG Greens (just enough to hold my job, not much more!). Every second Friday night a DJ by the name of Nigel would play out at the Woky, and that became the highlight of my social life. A bus ran from the Harvey pub to the Woky, so we could start in Harvey for happy hour then catch the bus and dance the night away to DJ Nigel. PJ either met us there or came out to Harvey to start off as well. By this stage, it was over a year since our Sydney trip, but we still talked about it often.

So, that's how the winter of 2000 progressed. It was a pretty sure bet that you would find me out at the Woky every second Friday night, dancing the hours away to DJ Nigel's awesome beats, always drunk by the end of the night and quite likely also a little stoned.

It was on one of these nights out at the Woky that I came up with the grand idea of heading to Bunbury after to go nightclubbing. I was a bit wary of losing my licence, so one of my friends agreed to drive us as he had slowed down his drinking quite a bit. However, before heading to town, we needed to go back home to Mylup to grab some clothes to wear out. Unfortunately, we didn't make it that far. We didn't even make it to Mylaup.

While driving out on Uduc Road just past work, my trusted skipper nodded off for a second and that is all it took for him to lose control of the VP. The car skidded over the road and slammed into a pole. Thankfully, we were all ok, but our driver was pretty shaken up. We walked back to Harvey and went to the police station to report the accident. My friend blew in the bag and was thankfully under the limit, so all was ok there. I rang mum, who came to pick us up. She wasn't angry, but just thankful we were both alright.

It took a while for the insurance money to go through and at least a few months before I would get another car, so once again I had to rely on mum and dad, for whom I am forever grateful that they were there for me while I was trying to find my feet in the world.

One Eye, One Ear – No Worries

As soon as the insurance money came through on the VP, I invested it in a white VL Commodore. I was now onto my third car at age 21.

In October that year, I started on a shift pattern at EG Greens. That meant working three days, having two days off, then working two days and having three off. I now had to work some weekends, depending on where the pattern fell. Having seven days off a fortnight was great, but for someone my age, that just meant more drinking time. Cozzo was on the same shift as me, so we spent a lot of time together.

That year, I was also lucky enough to be set up to buy a house as an investment for my future, alongside my brother, Frog. The house behind mum and dads was up for sale, so dad put in an offer of $90k and secured it. Dad then sold it to Frog and I for a great deal, so we would have been mad not to take it. Looking back now, it was one of the best decisions I made for my future and I am grateful to dad for the opportunity.

Not long after, nanna moved into the house with Frog and I rent-free. After years living on the farm, it was time for her to make a change, so dad included her in the house deal. She was to stay there for as long as she wanted, which we were perfectly happy with, we loved having her close.

With nanna moving to Myalup, that meant the farm was empty. By October, my cousin Lauren was getting ready to move in there to look after it. One night after our shenanigans at the Woky, Boo Boo, Cozzo and I were looking for something to do, so I suggested we go out to the farmhouse. They were keen, so I rang Lauren and asked her to meet us there.

She had yet to move in properly at that stage, so there wasn't much furniture, but that didn't seem to bother Cozzo. I have never seen anyone fall in love with a house so quickly. He loved everything about that old farmhouse. We all decided it needed a nickname, so it became 'The Farmstay'. When we left that night, I had a feeling we would be back before too long.

I was right; the following weekend, Cozzo turned 19 and wanted to celebrate his birthday at the farm. We loaded the VL up with vodka – our favourite drink at the time – and headed out for a few big days of living it up at The Farmstay. Lauren had moved in so there was a few more pieces of furniture to make it comfortable.

From then on, The Farmstay became our hangout for the summer. Cozzo and I were either working or boosting up at the farm with Lauren (now known as Lozza) – and it was fantastic. We often had visitors come out as well, including Cozzo's younger brother Brendon and his mate Begga. PJ and Bandy, and Adam and Jono made a few appearances too.

Before we knew it, 2001 was upon us. Scotty knew some people in Melbourne, so he left just after New Year's to try his luck over there, but returned a little later that year. We were all still carrying on our over-the-top lifestyles, but unfortunately that lifestyle caught up with one of the boys. At the ripe old age of 21, a good mate of ours suffered a heart attack.

A group of them had been walking down the main street in Harvey after a party to get some food from the local bakery, when one of the boys fell behind. The others shouted for him to hurry up without much thought, but by the time they all finally made it to the bakery, he had severe chest pains. They did the right thing and called an ambulance, which ultimately saved his life, and he spent a few days up at Bunbury hospital to recover. I'd like to say he learnt his lesson, but the first thing he did when he got home was go to the pub. It is a bit scary, looking back now, at the lack of care we really had for ourselves.

In winter of 2001, EG Greens had implemented a day and night shift pattern and Cozzo and I ended up on nights. That wasn't much fun, but by the end of the year we were back on days again with our much-loved seven day fortnights.

Sometime around October, a group of us booked a hotel room in Bunbury and went out nightclubbing. That was the first time I ever tried dexies (dexamphetamine) and boy did it boost me up. I think I met everyone in Bunbury that night and was still going strong, chatting everyone's ears off, by the time the sun came up.

We got back to Harvey and were all chatting, when our friend Calvin's name came up, so Scotty and I decided to go visit him. Calvin had left Harvey the year before to travel around Australia, but while in Karratha Calvin had been involved in an accident. Sadly, he sustained blood clots behind his eyes as a result which left him visually impaired. I have known Calvin for years and was so saddened to hear about his accident, but of all the people I knew, he was the one with the courage and character to overcome such an obstacle. True to form, he has done just that.

I did hear that during the early stages after his accident he thought a bit about me and what I had overcome, and that gave him the inspiration to push on. That meant a lot, that my story could, in turn, help others who faced difficult times.

Scotty and I headed over to see him, and Calvin reckons he heard Scotty coming from a mile away, yelling out "Rodger Dodger!" Calvin was still in bed as it was early on a Sunday morning, so Scotty just walked straight in and told him to get up and stop being a rude prick! He obliged, and the four of us – Calvin, Scotty, Calvin's mum Christine and I – sat out the back and had a good chat. Well, Scotty did most of the talking, Calvin was pretty quiet, but I put that down to getting woken up by a couple of drunken mates early on a Sunday.

The year 2002 began with some new friends to add to the mix, including Jolly, Jarrod, Ash, Josh and Begga's cousin, Andrew. Matt quit his job at EG

Green's to spend some time out at his mum and dads place in Cookernup. After a few months not seeing him at work, I went out to visit and we ended up having a heart-to-heart out by his old treehouse. We chatted through numerous things that were bothering us both in our transition from teenage to adult life and it was great to hear Matt was getting on top of a few of his concerns. I drove home happy that I had been able to spend the afternoon with him and listen to what he had to say. I knew he would always be there for me, and vice versa.

Nothing else changed much for the rest of that year. I was still living it up and just enjoying my youth with a bunch of good friends doing the same. PJ and Bandy moved into a flat up on the highway, so I was spending a lot of time there. My life was living for the next beer, the next laugh, and it was such an innocent and fun time.

PJ bought himself a new car, a high-powered V8 Commodore. One night when we were all drinking at Begga's place, someone came up with the idea of driving out to The Farmstay. So, Begga, Cozzo, Bandy and I jumped in my car, while PJ and Chase (another friend from Harvey) followed in the new V8. I made it safely, but after a while we realised PJ hadn't turned up. Bandy tried calling and eventually PJ answered. He sounded very shaken up and said he had just had an accident. He had come to an intersection at high speed, but couldn't brake in time. The car had jumped a drain, slammed through a fence and ended up in a paddock. The two boys were both a little rattled, but thankfully neither was seriously hurt. Sadly, the car wasn't so lucky – it was a write-off.

PJs parents weren't happy he was speeding and driving dangerously, but they were relieved he was alright. We all should have learned our lesson that night, but I don't think we did. When I got home the next day, dad hit me up straight away.

"I heard that Paul had an accident last night and you were also drink driving!" he said. "What are you boys doing? Do you want to get yourself killed?" I just looked him in the eye, shrugged and said, "oh well, boys will be boys". Not the right response, but that is just how our attitudes were at that time. We were young and thought we were invincible, and even losing my license not long after for drink driving didn't have the impact it should have. How wrong we were.

In 2002, I also met Ryan who had begun playing for the Harvey Bulls Football Club the year before. He had become good mates with a few of my friends through footy, so I guess I was destined to join the pack at some stage. He became nicknamed 'Rhino', which was fitting for his big personality. He and I went out clubbing one night in Bunbury, but by around 3 am he had enough and drove home, but my night wasn't finished. At daybreak, around 6 am, I called him to see if he wouldn't mind coming back to pick me up. By the time he got to me, I had found a nice patch of grass to have a nap on and he couldn't see me, so rang to see why I wasn't standing outside the club as agreed. When he came back past, all he could see was my hand sticking out of the grass, and I have never heard anyone laugh as much as he did that morning! He helped me up, put me in the massive cruiser he drove around in, and took me back to Myalup where I found a more comfortable bed.

Thanks to my ever-struggling work ethic, taking days off whenever I wanted and never really working very hard when I did turn up, the bosses decided it was time for a stint in the tripe room. As anyone who has ever worked in the meatworks will tell you, the tripe room is the worst place to be stationed, by far. It is where all the stomachs from the cows are sent to be cut up, cooked then packed. It is disgusting, smelly work. So, my bosses decided this place would either make or break me – I would quit, or it would toughen me up and change my attitude for the better. Am happy to say I chose the second option – I'm no quitter!

The silver lining to my tripe days was that I met some of the most interesting characters I have ever known there. I guess anyone who was prepared to do that type of work is going to be a little different. One guy seemed to be drunk 24/7. He was only in his 40s, but the years of abusing his body added at least another 20 years to his appearance. Any chance he got, he would sneak off to his locker for another swig, plus he smoked like a chimney.

He was also one of the most negative blokes I have ever encountered – he just didn't like people at all. He thought the world was full of losers and basically, society sucked. He was not exactly inspiring to be around, but nonetheless entertaining at times. Perhaps it was the type of work we had been unfortunately assigned together, but for some reason or other, he seemed to have a soft spot for me. At that age, being liked by someone who seemed to hate everybody else was pretty cool.

I am happy to report that, at the time of writing this book, he had come out of his hole and cleaned himself up. I hope not too much damage has been done to his mind and body, but he has a much healthier future ahead regardless.

In that delightful tripe room, I also worked with another bloke that never failed to make me laugh. He was one of the funniest people around and always had a story to tell. He was a good judge of character and took great delight in impersonating other people, which always made me laugh. He had a different outlook on life to most other people I knew and was so tight with money, I swear he still had the first dollar he ever earned! Even though he had more money in the bank than he knew what to do with, he still came to work with holes in his socks and singlet. Classic.

While the work was pretty shit, spending time with these types of characters always made the day that much more bearable.

The end of 2002 was memorable for a few reasons. Firstly, after four years, Jono had finished his apprenticeship and was now a qualified electrician. He decided his future was not in Harvey, so set about heading off into the world to find his fortune. His first stop was Geraldton, which is about six hours north of Perth. I was happy for him, but knew I was going to miss him. Ever since our friendship had repaired after meeting up on the beach in Myalup back in 1997, we had spent a lot of time together and shared many laughs.

One of those great times was the AFL Grand Final day in September 2002. I was still going through a dexie phase, so had popped a few and went down to the bowling club with Jono where I proceeded to chat everyone's ear off and not take much notice of the game. We ended up in Bunbury nightclubbing with a few of the crew, including Adam, Luke and Mark. As often happened, I can't remember the end of the night, but I do remember waking up on someone's front lawn the next morning, lying there next to Adam. We had no way of getting home, so he rang Mark to come pick us up.

Unfortunately, not long after that night, it was time for Jono to pack his bags and set off on his new adventure. Before he left, we took the opportunity to catch up for a few more beers and sit around reminiscing about the past few years and all the fun (and mischief) we got up to.

His two favourite stories were from 2000, and he wasn't even there, but they are worth a mention. One evening, Boo Boo and I were walking the streets of Harvey after drinking all night. The sun was coming up and as we walked past the train station, I said, as a joke, that we should catch the train to Perth. The next thing I knew, we had sobered up and were in the city! It was already turning into a hot day and we couldn't get another train back to Harvey until 6 pm. It was going to be a bloody long day, and Boo Boo, who by this stage already had a bad heart, couldn't wait that long. He caught a bus back to his aunty's place and left me to wait it out. I finally got a train home and swore I would never do that again. I still made it back before Boo Boo though, who apparently took a couple of days to return.

The following Friday I was drinking with friends at Scotty's place and at sunrise the next morning, we were the only two still going. He came up with the great idea of catching the train to Perth to watch the Wildcats (basketball team), so off we went, only to realise halfway through the trip that they weren't playing until the following day. So, we got off the train at Pinjarra and started the long walk back to Harvey. Luckily, we got hold of Adam by phone and he came to pick us up. Thank goodness for mates, hey! Thankfully, I learnt my lesson after the second drunken train adventure and made sure I steered clear of train stations whenever I was drinking after that!

After catching up and retelling our favourite stories, it was time to say goodbye to Jono. He left a few days later and headed to Geraldton, and I was left wondering whether we would stay mates or drift apart – but only time would tell.

In December 2002, we celebrated PJ's 21st at the Woky pub. We all got pretty drunk, of course, and it turned into a pretty big night – but I wouldn't expect anything less from PJ!

Eleven

NOT 18 ANYMORE

By the following year, I was starting to feel a little flat from my full-on lifestyle and trying to stay 18 forever. It was all beginning to catch up with me. I had started catching up with Matt again after his time out from the party scene. Sometime in late January after another big drinking session, I told Matt I was thinking of taking some time off the booze. I was the happiest drunk you could meet, but I was starting to feel low mentally. Matt could somehow sense that and thought it would be a good idea to take a break. Also, since I was 17, I hadn't known what a quiet weekend was, so I wanted to see if I could lay low for a bit.

So, for six weeks in early 2003, I went cold turkey and learnt more about myself than I thought possible. I was still catching up with my friends on weekends, but while they got stuck into the beer and spirits, I stayed on water or soft drink. I wrote down a list of goals I wanted to achieve over the coming year. This was my first attempt at true goal-setting, and although these ones were a little half-hearted, it was a good start. After the six weeks, I was starting to feel better. I got my licence back during that little dry spell as well, so not only was I sober, but I was back on the roads too.

The end of March was Adam's 21st, so that was the end of my sobriety, but it was good while it lasted. That winter was pretty much the same as any other recent year; partying with friends over the weekend and working during the week, mainly in the tripe room with all the crazy characters it attracted.

Heading into spring, Adam told me he was planning a trip to the US and was due to fly out in October. I was a bit jealous, as it was a long-held dream of mine to see America, but at that stage of my life I wasn't as confident as Adam and not ready to travel just yet. I was sure I would one day though. I was going to miss Adam, but knew he would be back in a few months with some epic stories to tell.

On the 10th October we had Cozzo's birthday, so in the morning him, Luke and myself went for a drive to Bunbury. Adam's trip had inspired me, so while we were in town, I picked up a few brochures from the travel agent on America to read through. We decided to head back to Cozzo's and spend the afternoon drinking to celebrate his birthday. I was off beer at that point (maybe I should have picked up some brochures on Russia!) so I grabbed myself a bottle of vodka and got stuck into it.

Cozzo had moved house and was sharing with a guy named Darren and his girlfriend, PJ's sister Shazza (who later married). It was an old house on the outskirts of town, so it became known as 'The Ranch' and a bit of a party house. I was getting stuck into the vodka, then later in the afternoon Cozzo and I went out into one of the back paddocks to watch the sun go down. I was pretty drunk and started going on a rant about how the sun was going down on our youth and some of the best years of our lives were almost up. We had had fun, but I knew that time was almost over and we couldn't stay innocent and carefree forever.

I guess I could sense something that day in the paddock. What I didn't know was that behind that awesome sunset was a dark cloud.

Just over a week after Cozzo's party came the worst time in many of our young lives, as we suffered the horrific realisation of losing a close mate in a tragic accident.

The story began at the October Harvey Show, where the kids would flock to make themselves sick on lollies and rides, while the adults hung out at the bar and caught up on the gossip. For a small town, it was the event of the year and everyone looked forward to going to the Show. As a kid, I loved the chance to catch up with mates and go on as many rides as we could fit into the weekend, and as I got older, not a lot changed - except the bar became more of the focal point.

I finished work on the Friday and headed out to the Wokalup servo to meet Matt, who had begun working there part-time. After he finished, we went back to The Ranch for a few drinks before moving on to the Harvey Show.

We walked sideshow ally for a while then ended up at the bar, where I got right amongst it, chatting and catching up with people I hadn't had the chance to see much lately. I had a bit of a chat with PJ, but we were both doing the rounds so didn't hang out together for long that night.

One of the boys ended up getting arrested for swearing at a cop, but we thought that was about as eventful as the night was going to get. We went to a party down the road once the Show finished, then headed to Matt's parent's place in Cookernup for sleep. The following day around midday, Matt and I made our way back to the Show, where I gravitated towards the bar again after getting tired of watching Matt losing his money on the twenty cent machines.

PJ was working up at Worsley by this stage and was rostered on over the weekend, but had planned to head into the footy club to watch the band afterwards. I hung out at the Show until it closed at 5 pm, then moved on to the Harvey pub while I waited for the band to start at the club. I was, as you could imagine, fairly drunk, so I laid down on the grass by the pub with the intention of having a little sleep so I would be ok to listen to the band later. The pub owner saw me and offered to call a taxi, but I wasn't ready to go home and somehow managed to convince her I was ok to stay. Not sure how!

I made it to the club and met up with my mates, including PJ. The night is a bit of a blur, but one thing I do remember was throwing my arm around him and telling him that Sydney was just the start of our adventures. Next year, we were going to go to the USA together and I had already started doing the research. He seemed just as excited as I was.

After that, I called it a night in the back of Adam's car and slept it off until around 10.30 am the next day. I woke up feeling pretty seedy and had trouble finding my bearings, crammed into someone else's car and still at the footy club! I didn't have my phone on me, so I walked to the payphone on the main street in town to try to call a taxi, but I couldn't get through.

While walking back to Adam's car, wondering what I was going to do next, I saw someone walking across the oval towards me. It was the younger brother of one of the guys and we started chatting, but I could tell straight away there was something he was holding back. Finally, he said, "have you heard about PJ?" I hadn't had any human contact since the night before, so asked what he meant. I will never forget his next words:

> "He was killed in a car accident early this morning out on Hocart Road."

I felt numb. I don't remember much more of the conversation but headed back to Adam's car to try to get my head around what I just heard. My world had suddenly fallen apart, and not being able to find my phone was immediately so trivial.

Finally, a tractor pulled up and Adam jumped out. For a brief moment, I smiled at this unusual arrival, typical Adam-style, but that smile was short-lived as I snapped back into disbelief over the news. Adam and I started chatting and the topic of PJ came up pretty quickly. He had heard what happened, but no details, and the enormity of it all hadn't really sunk in for him yet either.

He gave me a lift out to The Ranch, although we were both really wary as out that way was where the accident had happened. He dropped me off and I walked into the loungeroom to find Cozzo sitting there on his own, sinking shots of tequila. I sat down next to him and all I can remember him saying was, "this is a massive reality check".

I finally got home and mum and dad were waiting, visibly concerned as they had also heard what happened. I put on a brave front and went straight to my room, where I was finally able to let go of my emotions. I curled up into a ball and cried my eyes out like never before. Nana arrived to try to comfort me, but it was no use, and eventually my well-meaning family decided the best thing they could do for me was to let me filter it all through myself. They turned off the light, shut the door and left me there with my tears for the next few hours. Laying there in the darkness of my bedroom, I thought about how PJ and I had first met six years earlier. I thought about all of the good times we shared and the memories we made over those years, especially Sydney.

I also started wondering about death and the afterlife, and where PJ was now. I must have eventually nodded off for a while because before I knew it, it was night time. I heard mum watching TV. I went out and joined her, Australian Idol was on and it happened to be the infamous episode where Dicko insulted Paulini about her weight, but that is not how I remember that night.

I took the week off work and spent most of it locked away in my room. Looking back on that time, the one regret I have is that I didn't have the courage to go and see PJ's mum and dad to offer my condolences and see how they were coping. As we go through life, I have learnt that we are all given tools to help us deal with difficult situations, but at that point of my life I felt enormously ill-equipped to deal with the heartbreak of losing a close friend and as a result, I didn't feel I had much to offer his suffering family either.

I was able to ring The West Australian Newspaper to put a condolence notice in with a heartfelt message to PJ, and mum and dad did the same. PJs funeral was to be held the following Friday and he was to be cremated at the Bunbury Crematorium followed by a wake at the Woky.

On Thursday night, I emerged from my bedroom to pick Cozzo up from The Ranch and head out to Cookernup to spend a few hours with Matt and Luke. Although I had needed time on my own, now it became important to reconnect with friends and support each other. We sat around chatting for a while, mainly just trying to make sense of what happened. Adam wasn't home as he was on his way to fly out for his big trip to the USA, and I wondered how he was feeling leaving in the midst of such a horrible time. But, we all agreed, PJ would have wanted him getting on with his life and enjoying this trip so long in the planning.

Cozzo and I headed back to Harvey around 9 pm, knowing the next day was going to be extremely difficult and emotional. Cozzo could see I was pretty quiet, and he offered to stay the night with me out at my parent's place. This meant a lot to me, and further reinforced the need for us to be there to support each other in this dark time.

Cozzo and I were pretty quiet the next morning as we got ready to head to PJ's funeral. Mum and dad were really supportive and made sure I knew they were there for me, but they were also glad I was going with friends and we were all dealing with it together. While I already had a close bond with many of the boys, a tragedy like this brought us even closer as we battled to understand how one of us could be taken so suddenly.

PJ drew a huge crowd at the crematorium, with pretty much the entire town of Harvey turning up to pay their respects. I held it together for as long as I could, but when they started playing Celine Dion's *Wind Beneath My Wings*, I lost it. Afterwards, lots of people came up and gave me a hug, knowing how close I had been to PJ, and I tried my best to comfort those around me as well through all of the tears.

After the crematorium, we all headed to the Hungry Hollow, a pub in Bunbury right near the beach. We drank to the memory of a great mate, before moving on to the Woky for the wake. I was amazed by the number of people here too, all sharing stories and reminiscing about PJ's life and what he meant to them. I was only halfway through my first beer when PJ's mum

One Eye, One Ear – No Worries

Leigh came up to see how I was coping. As I have said before, I have a few regrets about how I handled things in my younger years, and this was one. This poor lady had just lost her son, but went out of her way to see how I was doing. It should have been the other way around, but I just couldn't break out of my dark hole at the time.

As expected, it was an emotional night with everyone seeming to have a good time one minute, then crying and hugging each other the next – especially when PJ's favourite song, *The Gambler* by Kenny Rodgers came on. When we heard the intro to the song, a group of us formed a circle and one of the boys stood in the middle holding up a lit cigarette lighter. I remember thinking it was a fitting tribute, with the flame symbolising the essence of life and death. We are all burning brightly while we are here and when we pass, the flame is carried on by those people left behind. PJ may not have lived nearly long enough, but he certainly lived brightly.

By about 12.30 am I was totally spent after such an emotional day and headed back to The Ranch to sleep. The next day, dad picked me up and took me out to the Woky where I had planned to meet up with PJ's older brother Shaun to grab copies of the photos Paul and I took in Sydney. I had always planned on getting them from PJ himself, but never got around to it. I have since put them in an album so I can look back and reminisce whenever I want to reconnect with a friend lost too soon.

The next day I was back at work, ready to get on with life, as I knew that's what PJ would have wanted. But, little did I know that the tragic death of one of my best friends had triggered something inside of me, and that depression I had been harbouring for so long was about to be released in full force.

I had hidden how I felt for a while, even before PJ's passing. I had begun to feel sad on and off for no apparent reason, but I made sure no-one could see it. I would go to work during the day, then at night would jump in my car and drive down to the beach and park up, then just sit there for a few hours alone with my thoughts. I did this night after night, it was a very lonely time in my life. I was desperately trying to understand PJ's death and why he had been taken from us so young, as well as work out why I was feeling so sad. Up until that point in my life, I had never really been a deep thinker, but as I sat in my car during those lonely dark nights, I found myself contemplating life like I had never done before.

I thought about the way I was born and all the people I had inspired around Harvey and surrounding areas with my positive attitude. Was that the reason I was in this world? I wondered whether I would ever have the courage to travel like PJ and I had planned, and make friends all over the globe. There were quite a few tears shed during those long nights sitting alone in my car, but looking back now, I believe that's where I found myself and my purpose in life.

It was during my darkest hour that I found reason to live, but to get where I knew I needed to be meant a long road ahead. I came up with two major goals to strive for. The first was to improve my standing at work. Until now, I had been unreliable and always looking for an easy way of anything slightly challenging. I had been looked after at EG Greens because of my father's good name, but that's not how I wanted to be remembered by my workmates. I wanted to earn respect in my own right, just like dad had, and when my time came to leave, I wanted to be able to walk out the gate with my head held high. I knew I had a lot of work in front of me, but I was finally ready to start.

My second goal was to fulfil my dream of travelling the world. While I was alone during my nights at the beach, I decided the best way to overcome this depression (at least in the short term) was to keep myself busy and continue to live life to the fullest. Looking back now, I should have sought help, but at the time I was too stubborn. So, instead, my way of coping was to take a big breath and head back out into the party scene.

However, this backfired, every time. Unlike the old days where I would drink and dance until the sun came up, I had lost my stamina. I would be fine for a few hours and act up as the life of the party, but then I would reach one beer too many and I would become all emotional and break down crying. My friends were amazing though, and I was truly grateful for the love and respect those around me showed. But, despite the comforting of fellow party-goers, I always felt bad for distracting the attention away from the host.

I didn't want to deal with my depression, so whenever someone would ask how I was after one of my party break downs, I would just tell them that I wasn't coping too well with PJ's death. It wasn't a lie, but it wasn't the whole truth either. I was determined to work through it on my own.

One of the biggest lessons I learnt about life over the years is that while it is great to have a lot of friends, you only find out who the true ones are when you are at your lowest. At that stage in my life, Matt stepped up to the plate and proved without a doubt that he was one of those friends. He saw there was more to my moods than I was letting on, and he took the time to really be there for me. We had lots of great chats and heart-to-hearts. My older brother Kelvin also noticed something wasn't right, even though he had been going through a tough time himself. He would often come and find me down at the beach and just sit and chat, which helped us both a lot.

I have always had a very supportive family, but I realised just how supportive they were at that time. Dad came through in his own little way as well. He knew PJ and I had plans to travel together and at that stage in my life I wasn't confident enough to travel alone, so one night out of the blue he said if I would save up the money, he would come on an overseas trip with me. I was pretty happy to hear that, as it gave me hope and something to look forward to.

Twelve

THE WORLD TRAVELLER IS BORN

I had my heart set on travelling to America since I was very young, but the travel agent advised that there were strict rules in place regarding entry into the US, and since both of us had drink driving convictions, it would be a shame to fly all the way there to be told to turn around. So, we changed our destination to Canada. The tour we decided on started in Toronto, where we would then travel across the country over two weeks and end up in Vancouver. This included a three-day train ride, which I was quite excited about.

As I said before, this depression had a strong hold on me, but the trip gave me hope and something to aim for and hopefully pull me out of the darkness.

We booked to head away in July 2004, so for the first half of the year I had to keep working to save up while trying to keep my mood at bay. Sometime early in 2004, a new bloke started at Harvey Beef and as usual when I meet someone new, it wasn't long before he asked what happened to my face. I told him I was born like that, and I will never forget the sympathy in his eyes when he replied, "sorry to hear that. You must find it hard to get true friends."

I could understand where he was coming from and he was only trying to be comforting and friendly, but I still can't get over the small-minded attitudes of people. By taking just one look at my face, he decided my life must be a misery, but little did he know I was one of the most popular people around town! I had learned not to judge people so highly on looks, it is what is inside that counts – and I hope one day he does too.

In early March, Adam arrived home from the US and I enjoyed hearing about his overseas adventures. His stories made me all that more excited for my own trip just four months away.

Before long, July rolled around and dad and I boarded the plane for Canada. The first stop was Hong Kong where we had booked a night to break up the long flight. The flight went pretty smoothly and as we started the descent into our stopover, I was straining my neck from the middle aisle to try to see out the window. I was finally feeling that excitement that had been building since dad and I first decided to go away together. I was trying hard to take it all in, even before we had disembarked the plane! We got through customs and caught a taxi to our hotel. By this stage it was getting dark, so we opted to stay in and use our time the next day to explore the city.

The first thing we did the next morning was head down to the harbour, where I got some great photos. I took some awesome shots of the city skyline and I remember thinking how impressive it was, but then I thought back to that day PJ and I spent at Sydney harbour and how amazing I found that scenery as well. It dawned on me that no matter where in the world I travelled, any new experience would be inspiring and photo-worthy and I couldn't wait to find more.

Dad and I left the harbour and caught a taxi up to the Peak, a district in Hong Kong set atop a mountain, as I had heard it overlooks the entire city and I would be able to get more incredible photos. One of the first things I noticed when we got there was how much smog was covering the city, but it was still an amazing view. We spent about an hour up there just taking it all in; less than a day into the trip and my camera was already getting a good workout!

We caught a taxi back down to the city and had lunch, then spent the afternoon having a look around the Botanic Gardens. Before long, the day was drawing to a close and we had a flight to catch, so we went back to our hotel, grabbed our stuff and headed to the airport on the bus. We were on to the next exciting part of our trip – the long flight to Canada! It was about 17 hours on the plane, but thankfully I was able to sleep most of it.

We landed at Toronto Pearson International Airport at about 10 pm then caught a taxi straight to the hotel. We stayed at the Chelsea Hotel, right in the heart of the city. As it was quite late by the time we checked in, we decided to get some sleep and start exploring the next day.

We both got up and had some breakfast early in the morning, but dad was still getting over the long flight so he decided to go back to the room for more rest. I felt ok, so headed out into the warm Toronto summer to start having a look around. I walked a few blocks from the hotel when I came across the Hockey Hall of Fame, a museum dedicated to the history of ice hockey. I had heard the sport was big in Canada, so I decided to check it out. It wasn't until I was inside that I realised how big it was! The Canadians really love their hockey, along with baseball, but I guess it is the same sort of affection for sport that we have for Aussie Rules football! I didn't venture too far from the hotel on that first day, and after the Hall of Fame visit I took a leaf out of dad's book and headed to the hotel to sleep off some of the jet lag.

The next day we met up with the tour group to take a trip out to Niagara Falls. As it was basically the first day of the tour and none of us had met before, we pretty much sat in silence waiting for the bus. I wasn't very confident about meeting new people back then. I noticed most of the people on the tour were older, with a few younger couples who looked like they might have been on their honeymoon. For me, the main purpose of this trip was to get a feel for what life was like away from my comfort zone and see if travelling was really my thing, as much as I wanted it to be. If I came away from this trip with just one new friend, then that would be a big positive, but I was happy enjoying time with dad too.

As we boarded the bus I met the tour guide, Ken. He was aged in his early 50s and seemed like a friendly guy. The trip out to Niagara Falls took about an hour and a half, and once we got there, we got our tickets and waited in line to board the Maid of the Mist. That was an incredible experience. It is not until you are standing at the base of the falls that you realise how powerful they really are. Once again, my camera got a decent workout!

Unfortunately, we didn't have time to explore the caves behind the falls, but all in all it was a great day. On the way back to Toronto, we stopped at a souvenir shop where I met a nice young Canadian girl working there. She was more than happy to have a chat and even let me get a photo taken with her. It struck me how friendly the Canadian people were, especially as I was still quite shy and had my obvious differences. They certainly left a positive impression on me and I began to realise how valuable travel could be to growing my confidence again.

We got back to the hotel mid-afternoon and since it had been a big day, I decided to have another early night. I was doing pretty well – a few days into the trip ad I had hardly touched a beer, but I had a feeling that wouldn't last. Dad, on the other hand, was feeling refreshed, so decided to head down to the hotel bar for a few drinks. We still had a couple of free days in Toronto before we were due to board the train and head over to the West Coast, so before I fell asleep that night, I thought about what I wanted to do to make the most of my time there. I decided I wanted to check out the CN Tower, explore the Toronto Islands and have a few beers at the Hard Rock Café. If I did all those things, I knew I would leave the city satisfied.

The first quest off my list was beers at the Hard Rock Café. I headed down there the next evening and grabbed a spot at the bar and ordered a drink. I started chatting to a few locals who informed me there was a band due to play that night. I got pretty excited and was looking forward to hearing some local music. Unfortunately, probably due to still feeling the effects of a long flight and a few beers, I blacked out and can't' remember anything until I woke up in my bed at the hotel the next morning. I was relieved I made it back safe, but disappointed I didn't remember seeing the band – that's if I even stayed long enough to watch them at all as I had no idea what time I left. But, I couldn't dwell on that as I still had places to go and things to tick off the list during my short stay in Toronto.

I got up and put myself together and headed down to the harbour to catch a ferry to the islands. This place was magical, with views across the entire city skyline and the CN Tower overseeing the buildings below. It was awe-inspiring, and I managed to take yet more photos for my memories later. A friendly stranger took a photo of me standing by the water with the city in the background. I spent a few hours there, just wandering around, and I remember thinking how nice it would be to have someone to share that moment with. Little did I know that eight years later I would get another chance to visit the Toronto Islands, this time with a great friend I met in Europe.

It was late in the afternoon when I made it back to the mainland and seeing as I had a pretty big one at the Hard Rock Café the night before, I decided to call it a night early.

I rose early the next morning and after breakfast, dad and I walked a couple of blocks to the CN Tower. There was a big line of people that day, but before I knew it, we were up in the clouds looking through the glass panels at our feet to the city below. It was an unreal sight – and a little unnerving! After an hour or so we headed back to the hotel as we had to be up early the next morning to re-join the tour for the train ride across to the Rocky Mountains. Our time in Toronto was over, but I had seen the three landmarks on my list and was excited to head onto the next adventure.

The tour group met up at Union Station the next day and our tour guide, Ken, was his usual friendly and cheerful self. He came up and shook my hand with a big grin and asked if I enjoyed my time in Toronto. Once we had all caught up, we boarded the train and as I watched the outer suburbs of the city roll by, I remember thinking I would love to visit again one day (little did I know that, less than a year later, I would be back!).

The next few days on the train were pretty uneventful, besides looking out at the amazing scenery whizzing by. We passed many lakes and prairies, which were just spectacular to see. There was a small bar at the back of the train, but surprisingly I didn't take advantage of all that drinking time I could have had! Perhaps I had in my mind that I would never get the chance to see landscapes like this again, so I wanted to take it all in – sober.

We made a few quick stops along the way, including Edmonton and Winnipeg. I remember getting off the train at Edmonton station and seeing as it was only a quick stop, I only really had time to take a photo of the city skyline in the distance. It was a bleak and windy day, so I was happy to get back to the warmth and comfort of the train carriage.

We finally arrived at the Rocky Mountains after three long days of travelling. It was a great experience taking the train, but three days was long enough! When we disembarked, I was immediately struck by how spectacular the mountains were. We were in Jasper, a resort deep in the heart of the Rockies, where we would spend the night before heading out the next day on a coach.

After checking in to our hotel, dad and I went for a walk and had a quick look around. It is a bloody beautiful place, that is for sure. That night, quite a few people from the tour were having a few drinks down at the hotel bar and, seeing as I hadn't had the chance to really get to know everyone yet, I decided to head down to join them. Dad came along too. They were a pretty decent bunch of people and, as usual, Ken was right there amongst it, knocking back the beers and having a great laugh with everyone. I quickly joined him.

As the evening wore on, I realised it was still light outside, which I wasn't used to seeing in Australia. An English girl who I had been chatting to took a photo of me with the sun setting behind, shining over the Rocky Mountains. It was a beautiful shot, unforgettable, even though I was quite drunk by this stage! Back inside, dad decided to call it a night but I kicked on until one of the older guys from the tour helped me stumble back to my room.

The next day we were told we had an extra night in Jasper, so after sleeping off my hangover, I went out for another look around and a bit of shopping. That night I headed back to the bar, but no one else from the tour was there this time, perhaps they were all still recovering from the night before! I figured I may as well take the opportunity to mingle with the locals and further push myself out of my comfort zone, which was one of the main objectives of this trip.

I saw a bloke sitting at the bar drinking on his own so went up and introduced myself. He took one look at my face and turned his back to me. After trying to talk to a few more people and getting pretty much the same response, I realised this wasn't going to be my night and headed back up to my room. Dad was still awake and asked why I was back so early. I just told him I wasn't really into it. It took me a while to get to sleep, but I was determined not to let one bad night ruin my whole trip, which had otherwise been an awesome experience.

We boarded the coach the next morning and arrived in Banff early afternoon. To me, it looked a lot like Jasper, but bigger. We all went out for tea that night while the Canadians entertained us with a good show. The following day it was off to Kamloops, where after checking in I ran into Ken the tour guide in the hotel lobby. He asked if I was keen to join him for a few drinks at a pub down the road. I thought about it, probably all of two seconds, and agreed to go with him.

We took a spot at the bar and started knocking back the beers. It was great to spend time with him and get to know him better. We chatted for hours and a good friendship really started to form. Years later, Ken told me in a message that the night was one of his favourite from that trip, which meant a lot to me.

The next morning we were off again, bound for the metropolis of Vancouver. As the group gathered, Ken and I looked at each other as we both knew we were hungover and he gave me a big wink as if to say, "thanks for a great night, mate". We arrived in Vancouver where Ken took us on a tour of the city; Stanley Park, Lions Gate Bridge, Canada Place and so on.

We eventually checked into our hotel and while in the lobby I noticed a flyer on the wall advertising a live show that comedian Jerry Seinfeld was putting on that night in Vancouver. As I had seen him on TV and a few of my friends were big fans, so I thought it would be a great show to catch live while I had the chance. As luck would have it, I was able to buy a ticket from the hotel and seeing as the hall was only a few blocks away, it all fell into place.

Just before showtime, I got ready and headed to the hall. It was packed and Jerry put on a great show that left me really impressed. He looked small from where I was sitting at the back, but at least I got to see him live. Unfortunately, my lifted spirits took a little dive on the walk back to the hotel. I passed an alleyway where upon peering down, I could see people sitting and sleeping under blankets and it dawned on me that no matter how beautiful a city appears to tourists, every one of them has a dark underbelly. The homelessness saddened me, as I hadn't really seen anything like it back home.

The next day, the tour group gathered once more and we all took the Skyride gondola up to the top of Grouse Mountain for a day of exploring. This ended up being a great day and I couldn't have asked for a better end to my first ever overseas trip. To top it off, Ken asked dad and I if we would like to join him for a few drinks at a local bar that evening – his shout. We quickly agreed! Later that afternoon, not long after we got back to the hotel, dad and I met Ken in the lobby and off we went in search of a pub. We quickly found one and had another great session on the beer. I found out a little more about Ken's life; he was living in Hawaii when he wasn't running tours and seemed to have seen and done a lot. He was a really interesting character.

Ken must have bought a few beers, because I couldn't remember how I got back to the hotel. The first thing that came to me after our night out was waking up in our room to the phone ringing. It was Ken wanting to know if I wanted to go down the pub for lunch and a quick beer before we were due to head to the airport for the long flight home. At first I thought, "aren't we already at the pub", then I started to come to my senses and realised it was the next day and I was in bed!

Never one to knock back such an invitation, I told him I would clean myself up and meet him down at the same pub we were at the night before. Dad had a bit to do before we were due to leave, so I went on my own to catch up with Ken one last time. After our drink, I thanked him for a great trip. Being the person he was, he returned the gratitude for my friendship and offered his postal address in Hawaii so we could stay in touch (as Facebook was a shadow of its current popularity and I wasn't that great at email). We said our final goodbye and as I walked back to the hotel, I remember thinking I would see him again one day.

Dad and I caught a taxi to the airport and boarded the plane for Australia. It was the same route we had taken on the way over, including a couple of hours stopover in Hong Kong. To pass the time, I listened to music for most of the way. There are certain times in your life where you will hear a song for the first time that really touches your heart and can influence what you do with your life. On that trip home, I first heard one of those songs. It was called *I am* by Kid Rock.

> *Have you seen the northern falls*
> *Or the midwest seasons changing*
> *A Montana storm*

Or a warm Kentucky rain
Have you heard the love that sings
Over the inner city sidewalks
Have you risen above
All that leads to hate

These lyrics really resonated with me, especially after the trip to Canada, and became the inspiration for me to "go see all that I can see". I also had a lot of time to think on the plane. I mulled over what I had been through in the months preceding the trip; losing PJ, struggling with my own mental health, feeling lost. I also thought about the depression and that this trip with dad was a step in the right direction to overcoming it.

I thought back to earlier in the year when I was back in hospital for another operation, that time to get some work done on my chin. It was the first operation I had after PJ left us and as they wheeled me into the theatre, I wasn't as nervous as I usually got. I felt that, in some strange way, PJ was with me and gave me strength – or I like to think so anyway.

Thirteen

Oh, Canada…

Before I knew it, the plane landed in Perth and we were heading back to real life in Myalup. A few days later, I was back at work, which didn't help my lowered mood. But, I was determined to hang onto the inspiration Canada gave me to move onto bigger and better things.

Work was back on a seven-day roster and this meant I missed the AFL Grand Final party for the first time in over 10 years. The funny thing was, I actually didn't care this year.

However, some things don't change that easily. I still loved knocking back the beers on my days off, especially on the weekends. One of these weekends in December, Luke, a friend of my cousin's, had a 21st party at the Binningup Country Club and the whole crew was invited.

It was a big night and later on, as a couple of my friends were walking out, they saw a drunk person passed out in the garden. As they got closer, they started laughing because they realised that drunk person in question happened to be me! They helped me up and took me back to Luke's dad's place where we continued the party. Another fun night was had by all.

Not long after, I went to a party in Myalup with Adam and Rhino. I didn't know the girl who was hosting, but the other two did so I just tagged along. There was a massive beach ball on the living room floor and at one stage, I booted it and smacked the host square in the face. Oops. Everyone started laughing, but she didn't see the funny side of it. Luckily, I managed to talk my way out of it and was allowed to stay.

Heading into 2005, things were really starting to change. Adam had enjoyed his time in America and was planning on heading back overseas to work and try to make a go of life in another country. He had been chatting to some people online in Toronto, Canada, who played in a local Aussie Rules football team. Each team in the competition was allowed to recruit a few fellow Aussies, so Adam thought that would be a great way to meet people and settle into a new life abroad. He got organised and left Australia in late January.

Before he left, I told him I still had some holidays saved up from work so if all went well, I would be seeing him over there shortly. Rhino was also planning to move to Canada to work and play footy. He was due to leave in April so I decided to try to plan it so I could head over when he went. I got my holidays approved through work and less than a year after my first trip to Canada, I was going back!

I was getting very excited, but then in early March Adam rang me with some news. He told me things weren't working out for him over there and he wanted to come home. Even though I was a bit shattered that my holiday plans were up in the air (as he was the main reason I was heading back to Toronto), I had to be there for him as a friend. He didn't need to prove anything to anyone and had already shown great courage and fortitude in my book by at least giving it a go.

However, by the end of the conversation, he seemed to have a change of heart and decided to stick it out for a bit longer, but if things didn't improve, he would head home. As luck would have it, he ended up going out for a few beers that night, met someone who gave him the number of a person looking to hire and he subsequently scored a job moving furniture for a legend of a bloke I would soon have the pleasure of meeting – Lloyd. He would be on the road a lot, moving furniture across Canada and sometimes down into the US – what a great way to see the world!

With Adam now employed and settled, my trip to Canada was back on so Rhino and I booked our ticket for late April. The night before Rhino and I flew out was my old school friend Ken's wedding, so it was an absolute certainty that I was going to board the plane with a hangover. I also caught a dose of the 'flu for good measure.

The following night, mum and dad took me to the airport where I met up with Rhino and off we went on another new and exciting adventure. This time I took a different route to the destination. Instead of stopping over in Hong Kong, we had to transit in Sydney, Los Angeles and Minneapolis before finally reaching Toronto. It was a long journey, with Rhino elbowing me every so often because he thought I was sleeping too much, but we made it.

While on the quick stopover in Sydney, I remember looking out the windows at the city skyline and feeling a sort of nostalgia as I thought about that great day I spent in the city with PJ. It felt so long ago. When we got to LA, we had to go from the international airport to the domestic airport. I got to walk on US soil – just like I had dreamed of – but that moment was short-lived as we took off into Canada.

Adam met us at the airport and had a taxi waiting out the front with a few cartons of beer in the back for us to indulge in on the way to the hostel. We were staying at the Canadiana Backpackers in downtown Toronto. After we checked in, we found another five cartons of beer on ice waiting for us – Adam had really outdone himself and turned it on for our arrival!

We got stuck into the drinks, then headed out to a bar where we met Andrew, a fellow Aussie staying at the same hostel. I was still exhausted from the long flight, and, coupled with a few too many beers in quick succession, it wasn't long before I had another blackout.

One Eye, One Ear – No Worries

The next thing I remember was waking up in our room with the cleaner standing over me yelling abuse. She wanted to show me something, but as I climbed out of bed, I realised the sheets were wet and smelt of urine. I had pissed the bed, but worse was to come. As I followed the cleaner down the stairs, I noticed a trail that was obviously more urine that led to a massive puddle on the floor smack bang in the middle of the guestroom. It didn't take me long to work out what happened. I had gotten so drunk, that not only had I pissed the bed, but in my confused state I had hurried off in search of a toilet, only to find myself back in the guestroom where I finished the deed. I didn't realise it was humanly possible for someone to pee that much!

The cleaner was really unimpressed by my achievement, and as soon as Rhino and Adam woke up, we were told to vacate the premises. Not the best start to my second visit to Canada! The boys thought it was hilarious, but I was having trouble seeing the funny side as we walked the streets of Toronto on that warm summer's day, me still in my wet underwear. We eventually found another hostel and before I even had the chance to shower, off we went in search of another bar.

We found a nice place and started another drinking session that would continue for the next few days. I am pretty sure we hit every bar in downtown Toronto, just chatting to the barmaids and living it up. After a few days, I finally hit the wall and staggered back to the hostel to get some much-needed sleep. Adam and Rhino stuck it out at the pubs for a bit longer, before finally joining me back at the hostel.

The next day, Adam had to go to work for a few days, which was probably a good thing as we all needed to dry out. Rhino and I decided to do a bit of sightseeing; things normal people would do when travelling. We went back to a few of the places I had visited the year before, such as the CN Tower and Hard Rock Café. We saw a homeless person laying in a cardboard box, which reminded me of the night in Vancouver when I saw the homeless people in the alleyway and realised how different this city was to back home.

When Adam came back from working, we decided it was a good time to find somewhere more comfortable to stay, seeing as the other two were going to be living in Toronto for a while. We found a nice apartment to rent out in the suburb of Ishlington.

Rhino was going to play footy with Adam in the Canadian league, so one afternoon when they headed off to training, I decided to head downstairs to the bar at the hostel before we left for the apartment. While sightseeing with Rhino, I had purchased a Kid Rock CD and asked the barman to put it on and play the song that had inspired me on the plane the year before – *I am*. I listened to the lyrics while sitting at the bar getting happily drunk.

We eventually moved out to Ishlington and recruited Andrew, the Aussie, to move in with us to help with rent costs. One night we went out for tea and I met Adam's boss, Lloyd. He took a shining to me and called me his bregend (brother legend). On the weekend I went out with Adam and Rhino to watch them play footy and met their teammates too; Floppy, Hendy, Sean (Cable Guy), Mike, Disco Bill and Rob (RV). They are all great guys and I have stayed in touch with a few of them over the years. After the game, we all got on the booze, which gave me a chance to get to know them a bit better. They couldn't believe how much we Aussies liked to drink!

About three weeks into the trip, Adam scored another job with Lloyd. This one required them to go cross country and deliver a truckload of furniture to Prince Edward Island (PEI). He asked if Rhino and I wanted to come along, and I thought it was a great idea to get away from the bars and the temptations of Toronto for a while and see a little more of the countryside. We left Toronto one afternoon in May in Lloyd's semitrailer. At night we slept at truck stops or, if Lloyd felt up to it, he would sometimes just drive through the night. The man was a machine and had lots of great stories to tell as we manoeuvred our way across Canada.

We passed through the prairies and, just like I was a year ago, I was amazed at how beautiful the Canadian landscape was. To get to PEI, we had to cross the Confederation Bridge, which at the time was the longest in the world. It was quite a surreal experience. There wasn't much to see once we got to PEI, just some colonial houses and if I remember correctly, I don't even think they had a pub on the island (which probably was a good thing!).

We finished the job, stayed overnight, then early the next morning we left for the long drive back to Toronto. I was amazed at how flat the landscape was on the east compared to the west, which included the Rocky Mountains. On the way back, Adam was asking about my previous trip to Canada with dad. He noticed something I hadn't thought about before – Canada is one of the longest countries in the world, but on two separate trips by bus, train and semi-trailer, I was able top transverse the whole country from coast to coast, from Vancouver in the west to PEI in the east.

It was almost the weekend, and Rhino and I were contemplating getting dropped off on the outskirts of Montreal to spend the weekend there, but in the end common sense prevailed and we decided to go the whole way back to Toronto. We arrived back in the early hours of Saturday morning and, after sleeping most of the day, we decided it was time for our week-long dry spell to come to an end – so we headed out for a night on the town.

We began at a local bar downtown called Maddison's and started drinking in the outside area. We noticed two pretty Canadian girls sitting at the bar across from us and Rhino dared me to go over and start a conversation with them. I'd had a few beers by then, so I wandered over and I must have done alright because after the bar closed, we all ended up back at their apartment where we sat around drinking beer and blowing bubbles until the early hours. Around 4 am, I got up to go to the toilet and duly passed out in one of the girl's beds. Maybe in my drunken state, I thought she may have joined me later, but unfortunately when I woke up a few hours later, it was daylight and I was alone.

I met up with Adam and Rhino in the lounge room and off we went up to Floppy's cottage on the lake to continue partying and to finish off the long weekend in style. Or, in Adam's case, sleep off a hangover!

By the time we got back from the cottage, I only had a couple of weeks left of my trip, so to get the most out of my time there, Rhino and I caught the bus down to spend the day at Niagara Falls while Adam was at work. We took the Maid of the Mist boat ride, which brought back great memories from my previous visit with dad.

After the boat, we went to the Hard Rock Café for lunch and a beer. With Rhino and I together, anything could have happened, but luckily things didn't get too crazy and it ended up being a nice relaxing and enjoyable day. We caught the bus back to Toronto late in the afternoon for a quiet night.

A few days later, Adam, Rhino and I went up to Actan to stay with Rob (RV) for the night. Rob was very welcoming and although he wasn't a drinker himself, he seemed to enjoy spending time with us crazy Aussies. After dinner, we went to a local bar where we played up and got kicked out – sorry Rob!

It was not long after, probably well into the final weeks of the trip, when Adam and Lloyd had a job to move a load of furniture to a place just outside Montreal and asked if I want to come along to check out the city. This was a great opportunity to see a little more of Canada before I headed home.

To get from where Adam and Lloyd were working that day, I decided to hitchhike into the city. I was picked up by a truck driver, who not only had plenty of stories to tell, but in the 45 minutes it took to get to our destination, he also filled me in on the details of his recent divorce! He dropped me off in the heart of the city and off he went on his merry way. He was just one of those characters who pass through your life for a reason – and it seems his reasons were to get me to Montreal and to scare me off getting married any time soon!

After a bite to eat, I wandered around the city, trying to decide what I should do to make the most of my day there. As I was walking along, I looked up and saw a sign that read, 'hot girls' and I assumed it was a strip club. This got me thinking that while I was growing up, I knew that with my face being the way it was, I was just happy hanging around with my mates, drinking and having a good time. I didn't worry too much about girls and that included never really being interested in going to a club like the one I had just found on my travels. I'm not sure why this was, because as long as you have money at these places, the girls don't care what you look like, but up to that point in my life I just wasn't into it.

But, seeing as I was on holidays, I decided to see what all the fuss was about as the neon sign lured me in with it's 'hot girls' promise. Even though it was the middle of the day, the first thing I noticed was that it was really dark inside. A few near-naked ladies were on the stage pole dancing, while a couple of older men sat at the tables. I took a seat at the bar and ordered a beer. It wasn't long before a lady came up and asked if I wanted a lap dance. She was scantily clad, so I downed the rest of my beer and said, "hell yeah".

She took me upstairs to a private booth. I had heard that in Perth you are not allowed to touch the girls, but here in Montreal you could touch them anywhere except between the legs. So, for the next hour or so, I had a great time. I remember thinking, "why did it take me so long, plus a journey to the other side of the world, before I finally stepped inside a place like this?!"

I was in the middle of appreciating her boobs with my mouth when the phone rang. Talk about awkward timing. It was Adam and he asked how I was going, and I told him I was doing a bit of 'sightseeing'. He told me that they had finished the job and gave me an address to meet them. So, I had one last suck of her boobs, said goodbye and made a hasty retreat.

I caught a taxi to the address Adam gave me where he and Lloyd were waiting. I jumped in the cab and as we started the long journey back to Toronto, I couldn't wipe the grin off my face. Adam took one look at me and said, "you've been sucking tits all day, haven't you?" Bastard. How did he know?! Lloyd thought my escapades were awesome and started giving me high-fives. One thing was for sure, I was never going to forget my first visit to Montreal!

It was the final week of my trip and as I was due to fly home the following Tuesday, we decided the weekend needed a 'going home' piss up at Maddison's. Adam invited the footy players, so after the game on Saturday we went back to the apartment at Ishlington and commenced another drinking session that was destined to become legendary by the end of the night. It started off with just myself, Adam, Rhino and Andrew, but within a few hours, the outside balcony and most of the apartment was packed as the footy crew started turning up to join the festivities.

Around 8 pm, we all made for the subway to head to Maddison's where we were due to meet up with a few more players. Unfortunately, one of the boys was only 20, which is under the legal drinking age in Canada, but after a bit of smooth talking by Adam and Rhino, he was allowed to join us. We all congregated out at the back bar. The beer started flowing, and before long we were singing the club song and making a bit of noise. I was wearing a Canadian shirt and everyone started signing it as a memento. It ended up being a massive night, as after Maddison's we went to a Chinese restaurant for an early morning feed. They set up at a table, but we were all too drunk and our party was quickly told to leave after Rhino started a massive food fight.

A few of us ended up back at our apartment. Just before the sun came up, I passed out in my bed, so I missed more of the action. While I was out to it and the sun was coming up, one of the footy boys thought it would be a good idea to start throwing empty beer bottles over the balcony onto the pavement below. After a few goes at this new game, the noise somehow set off the fire alarms in the apartment. One of the others, who was asleep on the couch at the time, jumped up, grabbed a screwdriver and disconnected the alarms so he could go back to sleep. The bottle-thrower then quickly left the apartment after realising the nuisance he was being.

Later that afternoon as we sat around nursing our hangovers, we had a bit of a laugh but then wondered what the ramifications would be, as we were sure we hadn't heard the last of the evening's performance.

It was my last day in Canada, so that night Rhino, Andrew and I went out for a few quiet beers. We were still hurting from the night before, so we didn't last long before calling it a night. The next morning while Adam and Rhino were at work, there was a knock at the door. I opened it to a gentleman standing there with a stern look on his face. He must have been the owner of the apartments and he told me that what happened with the fire alarms was a very serious matter and they were looking into it. He also mentioned that the cops may become involved and to expect a visitor in a few hours. This was a good time for me to pack my bags and head to the airport. I did ask Adam about it later and he told me not much came of it, thankfully.

I was soon back into the swing of things in WA. One day, not long after my trip, I was in downtown Harvey and ran into a man named Frank. He was a local who had lived next door to gran for many years and was very close to her. He had heard through the grapevine that I had just recently arrived home from overseas and suggested it might be a good idea to take my photos around to show gran and tell her all about my trip. As it turns out, gran wasn't with us for much longer after that day, so perhaps it was fate that led me to talk to Frank and push me to go around and see her.

She was so happy to see me and enjoyed hearing all about my trip, although I was careful not to include a few of the crazier moments! She did comment on the number of times I had a beer in my hand in the photos though!

It was only a week or so after that our beloved Gran passed away. She was well-known in town and everyone was devastated. There was a huge turnout for her funeral and it warmed my heart to see the love all these people had for her. I didn't think much of it then, but during that time both of my brothers had girlfriends and of course dad had mum, so every other male member of our immediate family had a female standing beside them for support. I had to stand alone and – as always – stand strong. The wake was at the fire station, and while we all shared stories of gran, we drank.

Fourteen

Lend Me An Ear?

A few weeks later there was another 21st birthday celebration to attend, this one up at the old golf club. I ended up getting so drunk, I collapsed on the table in the middle of the hall and food and drink went over everyone standing too close. Not a proud moment on my behalf, but in the spirit of the night, everyone thought it was pretty funny. The next thing I remember was waking up on the couch out at The Ranch.

As I always do after I have a blackout from drinking, the first thing after waking was to check I hadn't lost anything. Wallet – check. Phone – check. Car keys – check. You beauty, they were all there! But, when I went to lay back down I felt a sensitive spot on the side of my head so I put my hand up to rub it. Oh shit…where was my fake ear? I ran into the bathroom to have a look and, sure enough, my ear was missing.

In a panic, I jumped in my car and went around to Josh's place, as I remembered I had been boosting up with him at the party, but he hadn't seen it. I went around to a few other places and it was the same story – no ear to be found. I was due to attend a friend's birthday out at the Woky that afternoon, but without an ear on my head, I thought I had better call it a day and went home instead.

I was a little worried about losing my ear, but was quietly confident that it would show up, given that I was the only one (from what I knew) in town with a fake ear! I was still a bit self-conscious about it, but as luck would have it, Harvey Beef had a shutdown that week so I didn't have to go to work. So, I sat at home for the next five days, waiting for the phone to ring to say someone had stumbled across my ear, but it never did.

By Friday, I decided I couldn't stay home and hide from the world forever, so I went for a drive out to The Ranch. I went into the front loungeroom where Cozzo was and we started chatting. About five minutes into the conversation, Cozzo suddenly stopped and said, "oh by the way, your ear is on the mantlepiece, someone found it and dropped it off here yesterday". You little beauty, I was so happy, I could have kissed him! I jumped up, did a little dance, then proceeded to get drunk to celebrate.

The following few months were quite uneventful, until the first week in October when I had a week to forget – but unfortunately, I never did. On the first Saturday of the month I drove out to Yarloop to catch up with my mate Mullsy. After spending the afternoon down at the local pub, I remembered I had heard there was a band playing at the country club in Binningup, which is a coastal town not far from Myalup. I knew a lot of people who were going to be there, so after suggesting it to Mullsy, we began debating who was going to drive. I decided to let Mullsy drive my car as he was slightly less drunk than I was, so with Kid Rock's *I am* (still my favourite song) playing full volume from the CD, we headed for Binningup.

We parked the car, went inside and as usual, I knew nearly everyone there and the night started off really great. Mullsy doesn't often leave Yarloop, preferring to drink instead at his local pub, so it was good to get him out and about too. The crew at Binningup were more of a surfie crowd, but back then I mingled with everyone. Mullsy in his black bogan shirt stood out a little, but a few people remembered him from school and he soon slid into the crowd.

As always, the night turned into a bit of a blur, but I vaguely remember towards the end of the night a kid about 10 years old standing staring at my face. I was having such a good night, so I raised my glass to him and said, "cheers!". He then turned and ran off. About 10 minutes later as Mullsy and I were walking out to the car, a big bald man of about 40 years old came running up. He got right up in my face and started abusing me, saying I had commented something rude to his son. A lot of people were still hanging around outside the country club and saw what was happening, so a few came running over.

A bit of a crowd gathered around as this guy continued to abuse me. I kept trying to tell him I didn't say anything mean, but he was having none of it. He grabbed me in a chokehold and I remember thinking, "shit, this is getting serious". A few people who were standing around rushed in and started smashing at his arms to make him let go of me, which he eventually did, but the abuse didn't let up even as he was walking away.

As we jumped in the car and drove away, I tried yelling some abuse of my own, but it was a bit weak on my behalf. I knew he couldn't get to me anymore. I was shocked by what had just happened and couldn't quite get my head around the whole situation. We drove back to Mullsy's place to sleep it off and I kept shaking my head and commenting, "what did I say?!"

The next morning I woke up on Mullsy's couch and, remembering what happened, I felt quite low. I hadn't caught up with the Binningup crew for ages and I felt ashamed they had to witness the whole scene, even though I was confident I hadn't done anything wrong. It certainly wasn't the best start to the week, which only got worse.

After a few bad days at work, I heard from my old mate TC so when I finished up on Thursday I headed up to his place for a few beers. Later on that night we ended up out at the Woky where I ran into Fishy. He was another of the town larrikins who was friendly with my dad and although he had his quirks, I always enjoyed his company. Sharing a beer and a laugh with him would really improve my week, I thought. How wrong was I.

The skimpy working behind the bar asked straight out what happened to my face, but before I could say anything, Fishy decided to answer for me. His answer, in my eyes, was extremely rude and offensive, and all I could do was shake my head and say to him, "I thought we were mates" before storming out. TC followed close behind.

While driving home from work the following day, something came over me and I just started crying my eyes out. I had to pull over to the side of the road and let the tears flow for a good ten minutes. It had been a tough few weeks and it had all finally got the better of me.

Fifteen

Moving Out Of The Fog And Into A New Year

A few weeks later, Jono rang to let me know he had a wedding to attend down my way and was going to spend a few days in Harvey to catch up with family and friends. Relaxing and chatting with my old friend over a few beers really helped lift my spirits and, since he was based up in Geraldton these days, I made a promise that I would come up and visit him one day.

I had thought a lot about Fishy's comment and decided to get his number and ring to apologise for my reaction, as I don't believe in holding grudges. He also apologised and explained that he only meant his comment as a joke, but it came out wrong and he could see why I got upset. That phone call put my mind at ease and I felt a lot better after that.

Looking back over the year, 2005 had, in whole, been a pretty positive year for me. There had been ups, such as the highlight by far – Canada – and downs – losing gran, losing my ear and losing my patience with unkind people. A new year was just around the corner.

Heading into 2006, I was pretty happy with where I was at that stage in my life. I was still spending a lot of time at work with all the colourful characters in the tripe room, so that meant plenty of laughs. The travelling I had done opened my eyes to the world, and I was excited about where my future could head.

One of my friends had broken up with his girlfriend after a long-term relationship, so I was hanging out with him more. This friend, Ash, was four years younger but we had been mates for five years now after first getting to know one another at a mutual friend's place for a Friday night bender. We had got up to a bit of mischief involving golf balls and trying to saw down a tree, and I saw a kindred spirit in this young guy.

I was driving down the main street of Harvey one morning and as I drove past Ash's place, I saw him kicking a football by himself. Five minutes later we were both perched on a bar stool at the Harvey pub, where we remained for at least the next eight hours. In the early days of 2006, meetings like that became a regular occurrence.

Around February of that year, my friend Caliopi was back home in Harvey to visit her family for a week. She had been living in Melbourne for a few years. One Friday night, I joined a gathering of her friends at her mum and dad's place for drinks. I met her boyfriend Sean and he seemed like a great bloke, so a little later on he and I headed down to the local pub. While we were there, we met up with Charger and after a few more drinks, he came back to Caliopi's. Charger was a bit crazy back in the day, but he knew Caliopi from school and still hung out with some of her friends, so she didn't mind at all (in fact, she thought it was funny we had found him at the pub and brought him back with us!).

By midnight I was quite drunk, so – as I often did back then – I started the long walk out to The Ranch. After a while, Caliopi started to get worried I may not make it, so with her mum driving, they headed out towards The Ranch expecting to find me passed out on the side of the road along the way. Eventually, they saw me walking in the middle of the road, so they pulled over and told me to jump in. I walked over to the driver's side window, grabbed the steering wheel and told Caliopi's mum that I would steer while running alongside the car.

Caliopi was beside herself laughing, but her mum was a little more worried about my suggestion. They finally got me into the car and took me out to The Ranch safely. Caliopi never forgot about that night and we still joke about it from time to time.

Mid-2006 I finally decided to honour my promise to Jono and booked a ticket to Geraldton for a few days. I was pondering whether to fly, which would take one hour, or drive, which would take about six hours. I couldn't be bothered driving for that long, so I took the flying option. Jono was there to meet me at the airport with another ex-Harvey bloke called Dino, who I was soon to discover was quite a character!

We detoured for a quick tour through the town on the way back to Jono's place, which reminded me a bit of Bunbury. As soon as we got back to the house, we cracked a beer and got stuck into it, ending up on a pub crawl sometime later.

The following day it was Dino's turn to drive us through a town tour, and this one was more thorough than the day before. They showed me a lot of the landscapes and took me out to neighbouring Greenough, where in 1993 a young man murdered an entire family – mother, son and two infant daughters. That senseless act of brutality sent shock waves across the state at the time and it felt surreal to be in the area where these horrors took place.

My stay in Geraldton was short and the last night in the town quite relaxed. We went to a local pub for tea, then grabbed a carton and went back to Jono's where we spent the rest of the night just reminiscing and chatting about old times. The next day it was back home and – unfortunately – back to work.

Sixteen

The Next Big Adventure

After my experiences in Canada, I had well and truly caught the travel bug. I yearned to see more of the world and had saved up enough holidays again to start planning the next trip, but I just needed to work out where I would go! I was still in regular contact with Adam in Canada and he told me he was planning on stopping over in Thailand on the way home. He loved Thailand, and at that time in his life, said it was his favourite place in the world. He suggested it could be a good idea for me to meet up with him and spend a few weeks there together before he made it all the way back to Australia for a visit in November. I figured, why not?!

I booked my ticket for the first week in November and started to get excited for what was hopefully going to be another awesome experience. But, before I left, I had a duty to have a few more drunken misadventures and create a few more stories for the people of Harvey to talk about!

There was a young lady of around 19 years old who worked in the office of Harvey Beef that I had developed a bit of a crush on. One weekend in August while I was drinking at the pub, I heard there was a party up at her mum's place that night. I decided to attend with the hope that sparks may fly and I may get lucky. As it turned out, sparks flew alright, but they weren't of the romantic kind. I ended up getting so drunk that she asked me to leave and I woke up a few hours later passed out on an electric fence on their property, so I'm guessing I didn't get too far. The fence quickly brought my attention back to reality as the volts exploded through my body and I took that as a sure sign I needed to move on. I decided against pursuing a relationship with this girl, after all, I didn't want to get burnt again!

Thailand

November rolled around pretty quickly and before I knew it, I was boarding the plane to Bangkok to meet up with Adam. It was an eight-hour flight and the whole way there I was a bit nervous, as I was still a fairly inexperienced traveller. I had heard a bit about Thailand and the corruption and danger it had become known for at that time, but I had faith in my travel companion to know what he was doing … but I just had to find him first. We hadn't worked out a designated meeting place in the gridlock that is the massive Bangkok airport and I spent a good hour walking through the sea of people, trying to spot Adam - which was akin to finding a needle in a haystack. I started to panic, but then, just like Moses parting the red sea, the crowds gave way and Adam appeared. I was rather relieved.

We hailed a taxi and had the driver drop us in the heart of Bangkok. Our destination was Khaosan Road, which hosted a strip of bars and guest houses that were popular with tourists. We checked into one of the guest houses (funnily named 'Wallyhouse') and found it to be a bit of a dump. The squalor was unnerving to me, but Adam was always on a budget back then and was quite comfortable staying in those sorts of places as he believed living a bit rough was the best way to experience travelling. He was the more experienced in these things, so I just went along with it.

After we checked in, we went for a walk to explore Khaosan Road. I was amazed by the number of people, mostly tourists, but I also noticed a lot of little local women walking through the crowd selling large wooden frogs. The women would rub a wooden stick up and down a frog's back, which would make a sound that echoed all down the street. I knew I wanted to buy one, just not on the first night.

We walked to the end of the street where we bought chicken sticks from a street vendor. They tasted awful, but it was not a fancy restaurant, and I'm not sure what I expected. After that, we decided to head back to Wallyhouse and call it a night.

One day early on in the trip, Adam and I took a bus out to Pattaya beach. On the ride, we met a guy who called himself Trip Daniels and claimed to be an aspiring musician. He looked to be in his later forties, so I'd say he left his run at rock stardom a little late. But, he seemed like a nice bloke and was easy to talk to.

While we were walking down the main street of Pattaya, we passed a line of bars where ladies were calling out and giving us the wolf whistle. As Adam was a lot more experienced than I, he could spot a ladyboy from a mile and began pointing them out to me. I couldn't believe how many there were! We checked into a hostel then went for a look down at the beach. It felt a bit surreal to be on a beach in Thailand.

After the beach, we had a look around the local markets where I showed how much I had to learn about travelling. I wanted to buy a towel and found one at a stall run by an elderly lady. As soon as I picked it up, she held out her hand and told me it was 20 baht. I thought the price tag said six baht, but figured it was wrong, so I handed her the 20. Adam was standing nearby and saw the whole thing, and started pissing himself laughing that I had just been ripped off by an old lady. No wonder she had a big smile on her face when I gave her the money! To this day, he still reminds me about the towel.

With my new purchase in arms, we headed back to the hostel and got ourselves ready for a night out in Pattaya. This place was nothing like I had ever experienced before. There were ladies of the night everywhere, and no matter where you looked, there was some action happening, it was all very loose. We walked into a bar where we bumped into our muso mate, Trip. He was taking a keen interest in the band that was playing and I have to give him credit where credit is due, he really wanted his dream to come true.

After a few beers, we left Trip to his music fantasies and went to another bar. I still couldn't get over how much the place was crawling with prostitutes. Ladyboys are an enigma to me, but hookers I can spot! As a single man, I was tempted to indulge, but there are some things I won't include in this book. I will leave it up to your imagination as to how the rest of my night panned out.

The next morning we headed back to Bangkok and the comforts of Wallyhouse to meet up with a guy named, Scott. He was another Aussie who lived with Adam and Rhino for a while and played footy with them in Canada. Scott was heading back home around the same time as Adam and one very drunken night just before they were due to leave Canada, Adam suggested Scott drop by Thailand and meet up with us for a few days.

As soon as Adam had sobered up the next morning and remembered his proposal, he regretted it as Scott was a bit of a handful on the booze – but it was too late. Scott had already changed his ticket!

He was a bit different, this bloke, but we got on well. I got chatting to him and he seemed alright, but back then I tended to get along well with everyone. We spent that first day checking out a few of the streets around Khaosan Road and Adam bought a new phone. Scott was still a bit jetlagged from his flight so wasn't up for too much that first day, so around mid arvo we went back to our rooms for a couple of hours sleep before heading out for the night.

Once the sun went down, we were rested and ready to go. We started our evening at a restaurant/bar with a nightclub upstairs packed with tourists. We sat down at a table and ordered our drinks – my favourite part of any holiday! Adam and I drunk the local brew, Chang Lager, while Scott ordered a bottle of bourbon. Bad mistake. After a few drinks he was quite pissed and boy, could he dribble some shit! The lies just seemed to pour out of his mouth quicker than the bourbon went in. It turned into a pretty drunken night, but Adam and I made it back to our rooms, whereas Scotty passed out on the toilet at the restaurant. So, I guess it was coming out of both ends that night!

The following morning we spent some time taking the piss out of Scott for his drunken misadventure, then went to book a tour out to see the bridge over the River Kwai the following day. Since we had to leave for the tour early in the morning, we tossed up whether to have another night out or concede to an early one so we could properly enjoy the tour (and actually make the bus). Common sense prevailed…and we decided to tear up Khaosan Road once again.

We went back to the same restaurant and this time ended up at the nightclub upstairs. As was the case with the previous night, Scott was drunk after a few bourbons, so I spent the rest of the night trying to avoid him and the shit he kept spilling.

The next morning, we made it to the tour but, as expected, were nursing massive hangovers. We boarded the bus and headed to Kanchanaburi, located 128km to the west of Bangkok. It was a three-hour journey and I started wishing I hadn't drunk so much the night before. We finally made it to the town and from there we caught the train that took us over the bridge. It felt surreal to be in such a historic place, made famous by the movie, *Bridge Over the River Kwai*. So much history took place around these parts, things we can't even imagine nowadays. Later on, we had the chance to walk onto the bridge and I was able to take some great pictures, which are still safely tucked away in my massive collection of photo albums.

After our bridge walk, we visited the nearby Kanchanaburi War Cemetery, where around 7,000 POW's who sacrificed their lives in the railway construction are buried. We then spent an hour or so at a gift shop, just checking out the memorabilia.

A Brazilian guy named Davi was also on the tour, travelling with his sisters. We got chatting and he seemed like a cool guy. After lunch, we visited a tiger enclosure where Scott got a photo between two tigers on chains. He was so close to them, I wondered why they didn't attack him, but I'm guessing they were drugged up to the gills. Scott was sober that day, so he was back to being a half-decent human being. Davi thought we were all crazy – and that was on one of our booze-free days! We finished up the tour by spending a few hours at a picturesque waterfall, just relaxing and continuing to nurse our killer hangovers as best we could. The scenery was incredible, and I took so many photos!

It was soon time to begin the long journey back to Bangkok, and we arrived on Khaosan Road around dusk. Davi asked if we wanted to meet up with him for tea at a bar later on and we said we would try to make it, but as soon as we got back to our rooms, Adam and I crashed out. Scott made it, so I hope he didn't bore them with too much of his shit. Davi was due to leave Thailand the next day so it is a bit of a shame we couldn't make the effort, but we were just so worn out.

We slept most of the next day but seeing as it was Scott's last day in Thailand, we decided to have another night out. We went back to our local – the restaurant with the club upstairs – and got stuck into it. We met a Scandanavian guy who was drinking something out of a small bucket and straw. Whatever it was, it must've been potent because all of a sudden, he jumped up on the table and casually started walking from table to table while startled onlookers stood gawking.

The restaurant staff began standing at the foot of the table he was on, trying to coax him into stepping down, but he just looked down at them with a huge grin on his face. I thought it was one of the coolest things I had ever seen and when we went up to order our next drinks, I pointed to the bucket and said, "I'll have whatever he is having!"

The following morning was pretty much the same; another day, another hangover. Scott had poked his head into our room sometime that morning to say goodbye, but Adam and I were both so out of it from the night before, it felt like a dream and we barely acknowledged him. By the time we started to come good later on, he was well on his way back to Australia.

In an attempt to kill our hangovers, we decided to go for a walk to explore a bit more of Bangkok. We didn't get too far when we walked past a five-star hotel that had a pool out the front with two hot chicks lounging about in bikinis. Seeing as it was hot and muggy that day and we were still both suffering, we thought we had stumbled across the gates to heaven. In we went and as soon as I dived into the water, I felt so refreshed. I mustered the courage to go and talk to the bikini-clad girls, but they weren't interested in hearing my story about the Scandinavian we had met the night before and told me of their disinterest in no uncertain terms.

As I strolled back to where Adam was sunbathing, I wondered about some girls who complain about men being pervs, but when you make an attempt to chat and get to know them, they brush you off. So, I spent the next few hours chatting to Adam and occasionally just having a perv rather than worrying about small talk.

Chiang Mai

Since we had been in Thailand a week, Adam and I thought it would be a good idea to leave Bangkok and make the most of our time in the country, even though it would have still been fun to spend the rest of the trip drunk in Khaosan Road. So, the following day, we caught an overnight train up to Chiang Mai. As soon as we boarded, I was relieved to see bunk beds so we could sleep through the journey, rather than riding it out uncomfortably upright.

I quickly grabbed the top bunk and settled in for the ride. It was dark by the time we pulled out of the Bangkok Central Station and as I laid on the bed looking out of the window at the blackened streets and alleyways, I thought about all the people out there and wondered what their stories might be.

As we travelled further out of the city and into the countryside, I found I had a lot of time to think. Finally, I fell asleep and drifted into dreamland, before waking the next day to the delicious smell of freshly cooked bacon and eggs as the train caterers served breakfast.

Around mid-morning, we stopped at a local village for an hour so just to break up the long journey. Adam and I went off in search of some locals to meet and came across a father and son playing pool on an old worn-out pool table.

As I took in my surroundings, I realised they must also live in this dusty old place which was a world away from the comforts we enjoy back home. I also noticed that even though they didn't have much in the way of possessions, the Thai people were always smiling and seemed happy. This taught me a lot about human nature and the incredible power of gratitude; the poorest can have the biggest smiles and seem at peace, while the richest amongst us can come across as sour and unhappy. I guess it all comes down to what is in one's heart.

Adam and I were lucky enough to be invited to play a round of pool with the father and son while we enjoyed a beer and a chat with these two amazing human beings. Before too long though, we had to head back to the station to continue our journey north to Chang Mai. Saying goodbye was hard and I even saw their smiles fade as we walked away, but I knew they would be back to their beaming selves in no time.

Once back on the train, Adam and I had a heart to heart and he too was touched by how happy they seemed, despite not having much. He told me that one day when he had a bit more money, he'd love to return and buy them a brand new pool table. That was Adam, always thinking about how he could help others and I'll always be proud to call him a mate.

It was just on dark when we finally arrived in Chiang Mai and went off to find a place to stay. After searching for a while, we found a nice comfy hotel not far from the town centre. We checked in and decided to get separate rooms this time (I think Adam needed a break from my snoring!).

The following day we had breakfast washed down with a few beers then went for a walk around the city. Chiang Mai is a city in mountainous northern Thailand that dates back to the 1200s. Its old city area still retains vestiges of walls and moats from its history as a cultural and religious centre. It is also home to hundreds of elaborate temples, including 14th-century Wat Phra Singh and 15th-century Wat Chedi Luang, adorned with carved serpents. It was fascinating, but after an hour or so having a look around, we did what we usually did back then and found a nice little bar on the main street and settled in for an afternoon of drinking. It was a nice spot with an awesome view of a few temples across the street.

After a few beers, I got chatting to a fellow Aussie at the bar who told me his story. I listened intently as he told me about his battles with drugs and his plan to come to Thailand to stay with his brother to get clean. Sadly, he had found the lure of heroin over here too and before long was back to being heavily addicted. That led to him having a massive falling out with his brother and he was now homeless. He had spent the past few months wandering around Thailand like a lost soul as he didn't have enough money to buy a ticket back to Australia. I took pity on him and bought him a beer, but at the end of the day, he had made his choices and his part in my story only lasted a few beers. I do hope he finally found his way and his own story took a positive turn.

Laos

The following day, Adam was keen to get on the move again. He was quite adventurous back then, the kind of person I would eventually become, but I was still in practice! We tossed up about heading to Vietnam for a while, but finally settled on Laos. We packed our bags and headed for the bus station, and were soon crossing the border into Laos. When we got to customs, I remember thinking how different it was to anything I had seen so far. It was very relaxed and so dusty. We filled out an immigration card and went through into this fascinating country. One of the first things I noticed was how untouched Laos was by modern demands, stress and pace of life that we experience back home.

From the station, we took a short bus ride to the capital, Vientiane. While on the bus we met another Aussie who was backpacking and surfing his way around South East Asia, Tim. He had masses of red hair and was a real go-getter, so we called him 'Big Red'. By the time we arrived in Vientiane, he was one of us – at least for the time being. Vientiane is a city with an estimated population of 760,000 people and is located on the banks of the Mekong River, not far from the Thailand border.

We were dropped off in the heart of the city and set about finding a backpackers or hotel to stay at. While walking around, I started to take in my surroundings. As I mentioned before, it was really dusty everywhere we walked and, for a capital city, I couldn't believe how behind the times they were; not an ATM or EFTPOS machine in sight. It was a world away from our state capital, Perth.

Despite the banking difficulties here, Adam had managed to secure us some cash and he gave me some to spend while we were here, I just had to pay him back once we returned to the world of ATM's in Thailand. Big Red decided to tag along with us and after a while we found a nice little hotel to stay at on another (yep, you guessed it) dusty street. After checking in, Adam and I in one room and Big Red in another, we found out there was a street market not far from the hotel. Around dusk and after we had settled into our rooms, we headed out to the market and spent around an hour browsing the stalls. Adam bought a few gifts for his family, but I was a bit lazy in that regard. Once it turned dark, we decided to head back to the hotel and call it a night.

The following morning we said farewell to Big Red, who was off to continue his travels. We planned to hopefully meet up again in Bangkok when I arrived back there in a week or so. I was amazed by some of his travel stories, especially when he told us he had been all over Vietnam on a scooter. I looked forward to hopefully hearing more over a few beers later on.

Big Red left us in a trail of more dust and Adam and I went for a walk to find a restaurant for lunch. We found one a few blocks from our hotel and I remember looking up and noticing what looked like live wires hanging dangerously close to the outside dining area. Perhaps we would eat inside here! When we walked inside, I couldn't believe what I saw. Instead of tables, they had comfy mats with pillows so you could really kick back and enjoy your meal.

After finishing our fried rice without falling asleep, Adam came up with the grand idea of hiring a motorbike so we could explore the outskirts of the city. I wasn't too sure about it at first as my uncle had been killed in a motorbike accident when I was only five years old, and I had been fearful of them ever since. Adam, on the other hand, had grown up with motorbikes, so I eventually warmed to the idea. Adam hired the bike, I jumped on the back, and off we set on another little adventure. We rode out of the city and into the surrounding countryside. Laos and it's expansive farming land reminded me of home in Harvey, but it was also very different.

All of a sudden, the horizon gave way to a massive temple resembling a mini Taj Mahal. We rode up to it and parked out the front as we marvelled at the size of the place. This temple had been converted into a museum and must have been a big deal in Laos, as I noticed a lot of children walking around in groups (perhaps on a school excursion). We had a look around inside, then gave up due to the sheer size and went back outside. There was another group of school children out there, who seemed more intrigued with the two crazy Australian's than the huge structure they were about to enter. They wanted a photo with this strange foreigner, so I agreed to jump in a photo with them and while the shot was being taken, I got them to give the thumbs up and shout 'g-day, mate!', which they did with great enthusiasm!

By this stage, it was mid-afternoon so we decided to call it a day and head back into the city. The children were still standing out the front and pointing as they watched us ride off into the almost-sunset in a trail of dust.

That night, we found a bar in the city where we got chatting to a Canadian fellow who told us he had just come from Vang Vieng. The town was a tourist-orientated spot about four hours by bus north of Vientiane on the banks of the Nam Song River. You couldn't wipe the smile off the Canadian's face as he told us about it, he was so excited. We asked him what the attraction was and he said that tourists flock from all over the world to go tubing down the Nam Song, where they have bars set up along the banks that you can stop in for a beer at. So, it is kind of like a pub crawl on water! While he was telling us this, Adam and I looked at each other and we both knew what the other was thinking – we were heading to Vang Vieng next!

Vang Vieng

The next morning, we boarded a bus bound for the town, arriving around midday. As we hopped off the bus at the other end, I took in my surroundings and was amazed by the scenery, especially the karst hill landscaping the buildings. Adam and I went through the same routine we had at every other place we had visited; found a hostel, booked in, then went to have a look around before it got too dark.

The following morning we rose early, as we were both excited and looking forward to a day of drunk tubing. We met up with the other tourists at the designated meeting point, paid for our tube and caught the bus to take us to the first bar. It was still early morning when we arrived, but it was already starting to feel quite hot and muggy, so everyone was keen to jump in and sail down the river – except Adam and I, who went straight to the bar and grabbed a beer. Everyone saw this and next thing, a few others were doing the same.

Back then, I found it easier to meet and get to know new people over a few drinks, so this was the perfect start to the day for me! There were all sorts of people with us that day; Canadians, Kiwis, Americans and a fellow Aussie by the name of Sean. After our beers, we decided to start our adventure downstream. The water was cold at first, but I soon got used to it. When we arrived at the next bar, the current was quite strong and running quick, so the barman had to reach out with a stick so we could grab hold and be pulled into the safety of the bar. A few more beers later, and we were off again.

Since it was a hot day, the beers were going down too quick and the rest of the day became a blur, but Adam was able to recall a little more than me. We ended up staying at the third bar for a few hours as it was pumping (this one was especially busy compared to the others) and there were some hot chicks in bikinis walking around. When we were finally ready to float down to the next bar, I thought up a neat trick to get onto my tube. There was a steep embankment, so I told Adam to put my tube in the water and let it float past, then I took a run up and tried to jump onto it. I missed completely, but I got a big cheer from the drinking crowd!

Unfortunately, I didn't even make the next bar. Instead, I passed out drunk and just floated on by. I even missed out on last drinks at the last bar, as I was too far gone. I would have floated all the way to Cambodia if Adam and a couple of other tourists from our group hadn't grabbed my tube and guided me to shore when we got back to Vang Vieng.

At the start of the day, we had been given a waterproof bag to hold our belongings. Ours had Adam's new camera in it….and I lost it somewhere along the way. Apparently, according to my ever-patient travel companion, we had a few words over the lost camera when we got back to the hotel.

As you could imagine, we were pretty hungover the next day, so were in dire need of a quiet one. It didn't help that I was also incredibly sunburnt from passing out on the river. Instead of a full-blown party session like we were prone to do, instead we chose to check out a few bars around the town and lay low. The bars here were very different from any other I had been to. They were more like wooden huts.

At one place, they were serving magic mushroom shakes. Seeing as we had never tried them before and were on an adventure, I decided we really should give one a go. I was quite excited and half expected Vang Vieng to turn into a fantasy land kind of like Alice in Wonderland with Adam and I as the main characters in some warped storyline, but sadly, I was sorely disappointed. It hardly seemed to have an affect on me at all. Aldous Huxley, we weren't! Adam did experience one change…an added power chuck as we were walking back to the hostel.

The following day we spoke about our plans for the rest of the trip and since Adam was starting to run low on money, he needed to get back to Australia shortly to find work. We decided it was best to slowly make our way back to Bangkok and begin looking at our options.

One choice was to take a short bus ride north to Luang Prabang. From there we would catch a wooden speedboat across the border and back into Chang Mai. We thought about this and the eight-hour speedboat ride sounded really uncomfortable but, to be honest, we couldn't really be bothered thinking up any other way. So, we caught the bus to Luang Prabang and as soon as I saw the old speedboat, I wondered what we had gotten ourselves into. It was a rickety wooden motorised boat that sat about eight people. We piled in with the other crazies with a death wish, and off we went.

We were right about it sounding uncomfortable – it was terrible. It was the worst ride I had been on in my life and by the time we stopped on the edge of the Mekong for lunch, my back was hurting something cruel. While having our respite and food, a dodgy Asian guy came up to Adam and I and offered us a hit of heroin. We politely declined, but I remember thinking that it must be so easy to score in South East Asia if you wanted to. As we got back on the speed boat, my back started hurting again and I thought that maybe a hit of heroin might not have been such a bad idea after all!

The return journey

After eight long and gruelling hours, we made it across the border back into Thailand. We caught the taxi ferry to Chang Mai and checked into our hostel, keen to hit the town again. We met up with an old English guy at a bar who, along with a couple of other dodgy-looking guys – took us to a place where there was a wrestling ring set up. We were all quite drunk, but I remember Adam putting the gloves on and having a spar at one stage. I'm pretty sure he came off second best.

I eventually called it a night and apparently got a lift back to the hostel on the back of a scooter, ridden (according to Adam) by a ladyboy. Adam kicked on and finally arrived back at the hostel the following afternoon.

The following night called for quieter shenanigans. We went out for dinner then checked out a local fair, followed by taking in a movie (James Bond) at the mall. We had a massive trip back to Bangkok planned for the following night; we were due to leave Chang Mai at 7 pm and arrive back in Bangkok around 7 am.

Just after dusk the next night, as we had done a few times now on this trip, we once again packed up our stuff and headed to the bus station. I settled into my seat and put my headphones in and started playing – you guessed it – Kid Rock! Even though I slept most of the way, I still felt quite lethargic when I hopped off the bus the next morning.

Joel Whitwell

Adam and I made our way back to Khaosan Road, where our adventure had begun a few weeks ago. We checked into Wallyhouse again, but the lady who ran the place didn't seem too pleased to see the two drunken Aussies back. She did seem to warm to us after a bit of a chat, though. We headed to our room and slept for a few hours, then Adam booked his ticket to fly back to Australia the next day. Seeing as it was our last night in Thailand together, we decided to have one last big night out on the town and boy, it must have been a big one, because to this day I still cannot remember anything about it at all.

We survived though and even made it back to the guest house, somehow. We woke up around lunch time and after the routine question of, "what happened last night?", Adam packed his luggage and got ready to head to the airport. I still had another week in Thailand, but it was going to be strange without Adam.

It was a great three weeks travelling through South East Asia together and we made enough stories to fill out a chapter in this book, that's for sure! We hugged as he left and promised to catch up again when I was back in Australia the following week. Once Adam was in the taxi, I headed back to my room to sleep off my hangover. I woke up around 9 pm that night and I could hear all the noise and partying happening along the road, but I was too tired and burnt out to go out, so I put my headphones on and fell back asleep.

The next day, I laid in bed thinking about how I was going to spend my last week in Thailand. Seeing as I was now on my own and had already seen quite a bit, plus I was still a nervous traveller, I decided to just stay put around Khaosan Road. I remembered Big Red saying he was hoping to be back in Bangkok around this time, so I found an internet café and sent him an email, but not really expecting much to come out of it.

There was an Irish pub called Gulliver's on the corner nearby and I told him he would find me there if he happened to be in town that night and wanted to catch up for a beer. I had no idea if he would be in town or if he would even get the email, but I had nothing to lose. I headed to Gulliver's around 7 pm and by 10 pm I had consumed quite a few beers. I had given up on the idea of seeing Big Red that night, so I thought I had better finish up my beer and head off to find another bar. But, just at that moment, like a scene from an old Western movie, the saloon doors swung open and in wandered Big Red. I couldn't believe it and I remember thinking, "what a bloody legend!". He saw me pretty much straight away and came over to get stuck into drinking and chatting like we were old friends, even though we had only met once.

It was a great night and I really enjoyed hearing all his crazy travel stories. I even got him to tell me about his travels over Vietnam on the scooter again. It was a massive night, and as a consequence, so was the hangover the next day.

Big Red and I caught up again a day or so later and spent some time checking out one of the biggest malls in Thailand. He flew back home to South Australia not long after, but we still keep in touch from time to time. He has now settled down at home, happily married and with a young family. I guess his crazy travel days are long gone, but, you never know, he may just rip all over Vietnam on a scooter again one day!

The day finally came for me to return to Australia too. I took one last walk around Khaosan Road, taking in the surroundings and watching the people, thinking I may never get a chance to come back (as it turns out, I did only three years later). On the flight home, as I often did, I found myself thinking about the trip I had just been on and the incredible experience it gave me.

While journeying throughout South East Asia, I learnt a little about another culture and how people in other parts of the world live. Even though I was still a bit green, I was starting to believe that maybe travelling was in my blood and I would get a lot out of life by choosing that path. Well, I knew I would get a lot more out of life by travelling than sitting down at the Harvey Pub every weekend!

I also thought about my friendship with Adam and how he had been such a great support in encouraging me to visit Thailand and Canada while he was there. It really did help having a friend like that, and I felt blessed to have so many good people in my life.

The first Friday after I arrived home from my trip, Ash wanted to hear all about my latest adventures, so I met up with him down at the pub. By the end of the night, I was so drunk that apparently I stood up on the top of the bar and started yelling, "I love Thailand!". Luckily, Spud, the publican, knew me well enough so he didn't kick me out, though he did tell Ash that he had to catch me if I fell.

Seventeen

ADMIRING SOME LOCAL SIGHTS

Denmark

Eventually, 2006 made way for 2007 and at the start of that year, I felt as though I was beginning to come into my own, not only as a traveller, but as a fair dinkum drunken larrikin! It was also the year that I, like the rest of the world, discovered Facebook.

Just before Easter that year, my old friend TC rung to ask if I was keen to head down south to Denmark and stay at his mum's place for the long weekend. I jumped at the chance, as the only time I had ever been down that way was a trip I took to Albany with mum and Kelvin when I was a toddler.

T.C's brother Christian also came along. I couldn't believe what I saw as we passed the tall jarrah trees one after another on the scenic drive. It was quite late by the time we arrived, so after having a quick chat with TC's mum and her partner, we decided to call it a night and crash out. The following morning, we woke early and went to check out a nice lake that was situated at the end of the street. It had a little pier that I was able to walk out on and take some photos.

After that, we drove around to a few of the beaches. The coast is beautiful down that way, but at Easter time it was very cold and the sea was choppy, so we didn't dare go for a swim. At one stage, we went for a walk out onto some rocks that had a cliff edge near the water and a massive wave slammed against it, sending foam and water high into the air. For a minute there, I thought I was back at Niagara Falls! Luckily, we only got a bit wet and we weren't drunk, otherwise the outcome may have been very different.

We went back to TC's mum's place, had showers and got her to drop us off at the local pub so we could check out the night life. We ordered a few beers and found a table in the corner where we could relax and take in the atmosphere. TC, Christian and I took turns buying rounds and whenever it was my turn, I noticed a man at the bar who kept staring at my face, kind of like the man in Sydney many years before.

I didn't let it get to me at first, but after a while I decided that if he was so intrigued by me, then he should at least have the chance to get to know me. So, I went over and offered to shake his hand as a friendly gesture, but he just shook his head and went back to his beer. I was determined not to let it ruin my night, so I just grabbed our drinks and made my way back to where we were sitting.

Not long after, a man and a woman came in and being the nice guys we were, we offered for them to join us at our table. They accepted and we got chatting and found out they were brother and sister from South Africa who were travelling around Australia. The lady was quite attractive and before long, her and I were engrossed in conversation. She seemed to take a shine to me and said if I ever find myself in her part of the world, I would be more than welcome to come stay with her. She wrote her email address down on a napkin and handed it to me, I couldn't believe my luck! When it was my turn again for the round, she came up to the bar with me, her arm around my shoulders. I quickly made eye contact with the bloke who had been staring all night and gave him a cheeky grin and a thumbs up. He didn't look too happy!

Near the end of the night, the lady and I snuck off and went across the road to a park where we just sat and chatted for ages, mainly drunk talk, and kissed a few times. We spoke about how much fun we would have if I ever did visit her country. Eventually, I heard someone call out and it was TC, letting me know the taxi had arrived to pick us up. Her brother also called out to let her know he had called them a cab too. We gave each other one last big hug and I promised I would stay in touch. We both jumped in our designate cabs and took off in separate directions. I couldn't wipe the smile off my face and I really looked forward to hopefully seeing her again one day.

I woke around lunch time the next day and straight away checked to make sure I still had her email address. I felt in my pockets and…no napkin. My heart sunk and I started to panic. I looked under the bed and all throughout the room, but I couldn't find it anywhere. TC drove me down to the pub where I searched the park and even asked the publican if someone had handed it in. He just looked at me like I was still drunk and shook his head. I couldn't believe it. Knowing my luck, the guy who had been staring at me all night probably found it, but I didn't want to think about that! After searching for ages, I finally gave up and realised it was a lost cause, so we left.

TC's mum's place had a spa, so that night, TC and I decided to hop in and chat to try to lift my spirits (don't jump to conclusions – we both had our shorts on!). I was feeling a bit low after losing the email address. The spa was very relaxing and we had a good talk, although I must say I would have preferred being in the water with my new South African friend!

The following morning, we said goodbye to TC's mum and started the long drive back home, still minus that email address. We stopped off at the treetop walk in Walpole, as we had heard it was worth a visit. After spending an hour or so there and taking a few photos, we continued on our merry way.

Hopetoun

Not long after my Denmark adventure, my old mate Jono rang me up and said he was doing some work in Hopetoun, which was also way down south but a bit further east from Denmark. So, I booked a Friday off work, grabbed a map, jumped in my car and started the long journey bound for

Hopetoun. There were two ways I could get there from Harvey; along the coast or inland through the Wheatbelt and Lake Grace. I chose the inland route, which ended up being a wise move.

It was a long drive, so to break it up a bit, I decided to stop for a rest at a service station just outside of Lake Grace. I was at the counter being served when someone walked out of the kitchen, took one look at me and said, "Joel!". I couldn't believe it. Here I was out in Lake Grace, hundreds of kilometres from home, and someone had recognised me. It turned out to be my cousin Jamie who I hadn't seen since I was a kid. He was a lot older than me and had travelled all over the world. He was a kind of hero to me when I was growing up because of all his adventures, perhaps that is where my love of travel started growing. So, you can imagine my surprise at bumping into him at a service station in Lake Grace! We got to have a quick chat, I would have loved to have stayed longer and hear more of his stories, but I had to keep moving.

I arrived in Hopetoun around five that afternoon and got directions to Jono's van at the local caravan park. It was great to sit down and have another beer with my old friend. We talked about our plans for that night and he said we had a few options. He knew a few people from work that were going camping and we were welcome to join them, or we could just hit up the local pub. I figured we had all the next day to spend at the pub so we should go camping.

Jono rang his mate to get directions to the campsite, which included some off-road. We finally reached the campsite and set up the deck chairs and esky, then got straight back into the drinking. We were camping with five others – three guys and two girls – and I found them to be a pretty good crew and fun to drink with. It ended up being a very merry night and for a while there I passed out in my chair as I was so relaxed by the fire. I eventually crawled into a swag on the back of Jono's ute.

We packed up camp early the next morning, then crawled back into our swags for a bit more sleep before heading to the pub for a pretty big afternoon session. We got down to the pub around lunchtime and straight away the beers started flowing. Jono was already like a local there and seemed to know everyone, so we didn't have a shortage of people willing to have a beer with us. I was in my element, drinking beer while meeting all these new and interesting people.

All of a sudden, an older man drinking at the bar looked over and called out my name. I couldn't believe it. No matter how far away from home I roamed, I kept bumping into people who knew me. I, on the other hand, had no idea who he was, so I decided to wander over and find out. It turns out he was the father of a guy I knew from partying back home, Chad, and I had met him a few times before at the Woky.

Before we knew it, Chad was on the phone and I was trying to convince him to drive down to Hopetoun to boost up with his old man and me. In my tipsy state, I thought that a spur of the moment decision to jump in his car and drive six hours south seemed like the best idea in the world, but unfortunately (or, perhaps luckily), he was busy that weekend. Instead, we made plans to catch up in the future. I continued drinking and getting merry with his old man and the other locals, enjoying a sunny day in Hopetoun.

The day ended up being another great drunken memory in my history bank. It was awesome to catch up with Jono again in a different part of WA and spend that time with him. The following day, he went off to work while I made the long drive back home, both of us with hangovers to prove a point.

Darwin

It was also around this time that I was starting to catch up with my old friend Marcus again. At that stage, his sister Emma, her partner Mark and their two children were living in Darwin, so he was going to make the drive up to stay with them for a while. This gave me another opportunity to check out a new place with another mate. I told him I would book holidays and head up there sometime in July for a few weeks. He headed off in his ute in late May and we kept in touch via phone until I boarded a plane in July. I landed safely in Darwin around 7 pm and Marcus was there to pick me up from the airport. It was just after dusk, but I could already feel the humidity – so different from the weather down south!

We stopped at a pub for a carton of beer on the way to Emma and Marks's house (of course) before getting into a few much-needed cold bevvies. We decided to head to the casino, but I was a bit worried I didn't have the right attire. Fortunately for me, Darwin is pretty lax, so thongs and a t-shirt were perfectly acceptable! We only stayed for a few hours, then back to his sister's house for some rest.

The following morning we jumped in Marcus's ute and went for a drive so he could show me around town. We visited the wildlife park and were able to pat a joey. We saw plenty of crocodiles in the enclosures, which were really impressive in size. We then headed to the wharf for lunch. After that, it was time to check out the Darwin museum where we saw memorials of World War II when the Japanese bombed Darwin harbour. The museum also showcased historical displays from Cyclone Tracy.

After all that sightseeing, we were in dire need of cooling off. Thankfully, Emma and Mark had a pool, and as soon as I hit the water…ahhhh….heaven. There was no way I was swimming in any of the local watering holes or the beach; there are way too many creatures in the water up there that will kill you without a second thought!

That night we headed back to the casino to try our luck. It turns out, I was in luck – I scored the email address of a very attractive lady I got talking to. The next morning, the first thing I did was check my pockets for that little piece of paper! I still had this one, but Marcus then informed me that the guy she was with was, in fact, her boyfriend. I figured she was a lost cause then and threw away her email details. Marcus had a good laugh at my expense, then told me to get myself together for another drive.

We jumped in the ute and headed to Mindil Beach for a look. The tide was rising, making little streams along the sand. It was an overcast day but quickly heating up, so Marcus suggested we have some lunch and a handful of beers at the Beachfront Hotel, a pub not far from Emma's. That sounded like a perfect idea, so before I knew it, we were kicking back with a cold beverage in the alfresco area, admiring the view of the ocean. I was really starting to like Darwin and the relaxed vibe here.

As often happens, one thing lead to another and suddenly it was getting late in the afternoon. We thought we had better head back to the house, then continued drinking there until about midnight when Marcus came up with the grand idea of going to the casino again. For some strange reason, the taxi driver dropped us at the wrong place, but Marcus said we weren't far away and he knew how to get there, so we decided to walk.

Instead of the casino, we ended up out in the scrub, walking along a fence towards some bright lights in the distance. We figured that must be the casino, so kept walking. The next minute we felt something underneath our feet and heard some moaning. Holy shit – we had accidentally walked right over the top of a group of Aboriginal people who had set up camp in their swags for the night! Marcus yelled, "run!", so I scurried over the rest of the sleeping group, leapt over the fence and didn't stop running until we passed the security guards at the entrance to our intended destination – we finally made it to the casino. However, feeling bad after our little scare, we weren't in the mood to gamble, so we caught a taxi right back to Emma's house.

The next few days were pretty quiet, spent mainly kicking back by the pool with a beer or over at the Beachfront Hotel. The quietness didn't last though, as one night just before the weekend, Marcus and I did a massive pub crawl up Mitchell Street, the area commonly known as the entertainment hub of town. We chatted up so many backpackers, and if by chance I scored any email addresses again, I certainly lost them all.

The following weekend was the Darwin Cup, a horse race known as "the richest race on dirt in Australia". The Cup is a massive event for the top end, with a huge influx of tourists turning up to enjoy the spoils of the racing carnival. Marcus, Emma, Mark and I donned some decent clothes and piled into a taxi, destined for the Darwin Turf Club for a great day of drinking and horse racing.

Sadly, we only made it for a few hours then abandoned the long queues, dust and humidity for the Beachfront Hotel. Once there, we all got quite boozy. We sat outside but it was still so hot, and as someone used to the cooler southern weather, I was really feeling it. I kept opening the door to the pub and standing in the air-conditioning for a few moments to cool down, then would join the group for a while before jumping back up to stand in the cool! Emma and Marcus thought this was quite funny, as I probably did it a dozen times over the afternoon.

We ended up back at Emma and Mark's place to continue drinking. The couple headed to bed not long after, but Marcus and I continued on and had a good chat. I confided in him that after being single my whole life, I was worried I would never find anyone and would be alone. He shared with me a bit of wisdom I have never forgotten; "We are born alone, and we die alone. It's the lives you touch along the way that count." These words meant a lot.

After a busy couple of days, it was time to quieten down again. Marcus wanted to lay off the booze for a while and I decided this was a good idea, but by mid-week, I was ready to party again. On the Thursday afternoon, I decided to walk down to the Beachfront Hotel and get on it. Marcus wasn't keen, so I went solo. It was just on dark when I left and I put a few beers in my pockets for the trip.

I was quite drunk by the time I got there and I don't remember much of the night, but from what I can gather, sometime in the early hours of the morning, I left the pub and started the walk back to Emma and Mark's place. About halfway there, I must have passed out on the side of the road. It wasn't long before the cops drove by and saw me laying there, thankfully. They tried to rouse me but didn't get much response. When they noticed my face, they thought I may have been beaten up, so were just about to call the paramedics when I somehow realised what was happening. I jumped up, gave them a high five and did a little dance right there on the side of the road so show them I was ok. I explained that I was born like this and was just a little drunk! They kindly gave me a lift to where I was staying, for which I am very grateful.

I didn't wake until late in the afternoon and felt a bit sheepish about my antics from the night before, so when Emma asked how I got back, I lied and said I caught a taxi. I never told anyone about my help from the boys in blue – but I guess that secret is out now!

For my last weekend in Darwin, we planned a day trip out to Litchfield National Park, which is 100km south-west of Darwin. The area is famous for plenty of picturesque swimming holes, nature walks and waterfalls over the incredible 1500 square kilometres. That Saturday morning, we packed up the car and headed for the park. Mark was away for work, but Marcus, Emma, her two children and I were looking forward to a relaxing day out. We hopped from swimming hole to swimming hole, keeping a close eye out for crocs as we cooled off in the clear water. I was able to take some great photos – but they never do the actual landscape any justice.

At the end of the day, we piled back into the car for the drive back to the city, marking the end of my adventures up north. The next day, we all had lunch at another local pub and then Marcus drove me to the airport.

Eighteen

WEDDING BELLS

After Darwin, the remainder of 2007 passed by without much fanfare. I worked, partied and just got on with life. Come 2008, two of my good friends were headed to the altar, and I couldn't have been happier for them.

Calvin's wedding was first. As I mentioned earlier in this book, the heart and character that he had shown after losing his eyesight in an accident was incredible. He went on to make a good life for himself despite the challenges, and I was honoured to be invited to share his special day with him.

Just a week later I also received an invitation to my friend Mark's wedding. I was so excited, but you wouldn't believe it – they were on the same day! Even worse, one was in Mandurah and the other was in Waroona, with the reception in Bunbury. I couldn't decide between them, so I made a pledge to attempt to go to both. It was going to be a very big day! The plan was to attend Mark's ceremony in Waroona, then head to Mandurah for Calvin's reception. Problem solved.

Before that though, there was Mark's buck's to survive. The best man, Adam, hired a bus to take a group of us down to Bunbury for a night out. For a laugh, one of the guys brought a wheelchair for the groom to sit in and be wheeled into each place, which I thought was a great idea.

Later in the night as we were all lined up to go into a night club, I noticed the chair was empty, so I jumped in and told one of the guys to wheel me up to the door. The bouncer must have thought the chair was a necessity, so he let me in without paying. I was wheeled straight to the middle of the dance floor, where in full view of the whole club, I stood up and started dancing. I think I stole the biggest cheer for the night with that one!

The big day finally arrived, so I dressed up in my finest wedding attire, jumped in my car and drove to Waroona to witness the marriage of Mark and his bride, Liz. She looked absolutely stunning and it was an emotional moment as she walked down the aisle. I was so happy to be there. After the ceremony, I hung around for a little while to catch up with a few people and had a nice photo taken with the newlyweds (which is still framed and hanging on the wall to this day!).

Eventually, everyone left for the reception in Bunbury, and I took off in the opposite direction, bound for Mandurah and the reception for my other good friend, Calvin.

Jono had come home to attend the wedding, so I met up with him and his brother before the reception. They were talking about the ceremony and I was disappointed I missed it, but I was no miracle worker! I was happy I made it to the reception and was looking forward to a big night of celebrating. The event was held at the Mandurah Quays, right on the water. It ended up being a fantastic night and, true to form, I was right amongst the celebrations. My old mate Aggie was also there and it was good to catch up with him, too.

It warmed my heart to see a good mate like Calvin getting married after everything he had been through after his accident. He certainly didn't let adversity beat him.

The next morning rolled around and I said goodbye to the guys and started the drive home to Myalup while nursing a wedding-sized hangover.

Nineteen

Memories.…Or Not

A few weeks later, on the eve of the Australia Day weekend, I was down at the pub having a few beers when my old mate Jarrod sent me a text to invite me to an Aussie Day pool party. I was stoked, and on-the-spot invited the two mates I was drinking with, Joshie and Brian, who were also keen. The following Sunday, I picked them up from Harvey, filled the esky with beer and started the journey to Bunbury. Jarrod had given me directions, but we still rocked up at the wrong party. Oops. We finally found the right address a little further down the street.

Even though it was still early in the afternoon, the party was in full swing by the time we arrived. Jarrod was happy to see us all and we settled into drinking and relaxing by the pool. We didn't know a lot of the other guests, but managed to mingle a bit. Heath Ledger had just passed away, so that seemed to be the main topic of conversation no matter who we chatted with.

Not long into the afternoon, someone brought out some ecstasy pills. Still in a reckless phase, I didn't hesitate to swallow one down, followed by a good swig of beer. Pretty soon I was off with the fairies and the next thing I remember was the sound of a car horn. I opened my good eye and looked up to see Joshie staring at me from the driver's side window of my car. He was cracking up laughing, saying, "get in, get in", with Brian also laughing at me from the passenger seat.

One Eye, One Ear – No Worries

I quickly jumped up and took in my surroundings – then realised I had been laying under a tree on the side of Ocean Drive, a busy street that runs along the beach in Bunbury. I did as he said and got in the back of the car, before Joshie took off (as he was holding up traffic). I had no idea what had happened and was shocked when they told me it was 2 pm on Monday afternoon. The boys tried to fill me in on the previous 24 hours, but they didn't know much.

Not long after I took the pill, we got a lift into town to go clubbing. I was busy telling everyone how much I loved them by this stage, so obviously, the pill was working its magic. As soon as we got to town, I spied a kebab shop in the distance and took off like a flash, and that's the last they saw of me.

Around 5 am I still hadn't shown up, so they decided to catch a taxi back to Jarrod's place and hopefully find me there, but no such luck. After a few hours, they began to get worried and tried calling my phone, but I didn't answer. Jarrod went for a drive but couldn't find me anywhere, then by lunchtime Josh and Brian needed to head back to Harvey so decided to take my car and see if they could find me on the way. Luckily for me, they took Ocean Drive instead of the other way through town.

Brian found himself staring out over the ocean and by impulse looked inland, and that's when he saw me under the tree. He pointed and yelled, "there he is" and the horn started blaring to wake me from my slumber.

On the drive back to Harvey, I tried to remember and piece together the previous 20 hours, but all I seemed to remember was standing in an apartment while the sun was coming up and talking to a Canadian guy about ice hockey. That's all that came back to me, that pill certainly did a number on me. If any young people are reading this – take my advice and don't bother with ecstasy. It isn't as fun as they say it is!

My brain was fried for a few days afterwards so I decided to go quiet for a while. The first half of 2008 was quite uneventful.

In June I began working in the tripe room with a guy from Japan, Hiro, who I got along with quite well. He was only in WA for a little while and was due

Joel Whitwell

to head back home, so he invited a few of us over to where he was staying for some farewell drinks. By that stage, Harvey Beef was operating two shifts, days and nights. We were all lucky enough to have scored the days, but the backpackers Hiro was sharing accommodation with were mostly on nights.

After a few drinks, we called it a night and I crashed in one of the spare beds. Not much later I woke to the sound of people making a racket. Apparently, the party was still going! Julien, a Frenchman who was also staying at the house, had invited some of the other backpackers around after they finished work that night. Back then, I was never one to miss out on a party and a good time, so I got up to join them. In my semi-drunken state, I forgot to put pants on and wandered out in my jocks. As you could expect, the guests were all quite shocked by this strange man coming out of the bedroom in his underwear, and I was probably quite lucky there weren't any ladies in the group. I did wonder momentarily why everyone had gone quiet. To put their minds at ease, I went around and introduced myself, then went to put on some pants.

As it turns out, the no-pants entrance was an effective ice-breaker. Once I was fully dressed again, I joined the group and had a great night and met some awesome new people. Two of the guys, Julien and David (Scottish Dave) told me they had planned a weekend trip to Perth to celebrate another guy's birthday. They invited me and another Dave (Davey) along too. It sounded like fun, so on Saturday night we met up in Harvey and caught the train to Perth to hook up with the others at a backpackers accommodation. Once we arrived, we checked into our rooms, then met up with the others for some drinks before heading out. It was a great night – but not without incident.

Around midnight, while walking between clubs, I somehow managed to get my foot run over by a car. Luckily I was well and truly drunk by then, so I didn't feel a thing and was still able to dance up a storm at the next venue. The following morning I jumped out of bed (as we had an early train to catch), but found I could not put any weight on my foot and immediately collapsed to the ground in a sprawling heap. Davey was quite concerned, but we had to get to the station, so helped me limp off down the road and we were soon back home.

The following Monday my foot was still very sore, so instead of going to work, I went to the doctor. To my relief, I was told it wasn't broken, but very swollen and painful. I ended up taking the rest of the week off. The talk amongst the backpackers at work that week was about the crazy Australian they took to Perth who got run over by a car.

I had become good friends with Julien and David (Scottish Dave) so found myself spending quite a bit of time with them. Davey was also around quite a bit, and we had many a fun night hanging out.

Ivy was another backpacker (from Taiwan) who was working at Harvey Beef. I began chatting to her often and found myself starting to fall for her. She came around to the backpacker's house a few times and I was always on my best behaviour when she was there. One day she sent me a message and we made arrangements for me to pick her up and spend the day together at Myalup beach. We spent the time strolling along the water, just chatting and enjoying each other's company, it was lovely. We took some photos and I could feel my heart pounding. I really liked this girl.

I dropped her back home later on, without making any moves (I was being a gentleman!), but as I drove away I felt confident our new friendship could lead somewhere. Unfortunately, I was wrong. Not long after our Myalup beach day, her Visa ran out and she had to go back to Taiwan.

Before she left, Ivy had a going away party at the house and I figured it was my last chance to see if there were any romantic feelings between us, so I didn't get as drunk as I usually would have and tried to chat to her every chance I got. She seemed distant though, not like at the beach. I decided to have one last crack, but just as I started talking to her, the front door opened, a guy I didn't recognise came in, grabbed her by the hand and lead her out to his car. They drove off, and I realised she was probably hooking up. I was shattered. Ivy left for Taiwan the following day and I never kept in touch, I figured there was no point.

'Mum, me and Kelvin. Back where it began. The future world traveller is born'

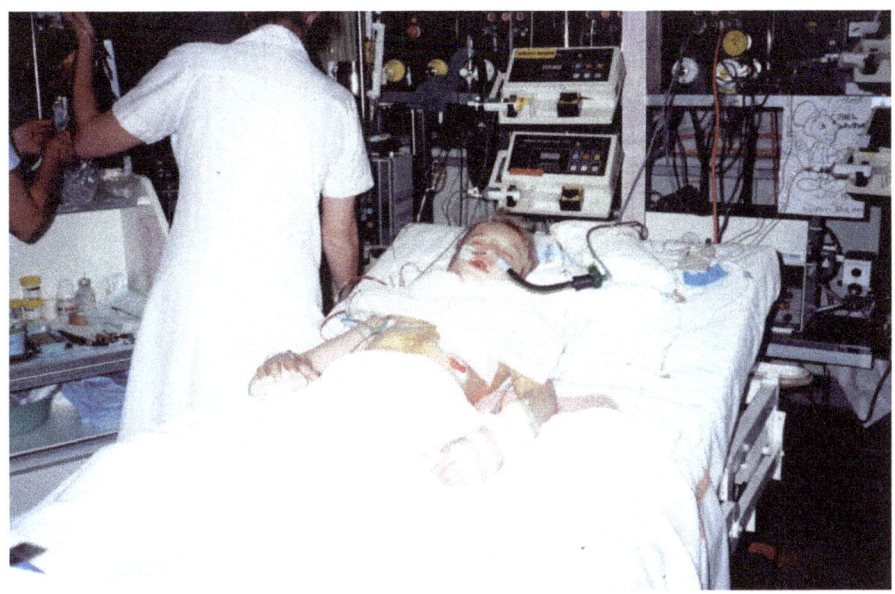

'During one of the many surgeries on my face in my formative years'

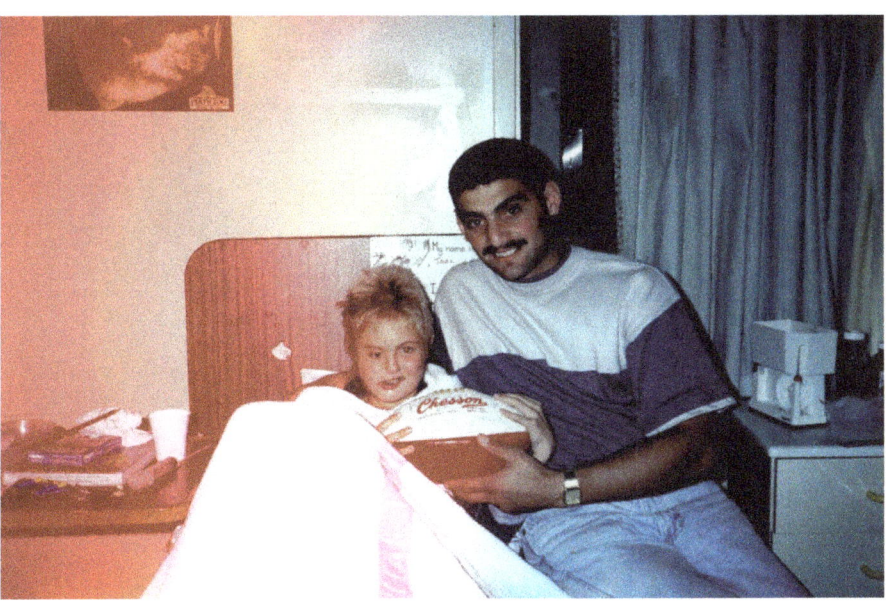

'With Ned during his visit while I was in hospital back in 89.
Will always appreciate what you did by coming to see me.'

Graduation day with my friend Coralee back in 1996. We are still good friends'

'About to head to the school ball back in 1998'

'With PJ. December 98. Forever in our hearts and memories my friend'

'In front of the Opera house during that awesome trip to Sydney back in Feb. 1999'

PJ in front of the Harbour bridge'

'Yes, Kidd Rock. I have seen the sun shinning over the Rocky Mountains. During my first visit to Canada with dad back in 2004'

'On the loose in Toronto with Adam and Rhino in 2005.'

'With Jono riding the Gondola in Venice during that epic World trip in 2009.'

'From Venice to Rome. With Jono again. We certainly covered some ground on that trip'

'Last tango in Paris. Visiting Jim Morrisons tomb out at Pere Lachaise'

'Thought I would try out with the band while traveling through Scotland.'

'With Adam in Toronto during World trip. 2009'

'Visiting Niagara falls with Adam and Nancy'

'In front of the Lourve. Paris. World trip two. 2012'

'With my good friends Mark and Liz on their wedding day back in 2008'

'Ushuaia harbour while visiting my friend Julian during world trip 3. Gateway to Antartica. Will never forget the chilly wind coming off the water'

'Reaching the summit at Machu Picchu. Such a special moment in my life'

'Finally living out my childhood dream of seeing the Golden Gate bridge in San Fran'

'First meeting Shaun Attwood in London. 2016'

'Got to love Copenhagen'

'With Tonia during the last night of our Topdeck tour through Spain. Another good friendship I made on my travels. Little did we know we would get the chance to catch up again during my visit to Sydney a few years later, but I will save that for my next book'

'At the canals in Venice. I miss that magical place'

'In the snow with Julian during my visit to Ushuaia'

'I felt free as a bird the day I got to visit the Grand canyon'

'Mum with her three boys'

'With my two brothers'

'With mum and dad'

Twenty

Dreams Taking Flight

Amongst the partying, meeting new friends, busted feet and broken hearts, I decided it was time to follow a childhood dream – to become a pilot. I started taking flying lessons out at Bunbury airport, and at $180 per lesson, I thought it was money well spent. I did my lessons in a Cessna, a two-seater. It was pretty daunting at first, but seeing as I was with an experienced pilot each time, I gradually began to feel less nervous. It was amazing to be so high over Bunbury, and after a few trips we were able to explore further along the coast and over Harvey and Myalup. It was surreal to look down at Harvey Beef and mum and dad's house. I felt as free as a bird and I could see why people chose to become pilots.

The instructor did most of the flying (of course), but each lesson I was given a little more control until I took over most of the flying while they told me what to do. To obtain my student's pilots licence, I needed to boost my knowledge base, so I often spent half the lesson in the air and the other in the classroom learning the basics like lift, drag and what to do when I encountered a cross-wind.

Luckily I learned that last part because the very next time I went up a tricky crosswind hit us on landing. The wind caused quite a lot of turbulence. I tried to line the nose up with the runway, but it was hard to control and I kept swaying side to side. I half expected the instructor to take over, but he told me to use what I had learnt to land the plane. I was shitting myself, but tried to remain calm on the outside.

Under pressure, I dipped the nose way too low and for a second it looked like we were about to do a nose dive straight into the runway, but at the last second I pulled back and somehow managed to land the plane and slowly bring it to a halt. Boy, was I relieved, and even the instructor seemed impressed that we were both still in one piece!

My flying dream was off to a great start and he said I was almost ready for my first solo flight, but as I was soon to discover, this couldn't last.

As I turned up to my next lesson, I felt safe in the knowledge that I was only a few steps away from my first solo flight and achieving my dream. I was with a younger instructor this time who I had done a few lessons with before. The take-off and flight went according to plan and I had everything under control. Then came time to land – and no tricky crosswind this time. I did what I had been taught and followed everything to a tee. I landed the back wheels down on the tarmac first, then slowly lowered the nose, but I must have gotten a bit excited and put a bit too much pressure on the stick and brought the nose down a bit harder than I should have.

We both heard a loud thump and suddenly sparks started flying everywhere. "Shit, the front wheel has come off", the instructor told me. I could see he was nervous, but tried to remain calm and told me to lift the nose back off the runway quick smart. He then took over and, using every bit of experience he had under his belt, managed to steer the plane onto the grass next to the runway and eventually bring us to a standstill without doing too much damage to the front end.

After we sat there for a moment to gather our thoughts, he turned and asked me if I was ok. He told me not to worry, as these things happen. I remember thinking, "yeh, wheels must come off planes all the time!" After inspecting the damage, he told me to wait by the plane while he organised for it to be towed back to the hangar. He handled it so well, I couldn't have asked for a better person to fly with that day. Before I left, he told me not to be discouraged by what happened and he hoped I would be back.

On the drive home, I was still quite shaken and thought about how realistic my dream was. I decided to give flying away for a while and concentrate on travelling and seeing the world – I thought that was a safer option! Sadly, I still have not been back to finish what I started up in the sky, but maybe one day I will.

I decided my real dream was to continue to experience the world – so that is where I set my sights.

By 2009, it was time to put my travel plans into action again. I decided I was going to go back to Canada to see Adam, who was still based over there, but then another opportunity came up. I had been keeping in touch with Jono over the phone and he asked me if I was interested in doing a Contiki tour through Europe with him – bloody oath I was! So, we set plans in motion for what was going to be another epic trip.

Before I took off jet setting again, I had a couple of goodbyes to get through. I had spent quite a bit of time hanging out with the backpackers over the past year, and there were two I had become particularly good friends with – Scottish Dave and Julien from France. We had a lot of fun times together at the house they were staying at, but their Visa's were due to run out soon. I caught up with them a lot before they were due to leave, and I was sad to see them go. As always, we had a great time with plenty of laughs, and Scottish Dave often reminded me of the time I dropped around to the house for a few beers and said I could only have half a carton because I had a flying lesson the next morning. He always had a good laugh about that one.

Julien left first in late February. Davey and I took him to the train station to see him off. We did the usual hugs and goodbyes, and I promised to catch up with him again for a few beers one day. Unfortunately, I still haven't been able to honour that promise, but I still plan to one day.

Scottish Dave left a couple of months later. Before he left, him and Davey and I went down to the Harvey pub for tea. He asked about my upcoming travel plans and if I was going to be visiting Scotland by chance. I hadn't thought about it, but seeing as Scottish Dave was going to be there, I thought it sounded like a great idea. Jono and I had planned to do a few extra weeks travelling after the Contiki, so heading to Scotland sounded good to me; Scottish Dave, bagpipes, haggis, Loch Ness monster – Scotland sounded like it had so much to offer!

We finished our meals at the Harvey pub and did the usual hugs and goodbyes. I told him I would see him in Scotland in a few months, as I was sure Jono would be happy with that idea too.

So far, I had planned two weeks travelling through Europe on the tour, two weeks in Scotland, five weeks in Canada and a week in Thailand on the way home. I also met a backpacker from Taiwan called Bogi, who told me if I was ever in his country, he would look after me and show me around. So, I decided what the hell. I may as well drop by Taiwan for a few days on route to Thailand. The trip was finally all set.

Twenty-One

Conquering The World

In July of that year the big moment finally arrived – my first world trip. I felt a huge sense of excitement as I finished up work on the Friday and spent the next few days catching up with people before I left. It was a big trip, but at the time I felt like I was never coming back! I organised a catch up at the Harvey pub with some mates the night before I was due to fly out. It was a pretty random gathering, but all who attended were great mates who I was thrilled to spend time with.

As I pulled up to the pub, I received a text from Jono who was at his brother's place in Perth, also getting ready to leave. It read, "get ready for a big month, Whitty". Now I wasn't only excited, but nervous too! Our little group of six had a great night, chatting about our latest antics and enjoying some good pub grub. I hoped it was a good omen for all that was to come as I travelled the world. We finished up tea and our drinks and I promised my friends I would catch up with them when I got back safe and sound in a few months.

I headed home (very responsible!) planning for a good sleep before leaving Australian soil to embark on the adventure of a lifetime. Unfortunately, the excitement and nerves had well and truly kicked in and I didn't sleep well, but that was to be expected.

I awoke the next morning to realise I hadn't started packing yet, but as always, mum came to the rescue. She was just as excited as I was for my first world trip. Because of everything we had been through together, I always had a close connection with mum. However, looking back, letting her help me pack probably wasn't the best idea! She kept pulling clothes out of the cupboard and saying things like, "here, you will need this as it would be freezing in Canada", even though it was going to be summer while I was there. Before long, I had a suitcase, large pack and a backpack filled with clothes and my mum standing there with a huge grin from ear to ear. I still had a lot to learn about being a world traveller – like minimalism!

We then packed the car and she gave me a lift up to South Perth where I was to meet up with Jono at his brother's place. We sat out the back chatting for a bit, then caught a taxi to the airport. We still had a few hours to spare before our flight, but Jono told the taxi driver we may as well get there early so we had time for a few cheeky ones (beers!). I was now starting to get very excited for the trip!

We checked in and settled at the bar for a couple of drinks before departure. Before long we were heading to the boarding gate, but just as we got there, I realised I didn't have my passport. Oh shit, I must have left it at the bar. I ran back to where we were drinking, but it was nowhere to be seen. My heart sunk and I couldn't believe it – here I was about to embark on a journey of a lifetime and I had lost my passport before I had even left Australia!

I started to really stress out, but Jono kept calm and told me not to panic. How could I not panic?! If I didn't have my passport, I wasn't boarding the flight! I would have been better off losing my clothes and boarding the plane naked as I might still have had a chance, but not without that critical document.

So, I took off all over the airport, trying to find it, all the while Jono tried to remain calm. As a last resort, I decided to check out the lost items room and guess what I found – it was there! Some good soul must have handed it in pretty quickly. Now we could board that damn plane and get on the way!

As soon as we settled into our seats and were in the air, we ordered a few more beers – as you do. We had a stopover in Singapore en route to London, where we took full advantage of Jono's QANTAS Club membership to enjoy a meal and another few drinks in luxury at Changi Airport. Apart from my passport mishap, the trip was nicely uneventful.

London

We finally landed in London and I couldn't believe how big Heathrow was. It was a maze. We collected our luggage and caught the tube to Russell Square, where we were to check into our Contiki hotel, The Royal. A few blocks from the hotel I started to struggle with all of my luggage and really cursing my decision to let mum help pack. But, we made it, and when we got there I found a storage room where I was able to stow half my luggage for a few weeks until after the tour.

Seeing as it was still morning when we arrived in London, we headed to a café across the road from the hotel for a late English breakfast. Following that, we decided to go for a walk to explore the area. A few blocks away, we came across a massive park, Russell Square. It is an enormous place, with a café on the corner and a beautiful fountain as the centrepiece. We sat down and relaxed for a few good hours in that park, soaking it up and enjoying being on solid ground after the long flight. Sitting there, we realised that all those times growing up we had said we were going to travel, and now it had become a reality – we were light-years from Harvey, sitting in a park in London, about to go on an amazing journey together. We weren't sure what to expect, but were pumped to find out.

After a solid sleep that night to recover a little from jetlag, we rose early to do a city tour on one of the classic London red double-decker buses. On the tour, we got to visit all of the well-known attractions the city had to offer, including Big Ben, London Bridge, Trafalgar Square, the Houses of Parliament and the London Eye. At one stage as we were passing Big

Ben, I stood up the front of the bus and pretended to be the tour guide. It could have been another career option one day if I ever lost my job at the meatworks! Unfortunately, the tour did not include Buckingham Palace but decided we would go for a walk to check it out the following day, as we still had a day to spare before the Contiki tour.

The sightseeing tour finished and the bus dropped us back at our hotel around lunchtime. We still had the afternoon to kill, and we both had that glint in our eyes that said, "it's time to get drunk". So, we found a pub right next to our hotel and settled in for a solid session of drinking. I ordered a typical English lunch of fish and chips, and I was already starting to feel like a world traveller!

The day before leaving for Australia, I had joined a Facebook page created for our Contiki tour. In that group were two girls from New York, who also happened to be sitting in that same pub as Jono and I. They looked over and seemed to recognise me, so one came up and introduced herself. Her name was Kathy. She excused her friend, Leigh, who was feeling a bit crook after their flight, so she stayed at their table sitting quietly and trying to muster the strength to carry on. We understood and knew there would be plenty of time to get to know her once she was feeling better. Kathy chatted for a bit then went back to check on her friend, while Jono and I continued sampling the local ales.

Needless to say, we were both a little hungover the next morning, but that wasn't going to stop us from checking out Buckingham Palace and exploring more of the city. We caught a bus into central London, where we hopped off not far from the River Thames. I decided it was time to finally step up and be the traveller I knew I was capable of being, so I took charge, grabbed the map and told Jono to follow me.

About five hours later and getting lost in a few pubs along the way, we were finally standing in front of Buckingham Palace. After ticking this landmark off our bucket list, we headed back to the pub near the hotel for one last drinking session before starting the Contiki tour.

While we had seen and done so much, we had also walked a lot over the previous few days – which was starting to play havoc with my busted foot. It was getting better after it's run-in with a car back in Perth, but being on the go was taking its toll. One thing I have learnt over the years is that beer is a wonderful anaesthetic, so I continued to ignore my foot and let the drinking work its magic. So, here we were, back at the pub, sinking more delicious English ales.

A couple from Rochester, USA – Jeff and Jamie – joined us at our table not long after we had settled in. They were also on the Contiki tour, so it was awesome to be able to meet some fellow travellers and make things more comfortable when it was time to assemble for the bus. Sadly, the beer was just not quite having the desired effect on my foot, so I had to excuse myself and head up to our room for an early night so I would be ok for the start of the tour.

I awoke the next morning with an excited feeling in my stomach. The only problem was that my foot felt a lot worse and I couldn't seem to put my full weight on it. It looked as red as a beetroot and I was a little concerned, but I decided that even if it had to be amputated, there was no way I wasn't going to live it up on this tour. Jono woke up not long after me and looked a little worse for wear. He said he had kicked on for a while with the American couple and was even dancing at one stage. I was spewing I missed out on seeing Jono dance, but I had a feeling it wouldn't be the last time on this trip.

Packed up and ready to go, we shot down to the foyer where we were scheduled to meet up with the tour group. We met Tom, another Aussie who we had bumped into in the preceding days. While we were waiting, we started chatting to three Canadian girls; Alara, Katy and Marcia. From that very first day, I found there was something about Marcia that really touched my heart. She had a really sweet nature about her, and I still remember that first conversation we had like it was yesterday.

Eventually, we all boarded the bus and – ever the cool kids – Jono and I headed straight for the back. Our Australian tour guide, Joey, stood at the front of the bus and as we pulled out of the hotel gates and headed towards the English channel, he began to describe what was to come over the next two weeks and what we could expect from the tour. He then invited us one by one to come up to the front and tell everyone a little about ourselves. I was shitting myself over this idea, as at this stage in my life I was still very nervous about talking in front of people. Thankfully, we only had a minute or two each, so it was kept very brief.

Joey then asked us to all swap seats every few minutes so we could get to know one another, kind of like a speed dating game. I decided to stay put and wait for other people to come to me, but I was able to meet some interesting people. There was one who especially stood out, a fellow Australian named Shaban. He was very outgoing, and I quickly warmed to his bubbly personality and charisma.

As we arrived at the Cliffs of Dover, everyone returned to their original seats and Ariel, the bus driver, prepared to board the vehicle onto the ferry for the trip across the channel. After the bus was loaded, Joey gave us some instructions on how to find our way back to the bus for our arrival in France. The journey across the water was going to take roughly an hour and a half, and seeing as the ferry was massive, he didn't want anyone getting lost or left behind.

He was right – the ferry was incredible. Jono and I started to explore and met up with Amy, who I recognised as the creator of that Facebook page I joined before leaving home. She was a school teacher from South Australia and very friendly. The three of us went up on deck and took in the view as we pulled away from England and watched the cliffs get smaller and smaller. It was a spectacular view, and I couldn't believe how white the cliffs looked against the blue sky and ocean, kind of like a wave. It was very surreal. I had a great chat with Amy on the ferry ride. As it turns out, she had also done a bit of travelling and had spent some time in Canada, so we had a few things in common.

Eventually, it was time to make our way back to where the bus was parked, but being me, I somehow managed to get lost on the way, and when I walked into the loading bay all I saw was a heap of buses that looked just like ours! I remember thinking, "shit, I could be in a bit of trouble here. I could have just broken the record for the shortest time to get lost on a Contiki tour!" So, I thought the best option was to head to the front of the loading bay where all of the buses had to exit in the hope that Joey would recognise me as they passed through. After about five buses, I was starting to panic, but just as I was about to give up and was wondering how I was going to get to Amsterdam, I heard the sound of a horn and looked up to see our bus with Joey at the front, waving for me to jump on board.

Amsterdam

Growing up, I had heard all about the legend of Amsterdam, so I was really looking forward to this part of the trip. My foot was still giving me a lot of grief, but I didn't care – I was not missing this. After checking into our hotel, we all met in the lobby and headed out for our first big night together as a group. Joey had planned a cruise on the canals, and then we were free to do our own thing before meeting up later on to take in a sex show at a local theatre if we so wished – which of course Jono an I did as we wouldn't see something like that back home in Australia.

After boarding the cruise, Joey stood up and told us a bit about the night and what we could expect. He laid down a few rules to follow while on the boat, but I was confident that as long as I didn't fall overboard or get caught pissing everywhere, I would be fine. Contiki was all about partying, and boy – was I ready to party. We all sang happy birthday to one of the girls, then Joey said a final few words before getting the party started with a big cheer.

I made my way around the boat, chatting and getting to know all the different people on the tour, always with a beer in my hand. There were the two Robbies from Melbourne, Reane from South Africa, Jake and Francie from New Zealand; a real mixed bag. It was a fun cruise, and a great way to start the tour. Joey was pointing out places of interest as we passed by, such as the Anne Frank house. I was lapping it up and I remember thinking, "this is what travelling is all about". Whenever we passed another boat full of party-goers, we would all yahoo and start cheering. Travelling at it's finest – partying on the canals in Amsterdam!

One Eye, One Ear – No Worries

After we docked, we made our way to the theatre for the promised show, but not without stopping at a few bars along the way. We settled into our seats at the theatre with our beer and popcorn as we prepared to sit and watch people have sex on the stage. Not exactly a Hollywood blockbuster, but certainly something different. After the show, we ended up at a nightclub. I'd had a great day, but by this stage I was getting a bit over the pain in my foot. It was time to call a taxi and head back to the hotel.

The following morning we woke up excited about how good the day before was and thought if that was anything to go by, this trip was going to defy even the highest expectations (providing we survived the next few weeks!). Jono rummaged through his pockets and pulled out what looked like a ball of hash he scored the night before. So, we had half each and a few shots of schnapps we had bought earlier, and boarded the next bus with a nice little buzz going on.

We had a free morning to spend in Amsterdam before moving on to Germany. While most of the tour wanted to check out the Anne Frank house, Jono and I were more interested in visiting the coffee shops and I wanted to do a bit of window shopping. So, off we set into the maze that is the red light district and I did my window shopping. I did select a purchase and told Jono I would meet back up with him in an hour or so after I had finished doing business.

Jono and I hooked up again not long after and set out in search of a coffee shop. We found the perfect place, bought a stick of Black Widow, and went upstairs to a lounge area that had a great view overlooking one of the canals. Paradise. We smoked our joint and straight away I fell back into the chair as the whole world seemed to slow right down, almost coming to a standstill. I looked out of the window and up at the sky, staring at the clouds.

Up until that point in my life, I had never really been that interested in clouds, but that day in Amsterdam I was quite fascinated by them. I watched the clouds glide through the sky like they didn't have a care in the world. Compared to the slow pace that seemed to be going on down here on the ground, the clouds, by comparison, seemed to be moving at quite a pace. I suddenly felt like I was up there amongst the white, fluffy masses, flying alongside them without a care. They were moving so fast though, I had trouble keeping up, so I changed course and flew right through them. I felt so free. I could hear Jono's voice in the distance, but I couldn't see him. I guess he wanted to enjoy the experience down there instead of joining me in the clouds. Oh well, his loss.

Eventually, I heard my name and thought whoever it was must have wanted me in the conversation, and I didn't want to be rude. So I slowly started to drift back down to Earth to try to partake in the discussion. It felt like it took forever to come down from the clouds and re-enter my body, but Jono and whoever else was there was patient.

Finally back on the ground and somewhat coherent enough to take in my surroundings, I saw Jono was talking to an older couple from England. I was still too spaced out to give much to the conversation, but I tried. Before long, it was time to head off to meet up with the rest of the Contiki crew for the road trip to Germany. We said goodbye to the English couple and started walking down the streets of Amsterdam once again. I was still a bit dazed and confused and everyone just seemed to float by, kind of like my clouds.

While we were waiting for the rest of the group, Lily, one of our fellow Contiki travellers, asked Jono and I what we had been up to over the day. We briefly explained how our day went, and she commented, "wow, you guys really didn't do much". Maybe we did. Maybe we didn't, but I enjoyed it anyway.

Germany

It was time to say goodbye to Amsterdam, and hello to Germany, where I couldn't help but notice how lush and colourful the landscape was. We stopped in a small town in the Rhine Valley, where we were due to stay the night. After dinner, everyone went on a wine tasting tour, but my foot seemed to be getting worse. By that stage, I could hardly walk and was starting to feel sick. I decided instead to play it safe and have an early night in while I could. I wasn't a big wine drinker anyway, plus the next night we were bound for Munich – so there was no way I would be having a quiet night in a beer-hall filled city like that!

After a good rest, my foot felt heaps better. On the journey to Munich, Joey stood at the front of the bus and went over the history of Germany, a history we all knew too well, especially the dark days when Hitler and the Nazi's were in power. I admired how Germany as a nation was able to move forward, not forgetting, but not dwelling.

After arriving in Munich, we checked into our hotel, then early evening we headed to the city centre. We gathered together and Joey gave us the option of doing a bike tour, or just exploring the city at our own pace for a few hours before we were due to meet up again around 6 pm for drinks at the Hofbrauhaus (one of the famous beer halls in the city). I was really thirsty by that stage, so I took neither option and instead grabbed myself a map and headed straight to the Hofbrauhaus so I could get a head start on the drinking. After a quiet night the day before, I was ready to cut loose.

I made it to the beer hall and ordered myself a stein as I took in the surroundings. These places were certainly different to any pub I was used to. The Hofbrauhaus is one of Munich's oldest beer halls, founded in 1589 by the Duke of Bavaria, Wilhelm V. The night I was there, a band was playing in the corner and the room was set with long wooden tables where people sat – locals and tourists alike – happily swilling their beer from one of the massive steins. There was a lot of singing, chanting and clanging of glasses together for 'prost', which I later discovered meant 'cheers' in German. I loved the atmosphere and quickly made myself at home.

I found out a little more history about the place as I chatted to the other drinkers. The Hofbrauhaus upstairs area was once used as a meeting venue for Hitler and his cabinet. It felt surreal that within these very walls once lurched a man who caused so much devastation and destruction in the world. I couldn't help but think that even though evil had once been here, it was now such a lively and happy place, filled with good cheer.

After a few hours, Jono and the rest of the Contiki crew arrived and the atmosphere went up a notch, if that was even possible. Our new Aussie mate Shaban was living it up and being the classic larrikin that he was. Jeff, Jamie, Jake, Francie, The Two Robbies, Alara, Katy, Marcia, Reane, Leigh and Kathy – everyone was having a great time. Every so often I went outside for a smoke, which was weird as back then in Europe you were still allowed to smoke inside most places. Maybe I just did it out of habit.

While I was on one of my smoke breaks, I started chatting to three Brazilian chicks who told me they were about to head to a basement nightclub to continue partying. They were pretty hot, so I didn't need to be asked twice – I was joining them. By this stage, the rest of the tour had also gathered outside to wait for the bus to take them back to the hotel. All of a sudden a taxi pulled up out of nowhere and the three Brazilians hopped in, followed closely by yours truly. I yelled out to the group, "prost!" as we sped away to looks of confusion and concern from my fellow travellers.

When Jono finally exited the beer hall and joined them, they filled him in on what they had seen in the taxi and he just cracked up laughing. He assured them that I was always doing stuff like that back home and he had no doubt I would be back in time to catch the bus in the morning for the trip to Austria. Joey was worried and probably wondering if this crazy Aussie with one ear and one eye was actually going to make it through the trip.

Meanwhile, in a different part of the city, the taxi had dropped me and my new friends off at the basement nightclub. I took my post at the bar as I watched the girls and the crowd around them dance the night away. They tried to get me to join them, but I was happy to remain at the bar thinking how lucky I was at that moment (in other words, I was too drunk to entertain the thought of dancing). After a few hours, I decided I had better call it a night and said a slurred goodbye to my companions. I staggered outside to a waiting taxi just as the sun was starting to rise over Munich. We sped through the early morning traffic to try to make it back in time for me to catch the Contiki bus. We made it in time and I quickly paid the driver and dashed upstairs to pack up my things.

Jono had already packed up and was heading down to the bus. He had started to get worried, even after his assurance to Joey and the tour, and thanked me for giving him a bloody heart attack. I chucked my things into my bag and made my way downstairs to the lobby where everyone had gathered for the next stage of our journey. While looking around at everyone through a haze from the night before, I realised I was still quite drunk. The story had already started to spread throughout the group about the Aussie who had just arrived back at the hotel less than an hour before.

Austria

After boarding the bus, I found my seat and hoped to fall into a deep sleep, but Marcia showed up and sat in the empty seat beside me. I couldn't believe my luck and figured it would be rude if I fell asleep straight away. After our first chat in London, I was starting to develop feelings for this girl. So, we talked for a while and I told her a little about the rest of my night in Munich. Then she asked what I got up to in Amsterdam. I didn't want to scare her off with the cloud story, so I just said Jono and I had a look around and took in all the culture of the city.

After having a nice conversation, I finally put my head against the window and fell into a deep sleep. I must have been really out to it, because when I woke up it was to a stationary bus with no-one else in sight. After getting my bearings, I noticed a café so in I went to order myself a strong coffee and wait there so I didn't miss the crew when they came back to the bus. Eventually, people from our tour started turning up and told me they had just been white water rafting and how much fun it was. I was disappointed, but I had such a great time the night before with the Brazilian chicks, that I guess I couldn't complain too much – plus, I really needed the sleep!

Our next destination was the state of Tyrol in Austria, where we were to stay overnight in a small town located at the base of the Alps. It was very scenic and reminded me of the movie *The Sound of Music*. After checking in to the hotel, we had a free afternoon to do as we pleased, so I went for a walk to check out the town. I was in awe of how beautiful this part of the world was.

I met up with Jono later on at dinner and he informed me that he and a few of the others had been at one of the local pubs all afternoon. I was initially dirty at him for not coming to get me, but figured I may never get the chance to see scenery like this, so it was a good choice to go for a walk instead of staring at the four walls of a pub again. The night was still young after dinner, so most of the Contiki group went out in search of another pub, lead by Jono and I. We seemed to have an uncanny knack of sniffing out the best pubs.

We found one in record time and the group piled in the door. This one even had a pool table, so Jono was in his element. As usual, I started knocking back the beers and mingling with everyone. Our new Contiki friends couldn't believe I was ready to party again already, considering the state I was in when we last boarded the bus. But, this was my first tour like this and nothing was going to stop me from living it up. Legends are made on Contiki, and I was hell-bent on creating my own! The night was awesome and ended with Jono, Amy and I staggering back to our hotel while singing the theme song to *The Sound of Music*.

Venice

The next day was exciting – we were headed to Venice. Ever since I saw Venice on Indiana Jones as a kid, I had always wanted to visit. Now, here I was, finally about to get that chance! We arrived in Venice late morning, which meant we still had most of the day to explore this enchanting city. As Venice is built on more than 100 small islands in a marshy lagoon in the Adriatic Sea, we had to catch a ferry to get there from the mainland where we disembarked at the Venice pier not far from St. Mark's Square.

One Eye, One Ear – No Worries

We gathered as a group and Joey told us we had a few hours free time to explore before we had to meet up again for the Gondola rides. Jono, The Two Robbie's, Tommy and I took off to check out this iconic city. We saw St. Mark's Basilica, Piazza San Marco, crossed the Rialto Bridge over the Grand Canal, and generally just wandered aimlessly around the canals and alleyways. I have to say, as much as I was looking forward to seeing Venice, the reality of the place did not live up to expectation, but it was a thrill just to have ticked the place off my bucket list and see first-hand what it was like.

We made our way back to St. Mark's Square where we met up with the rest of the tour for the Gondola ride. Jono and I shared a Gondola with the three Canadians; Alara, Katy and Marcia. Again, I couldn't believe my luck, I had never met anyone who touched my heart quite like Marcia and we were about to do a Gondola ride together (even though there were also three other people, but anyway!). Jono wanted to ride in style, so he brought a bottle of sparkling wine for us to enjoy as we floated through the canals. So, there I was, kicking back on a Gondola in Venice, sipping bubbles with one of my best mates and three pretty Canadian girls – it didn't get much better than that! We chatted and relaxed, at one point Katy stirred Jono and I up by reminding us that this wasn't Australia where all the convicts came from. We all had a laugh.

The Gondola passed under the Bridge of Sighs and I was amazed at the architecture of the place. I took some great photos to add to my travel memories. Sadly, all good things must come to an end and we arrived back at the pier a short time later. By this stage it was late afternoon, almost on dusk, and Joey had booked us all into a restaurant for dinner. We stopped by to witness a glass-blowing demonstration along the way, which was quite popular in Venice (especially with tourists). It certainly blew my mind, the way the artists could create such incredible shapes from such a seemingly unpredictable medium.

We arrived at the restaurant and took our seats. I was with Jono, Jeff and Jamie, as well as two other girls from Canada – Steph and Christine. I hadn't really had a chance to meet them properly, but that night at dinner, Steph and I really hit it off. She was easy to talk to and, even better, enjoyed a few glasses of wine. All of a sudden, the theme song for the St Kilda Football Club came on, *The Saint's Come Marching In*. Seeing as I happened to be wearing a Saint's shirt that night, it was a fitting moment to sing along. The Aussies were at it again!

After dinner, we made our way back down to the pier to wait for the boat to take us back to the mainland. While standing on that pier, we saw one of the brightest sunsets I have ever experienced in my life. It was spectacular. As I stood there watching the golden orb sink into the horizon, I felt blessed that I had this opportunity to enjoy a moment like this with some of the greatest people I have ever met on my travels. I knew that moment would stay with me for life as one of the most special memories I made along my journey. It was the perfect ending to a magical day.

Italy

Few cities rival Rome's astonishing artistic heritage and history. The city is full of world-class museums, adorned with ancient statues, and the architecture is nothing like I have seen anywhere in the world. I was lucky enough to spend a few days there on Contiki exploring the city and viewing some of the icons, such as the Colosseum, Pantheon, the Vatican and Trevi Fountain.

As legend has it, if you throw a coin into the Trevi Fountain and make a wish, it will come true. So, naturally, I had to try it. Unfortunately, to this day, I am still waiting!

Seeing inside the Colosseum was an awesome experience and it felt surreal to be in a place where so much history occurred. Centuries before, gladiators had battled it out right there on the grounds.

The food in Rome was also amazing. I indulged in a gelato a couple of times, the heat made it melt all over my hands – but it was worth it!

After a few days exploring the wonders of Rome, it was time to move on to the next destination. Florence (or Firenze) is the capital city of the Italian region of Tuscany. It is known for its Renaissance art and is a city steeped in culture. It is located on the river Arno, which cuts through the old part of the city. It was on the banks of this river that our bus driver, Ariel, dropped us off for our next adventure.

Joey took us to a place where leather wallets were made, then we had some free time before Ariel picked us up to take us to our hotel. As usual, Jono, myself and a few others from the tour found a nice bar and relaxed out the front while enjoying a few local beers. Joey had a big night planned for us with a Tuscan dinner in the mountains, before heading out to a nightclub in the city called the Space Club.

We thought we should get a head start on the festivities (it was a Contiki tour, after all), so we had a few beers under our belt by the time we checked into our hotel. We got ready and met everyone else down in the lobby for our big night out. On our way to dinner, we stopped at a lookout with great views overlooking the city.

The place we had dinner at was beautiful. We sat at two long tables in an outdoor area while Meatloaf played for us on his keyboard in the corner. Well, he looked like Meatloaf, sounded like Meatloaf and played Meatloaf songs – but no, it wasn't actually him. Nevertheless, he was good and kept us entertained. Even better was that he seemed drunk as a skunk, which we thought was awesome. He played his drunken heart out and even managed to spill wine everywhere, which I thought added to the performance perfectly. After dinner, we all gave him a standing ovation, but by then he was just about asleep on his keyboard.

We headed back into the city to hit the dance floor at the Space Club. We were all quite loud by this stage, with some of the crew feeling the need to practice their dance moves in the bus aisles. My dance moves were fine, so I stayed in my seat. Besides, I had better plans – to find myself a spot at the bar and start knocking back the drinks.

True to form, once we got to the club, I perched on a stool and made myself comfortable. As was often the case, the night quickly became a blur and I didn't remember anything until Jono woke me up the next day and told me to hurry up as the bus was about to leave for Switzerland. I still felt drunk as I stumbled out of bed and, seeing as I didn't have time to shower and get changed, I quickly grabbed my bag and followed Jono downstairs and onto the bus.

Joey didn't look too happy when he saw me, and word quickly spread that someone had gotten so drunk the night before, that they had passed out in the hotel lobby. Straight away, I figured that was me and the reason our tour leader was not too impressed by my presence.

Switzerland

On the way to Lucerne, Switzerland, we stopped off so we could take a gondola ride up to a lookout that gave us some incredible views of the Swiss Alps. On the way up, I suddenly started feeling quite nauseous and regretted drinking so much, but once we got to the top, it was worth riding it out. The view was spectacular, and I felt overjoyed to be given the chance to experience it. After taking a few photos and posing with some of my Contiki friends in front of the Alps, we made our way back to the café where the gondola left from.

While sitting there waiting, I asked Jono to fill me in on the events from the night before, and he happily obliged. Apparently, I was so drunk by the time we arrived back at the hotel after the club, that instead of heading upstairs to our room, I made a beeline for the couch in the lobby, where I threw my phone, wallet and smokes on the floor and promptly passed out.

A short time later, the receptionist working behind the counter looked up and saw me laying there. Seeing as I wasn't moving a muscle and whenever I sleep, my glass eye stays open (which is quite unnerving for the uninitiated) she thought I was dead. She started to freak out and called Joey's room. He came down, saw it was me and went up to get Jono. However, Jono wasn't impressed with being woken up from his own drunken slumber at three in the morning and showed his disdain by slamming the door in Joey's face. So, poor Joey had to go back to the lobby and wake me up to prove I wasn't dead (as the receptionist was still freaking out) and managed to send me up to my room.

One Eye, One Ear – No Worries

After hearing the tale, I went to apologise to Joey and we ended up having a bit of a laugh about it, but he admitted I came very close to being kicked off the tour. I can understand that, as being woken up by a scared receptionist at three in the morning, convinced one of his travellers was dead, was not in his job description.

After a few more hours, we made it to Lucerne and were thrown into our prison cells. Well, it was actually our hotel, but it used to be a prison and it still felt a bit like one. The place is called Barabas and was built in 1862, and still operated as a prison until 1998. Although it has been significantly upgraded to accommodate tourists, the narrow spaces, heavy doors and barred windows are a constant reminder (and interesting feature) of its dark history. Nonetheless, it had all the creature comforts we needed, including hot showers, soft beds and flushing toilets.

After tea, we went for a cruise on Lake Lucerne and, seeing as it was just on dusk, we were able to get some amazing views of the city lit up. While the skipper steered the boat, his right-hand man came out on deck to enjoy a few beers with us. I found him to be a strange one who reminded me of the character from Bram Stoker's novel, *Dracula*. On that cruise, I was able to learn a little more about the city.

Lucerne, situated on Lake Lucerne, is surrounded by an impressive mountainous panorama and is known as the gateway to central Switzerland. Complete with gable paintings, the covered medieval Chapel Bridge forms the centrepiece of the city's townscape and is considered to be one of the oldest covered wooden bridges in Europe. It is a city of town squares and churches…and a few vampires lurking in the shadows…

After the cruise, everyone was tired (especially so from the big night before), so we all headed back to our prison cells for an early sleep. Not long after we were all safely locked away in our cells, all the lights suddenly went out and I heard the loudest scream I have ever encountered in my life. It turns out it was Anastasia, another Canadian on our tour.

Paris

The next morning after we were released, we left Lucerne for an exciting journey to Paris. What made it extra special was that the day of our arrival coincided with Bastille Day, also known as French National Day, which is celebrated each year on July 14. The French National day commemorates the Storming of the Bastille on July 14, 1789 as well as the unity of the French people in 1790.

After checking into our hotel, we again boarded the bus for a city tour to take in some of the well-known attractions, such as the Louvre, The Avenue des Champs-Élysées, Notre Dame and the River Seine. We hopped off our ride not far from the Eiffel Tower to witness a spectacular fireworks display over the city.

The following day allowed us free time to explore the city as we wished, so after breakfast, Jono and I teamed up with Steph and her friend Christine to go for a wander. After catching the subway, it was a short walk to the base of the Eiffel Tower, where we kicked back for a while and laid on the grass, admiring the magnificent structure before us. After posing for the obligatory photos, we started making our way along the River Seine, ending up at a café for a caffeine hit and more chatting. Seeing as the tour was almost at the end and we only had one or two days left, it was great to be able to spend that morning in Paris with the girls and share that memory before we all went our separate ways.

After the café, Steph and Christine went off for a spot of shopping while Jono decided to head back to the hotel to rest up, as that night was going to be the last night we would all be together. Half of the people on the Contiki tour were flying out of Paris instead of returning to London, so it was shaping up to be a big night, a last 'hurrah'.

I probably should have taken Jono's lead on resting, but after watching The Doors movie as a child and reading all the biographies on Jim Morrison, I had to go and visit his grave while in Paris. So, I took the map and caught the subway out to Père Lachaise station in search of Jim's grave. When I hopped off the subway and stepped out into the bright sunlight, I took a look to the left and saw the massive wall surrounding the cemetery. You can't miss it.

One Eye, One Ear – No Worries

I grabbed a map from the flower shop near the entrance and made my way inside the maze of tombstones. The cemetery is huge, the largest in Paris, and was established in 1804. It is the final resting place of not only Jim Morrison, but names such as Oscar Wilde, Edith Piaf and Fredric Chopin.

I managed to find the spot I was looking for quite easily – division six – and was amazed to find a very clean and well-kept tomb, not covered in graffiti as the movie and biographies had said. It was lovely to see that it had been taken care of in the end. After spending a bit of time kicking back with Jim, I decided to make my way back to the hotel as it was starting to get late and I needed to allow enough time to get myself ready for our big night out.

I managed to get in a quick nap before donning my party clothes and heading out with the rest of the Contiki crew for our last night together. What better place to celebrate a fantastic holiday than the wonderful city of Paris! After another impressive drive through the city, we finally hopped off the bus in front of the cabaret club that Joey had booked for dinner and a show.

The cabaret club was right across the road from the Moulin Rouge, so a few of the girls in the group got quite excited and ran over to pose for photos there. I must admit, it is a pretty impressive structure with the red windmill protruding from the roof. Co-founded in 1889 by Charles Zidler and Joseph Oller, the Moulin Rouge is known as the birthplace of the modern can-can. It is now a world-famous tourist attraction, offering musical dance entertainment and iconic photo opportunities.

The cabaret club we dined at was also pretty spectacular. Even though my dinner consisted of the smallest piece of chicken I had ever had in my life, the food was delicious and the show was entrancing, quite a spectacle to behold (but I didn't expect anything less from a city like Paris!).

After the performance, the dancers asked if anyone in the audience wanted to volunteer to jump up on stage and join them in an act. Shaban, being the Aussie larrikin he was, decided it was his time to shine and immediately put his hand up. The performer had him sit in a chair in the middle of the stage and asked if he smoked, which he did. He put a cigarette between his lips and sat there nervously wondering what was going to happen next.

Then, the two performers stood at either side of the stage and started tossing flame throwers to one another as part of a juggling act. The flames went over, behind and in front of Shaban's head. Then, in the blink of an eye, one flame thrower went swiftly past the back of Shaban's head and the other straight past his face, taking the smoke with it. Man, that was quick. It was a great act, and everyone gave Shaban a massive cheer – what a legend.

Curtain call on Contiki

The curtains fell and the show was over, so it was time to head over to an Irish bar a few blocks away for drinks to finish off our adventure as one big group. We arrived at the bar and it was all cheering, high-fiving and drunken rambling about how we were all going to meet up again one day. I had grown quite find of these people and I was going to miss them, so for me, it was an emotional night.

The festivities continued until the early hours, I guess we didn't want the night to end. I remember making a promise to Jeff that one day I was going to visit him and Jamie in America. I am yet to make good on that promise, but there is still time!

The following morning, we dropped half the tour group at the airport for their flights home, then the rest of us made the long journey back to London, nursing massive hangovers. We spent our final night together having dinner at the pub near the hotel where we started the journey just two weeks before. I remember giving Marcia a big hug as the time had come to say goodbye before we all scattered in the wind to our own corners of the world.

Twenty-Two

Lads On The Loose

Scotland

A few days later, Jono and I had somewhat recovered from our Contiki adventures and caught the train up to Edinburgh to start the next stage of our journey. The trip took two hours and I remember looking out the window at the lush, green English countryside whizzing by. We arrived at Waverley Station and went to find a hostel, which we did just down from the Royal Mile, buoyed by the sounds of bagpipes in the distance.

Edinburgh was another amazing place I am so blessed to have had the opportunity to visit. We spent the next few days checking out the area, including iconic Edinburgh Castle, which sits atop a hill in the middle of the city. We also did a pub crawl (of course!) and ate a shitload of haggis!

I used one of those quaint red payphones to call Scottish Dave and planned for Jono and I to head to Dave's home town of Kelso for the weekend. Dave was kind enough to come down to Waverley Station to pick us up and drive us the hour and a half to Kelso, with his mate Iain in the passenger seat. On the drive to Kelso, we stopped at a pub for a beer, then ended up at Iain's place in the middle of town which they called the 'mancave'. We put our beer stash in the fridge, made ourselves comfortable and started drinking. Unfortunately, Dave had to work at a bar later, so he only had a few, while the three of us were happy to knock them back like there was no tomorrow.

We found ourselves at a local pub, where Dave was able to join us for a few hours before heading to work. Poor lad, he was going to be on the wrong side of the bar for a while! It was a great start to what was to become another epic – and very messy – weekend. Dave and Jono got along fantastically and Iain was just like us as well – although his party animal status seemed to exceed even our seasoned reputation! I watched as he downed three shots of whisky, spilt his beer everywhere, then the barman happily poured him another while he finished his drink quicker than I could say "holy shit". The man was a machine.

The night ended with a sober Dave picking us up after his shift as we staggered through the streets of Kelso. He took us back to his parent's place, just on the outskirts of town. The following morning, we were understandably feeling a bit rough, but decided to take a walk around Dave's parent's farm while our friend ran some errands. We came across a river with a little wooden bridge over it. Jono was amazed by this little feature, and as Dave recalled even a few years later, the first thing Jono said when we walked back into the house was; "there's an actual river by your house", which Dave thought was quite funny.

After a feed, we jumped into Dave's car and headed into town to Iain's place to embark on one of the biggest pub crawls I have ever experienced. We took the term 'Sunday sesh' to a whole new level and it was debauchery at it's finest. Kelso certainly has it's share of pubs and they all seemed to be named after a colour; 'The Black', 'The Red', and 'The White Swan', for example.

Walking along the cobblestone streets to the first pub, I found the small-town atmosphere of Kelso quite refreshing. We started off at 'The Red' and were pretty soon pickled – and it was only lunchtime. Iain was leading the way, and I don't think I have ever laughed so much in my life. At one stage, on a walk between pubs, Jono, Dave and Iain had a play wrestle on the lawn next to the cemetery while I happily stood back and took photos of the three of them rolling around on the ground. Jono lost his sunnies at one point, which we stumbled across on another trip between venues, just laying there on the grass. Looking back now, I am surprised we were even able to find the next pub by that stage, let alone a pair of sunnies!

We ended up at a nightclub, where the other three took off their shirts and wrapped them around their heads like bandanas. They were spilling their drinks everywhere, but still managed to get served, and I remember thinking, "only in Scotland".

Next minute, the night was over and the next day saw me waking up in bed next to Iain. I did a quick check to happily find my pants were still on, and breathed a sigh of relief. I was already feeling pretty crook, and waking up next to another man didn't make me feel any better! I found my shirt, which had a few patches of dried spew stuck to it, and saw Jono passed out on the couch. He was looking just as bad as I was feeling, so at least I knew we were all in this together.

Suddenly, there was a knock at the door. It was Dave, who had somehow made it back to his parent's place and had come to pick us up and take us back to Edinburgh. We had pre-booked a tour of the highlands, due to leave at 9 am, so we had to get moving. We made it to the bus just in time, said goodbye to Scottish Dave and settled back into tour mode. We must have looked (and smelled) a sight though, especially with the spew still on my shirt.

Jono did the old trick of covering his bloodshot eyes with sunnies. I wasn't so lucky. My glass eye was it's usual crystal clear colour, but my other eye was as red as could be and on show for everyone who had the pleasure of meeting me that day.

This tour was set to extend five days, and it was shaping up to be a long haul if we didn't start feeling better. We thought about bailing on the trip and even heading back to Australia early. The weekend in Kelso had destroyed us, even more than Contiki! However, we decided to stick it out and see what happened. In the end, we were glad we did. The highlands are a magical part of the world and it turned out to be another incredible experience that I am so glad I had the opportunity to pursue.

We were booked in to stay in a massive castle for the first night. Like Lucerne, it had an eerie vibe, and to this day I swear it was haunted. Luckily, we were in shared rooms, so I didn't have to sleep alone!

The next day, we headed out to the famous Loch Ness. I had my camera ready in case Nessie made an appearance and was convinced I could be the next person to capture an image of her (yes, I have a vivid imagination!), but alas, she was nowhere to be seen that day.

That night, we were ready for more drinking with our new tour friends at the bar in the hostel. After the bar closed, a few of us went for a walk down to the Loch again to see if we could spot the monster. In our drunken state, there were a few scattered sightings, but no pictures to prove it! I was busy staring out at the still water when I heard a splash and Jono yelling, "FREEDOM!". He certainly was in fine form that trip.

Before leaving Loch Ness, our tour guide told us that the lyrics to Led Zeppelin's *Stairway to Heaven* were written while the band was sitting in a boat on Loch Ness. I'm not sure how accurate that information is, but truth or not, it is a magical place.

Over the following days, we explored much more of the highlands and, despite initially wanting to pull the pin on the trip, I loved every minute. The weather was gloomy and overcast, but that just seemed to add to the mystique. We went out on a few hikes, which took the wind out of me, but there was no way I was going to miss out on the experience. We got to see the bridge where the Express, the train made famous by the Harry Potter movies, went across and yes – we happened to be there right at the time the train went by!

We finally made our way to Oban, where we were to spend our last night on the tour. Oban is a small resort town on the south coast of Scotland with a population of approximately 8,000, but during the tourist season it can host up to 25,000. The bay is a perfect horseshoe shape and the town is also well-known for its whisky distillery. Naturally, we had to partake in a tour of the distillery while we were there.

The tour group was booked for dinner at a local restaurant and the dress code was tartan. We all looked a treat in our outfits, certainly a Scottish night to remember. Jono and I decided that seeing as we had done pretty much everything else on this trip, it was time to break out the dancing shoes. However, after busting out a few moves, I was worn out, so I took my usual spot at the bar. Jono, on the other hand, was on fire, bringing out dance moves I had never seen before. It was fantastic to see him, and everyone around, having such a fun night.

The following day we departed Oban to make our way back to Edinburgh to finish the tour. The sky was still gloomy, but that didn't dampen our spirits. On the way, we stopped to check out a Sir William Wallace monument. To get there, we had to walk up a steep road, but seeing the monument at the top made it worth it. Sir William Wallace was a Scottish knight and a renowned leader of the Scottish Independence, leading the resistance fighters in a bid to free Scotland from English rule. He was knighted for his service in 1297, before being captured, hung drawn and quartered by the English in 1305. Wallace is portrayed by Mel Gibson in the movie *Braveheart* as he led the charge in the First War of Scottish Independence against King Edward I of England.

We finally arrived back in Edinburgh, where Jono and I booked into dorms at a university to spend our last few days in Scotland. That night, we met up with a few of the crew from the Haggis tour at a bar on the Royal Mile to say farewell and have a few drinks. In all fairness, I found it to be another great tour with friendly people, but it didn't quite live up to the Contiki! We all partied hard that night before the winds came by and we all scattered off on our own journeys.

Jono and I still had a couple of days in Scotland, so we enjoyed some downtime, taking walks, exploring the city and relaxing in the local green spaces. It was during one of our lazy afternoons while we were sitting in a park, talking about some of the things that had happened in my life, that Jono suggested I write a book one day. Well, here it is – I have finally done it!

We had some great chats over those days. It felt like the last time we were going to spend time together for a while and I wanted to make the most of it. Unfortunately, that feeling proved to be right as Jono settled up in Darwin after the trip, so it was many years before we were able to catch up again.

The final stage of our adventure was a train back to London, where we booked into a backpacker hostel to spend our last night together. Surprisingly, we were pretty tame and didn't cause any trouble that night! The following morning, we had breakfast at the same park where we had sat before on the first day of our trip. It felt surreal to be back there after all we had seen and done in the whirlwind five weeks away. We then made our way to the station, where we said our goodbyes and I caught the tube to Heathrow to continue on to Canada, while Jono still had another half a day in London before his flight back to Australia.

Twenty-Three

Canada's Comforting Soil

While killing time at the airport waiting for my flight, I decided to use the internet to check my Facebook account. It was good to hear from Alara and Jeff, two friends I made on the Contiki tour, but I was even happier to receive a friend request from Marcia. Even if I wasn't able to catch up with her on this trip, I knew I was going to keep in touch with her when I returned home to Australia and maybe one day we would get the chance to meet up again.

The eight-hour flight to Toronto was a smooth one. I was looking forward to catching up and spending time with Adam again. I caught the airport bus shuttle to Bond place, our designated meeting spot. It had been two and a half years since our travels through Thailand and a bit had happened in Adam's life since then. He was still happily based in Toronto, but had met a lovely lady called Nancy who had grown up in the area. It had also been four years since I was last in Toronto and in that time, Adam had moved away from Ishlington and was now living in the suburb of Davisville with two Irish lads and a Canadian guy.

We headed to Adam's place and he introduced me to his housemates – Boyd, Aiden and Matt – who were very friendly and welcoming. That first night, Adam and I went for a walk to chat and catch up, and I remember him telling me something that has stayed with me ever since. He said, "you can never stop learning in life." Such wise words, which I have endeavoured to live by for my remaining days.

The following day, while Adam and the other lads went to work, I went for another walk where I stopped in at a local pub for a beer. I found myself turning to say something to Jono, expecting him to still be with me, and I realised I missed him. After five weeks travelling side-by-side, that moment was over and I was solo again for a while, but it was nice to be back in the somewhat familiar streets of Toronto.

One of the first weekends I was there, I went to watch Adam play football with the Mississauga Demons – and he somehow talked me into playing. I hadn't pulled on the footy boots in years, and it showed as I only got one kick in for the entire time. But, we all had a blast, and it was an awesome way to spend the afternoon.

That night we all went out to a local bar, Whelan's Gate, for a few drinks. It was great to catch up with Hendy, Floppy, Dahm and all the other guys again. They had booked a private function for the footy club, complete with tickets sporting the silhouette of Adam passed out in the toilets! He had certainly made a name for himself there in Canada.

We all got quite drunk, and at one point I was dancing on the tables and thinking how great it was to be back here. Next thing, I woke up in a strange place, thinking, "I've got to stop doing this". As it turned out, I was at Boyd's girlfriend Linda's place. Later that day, after I had recovered a little, Boyd and I caught the subway back to Davisville. Boyd worked a lot from home, so I was able to see him quite often during the day and we got along well. So well, in fact, that Adam started calling him my Boydfriend.

One night, I went to a baseball game with Boyd and Linda to watch the Blue Jays play at Rogers Centre. Originally known as SkyDome, Rogers Centre is a multi-purpose stadium situated at the southwest base of the CN Tower. Growing up in Australia, I had always found baseball to be a boring sport, but seeing as I was in Canada where baseball is almost a religion, the atmosphere was electric and anything but boring. If you are ever in Canada, I highly recommend checking out a game.

The East Coast

Since my first overseas trip to Canada back in 2004, I had kept in touch with Ken. He had sent me his number and told me to give him a call while I was there. So, a few days after the baseball, I found a payphone and rang him. He told me he was back living in his hometown of Harvey (coincidence!), which is located right over on the East Coast of Canada, not far from the US border. Nevertheless, I figured it was time I made good on my promise to catch up with him for a beer, so I booked myself a ticket and flew over to the east. I landed in Fredericton, which is the capital of New Brunswick, and Ken was there to pick me up from the airport. We had a good chat on the drive back to Harvey and it was great to see him again after nearly five years.

After a quick tour through town, including visiting the cemetery where his parents were buried, we made our way to his house on the outskirts. It was a cosy little house that he had recently built. Ken had a friend staying there, Don, who was from Arkansas and exuded a laid-back hippy vibe. Don also loved a drink, so it was good to know there was someone else around I could get stuck into it with! That first night, the three of us sat out in the garage, drinking and telling stories.

One tale I particularly enjoyed was how not long before I arrived, Ken and Don decided to take a trip across the border into America. After hearing stories about how difficult it can be to cross lines, Ken decided it would be easier to drop Don off by a river to get back into Canada, so he could swim upstream into the country instead of risking no re-entry at the gate. The plan was for Ken to then pick him up at a designated spot, and they opted for executing the plan at nightfall so there was less chance of Don being spotted as he paddled along. Seeing as Don wasn't the best swimmer and by the time he hit the water he was quite drunk, it was a very risky operation. However, somehow they managed to pull it off and Don made it safely back into Canada without too much drama.

The following morning I went for a walk to explore the area surrounding Ken's place. Just down the road I came across a creek that offered a good view from Ken's window. It was a very peaceful place and it felt good to be out of the hustle and bustle of the city and to explore a bit more of rural Canada. When I got back to the house, Ken told Don and I to jump in the car for a camping trip up to Lake Magaguadavic to catch up with his friends Bruce and Brenda. We arrived at the lake about midday and one of the first things I noticed was how beautiful the water was and how friendly and accommodating Ken's friends were. They had a cabin overlooking the water that they called their home each summer, and it was magical.

Soon enough, the esky's were opened, the beers were going down a treat and we sparked up a lovely campfire to add to the ambience. At some point during the night I passed out in the spare room in the cabin, where I awoke in the early hours of the morning. Everyone else was asleep and it felt so peaceful. I made my way to the water's edge where I just sat for the next couple of hours alone with my thoughts as I waited for the sun to rise.

I had my camera with me and I took the opportunity to look through my photos of our recent Contiki tour and I realised how much I was already missing that time. Everyone else was now back in their home countries, at work or studying, while I had the opportunity to be still travelling. How lucky I was!

I made it to sunrise then stumbled back to bed, where I stayed all morning. Later that day, Bruce took Don and I out on the boat to go fishing. Even though I grew up at the beach, fishing was never my favourite pastime. I am reluctant to now admit that the only fish I have ever caught in my life was while sitting in the middle of a lake in rural Canada while coming down off a massive hangover. I am happy to report that I was the only one that day to land a fish, so that is a positive!

After our afternoon on the lake, we made our way back to Ken's place for a good night's sleep. Over the next few days, Ken continued to show me around the area. On one of my last days, Ken, Don, Bruce, Brenda and I piled into two cars and went for a drive down to St. Andrew's, a small coastal town on the Canadian/US border. It is a town known for its whale watching and golf courses. The massive Algonquin hotel was also worth checking out and Don and I happily got lost in the maze of rooms and hallways. Growing up reading Stephen King novels, I was amazed to discover that the American state we could see across the river from St Andrew's was Maine – home of the famous writer.

The following morning it was time to say goodbye to my new friends and Ken drove me to the airport to catch my flight back to Toronto. It was another emotional goodbye and I was starting to get tired of farewelling people, but as I was beginning to realise, this was a small price to pay to be able to travel as freely as I was.

Toronto

The Irish lads, Boyd and Aiden, played Gaelic Football and they were playing in their league's grand final on the first weekend back in Toronto after my East Coast trip. Adam, Nancy and I went along to support them. They ended up winning, so the celebrations soon began in earnest. Adam and Nancy had to work the next day so left after the final siren, but I stayed on to celebrate with the team. I didn't know anyone except Boyd and Aiden, but that had never stopped me having a good time before! By the end of the night, we were all singing, *Don't Stop Believing*, and *We are the Champions'* at the top of our lungs.

Seeing as I only had a few weeks left in Canada, Adam and I decided to plan a few trips over my last two weekends to make sure I got the most out of my time there. The first outing was down to Niagara Falls where we planned to stay the night. The second trip (and super exciting), was a three-day tour to cross the border into the US where we would visit New York and Atlantic City. I wondered how I would go getting into the country, with drink driving conviction on my record, but we were soon to find out. Was I finally going to live out my childhood dream and visit the United States of America?

But first – it was time to experience the raw power of Niagara Falls again. Even though I had visited there on my last trip, I was thrilled to be back; this place never disappoints. We hired a car and headed down on a Saturday morning, where we checked into a cheap motel. We spent the afternoon visiting a few wineries and partaking in a wine tour, which is quite popular in the Niagara region. That night, we went to view the iconic falls. As I had only ever seen them during the day, it was quite a spectacle to witness them flowing in the darkness, illuminated under bright lights with the roar of the water in the background. Afterwards, the three of us went into town for a few drinks to finish up another great experience.

US of A

The following weekend was our much-anticipated crossing into the US. We rose early to catch our tour bus for the trip and, much to my relief, the customs officers didn't probe too much into my history so I was allowed to enter the country. You little beauty – I was finally stepping foot on American soil!

I got the feeling this tour group was much different to the Contiki and Haggis tours and Adam, Nancy and I would more-or-less stick to ourselves. The first night we stayed in New Jersey, then the next day we were off to explore New York City. As the bus headed towards the immense buildings, I was amazed by the sheer size of it all as the NYC skyline loomed large on the horizon. When we arrived, our tour guide gave us a designated time to meet back at the bus for our onward journey to Atlantic City, which meant we had the entire morning to explore New York City.

The first thing we did was journey to the top of the Rockefeller Centre, where we were able to take in some awesome views of the city, especially of

Central Park. We then headed to a boat cruise on the Hudson River and as we passed the Statue of Liberty, the boat stopped and the crew played *God Bless America* over the loudspeakers. It was such a surreal moment in my life, and as I stood there on the boat listening to the music, I felt a tear leave my eye. I had finally had the chance to live out a dream from childhood and visit the US of A. It meant a lot.

After the cruise, our free time was up and we boarded the bus to Atlantic City. It was late afternoon by the time we arrived. Nancy opted to stay at the hotel, while Adam and I went for a stroll along the boardwalk. To one side of us was the Atlantic Ocean, while on the other there were casinos everywhere, reaching for the sky. In my mind, it was 'Vegas by the Sea', and I'm sure many dreams were made and lost in this city too. Adam and I chatted as we walked along, talking about how unreal it was that two good friends who grew up in Harvey, WA, were now walking together along the Atlantic City coast.

We met up with Nancy a little later and checked out a few of the casinos, then went for a few drinks at one of the beach bars. The next day we made the journey back to Canada as I started to prepare for my long trip to my next destination – Taiwan.

Taiwan

The day before I left Canada, I messaged my Taiwanese friend, Bogi, and he replied that he would be there to pick me up from the airport. So, after my usual goodbyes to Adam and the crew, I was on my merry way to the island of Taiwan.

I arrived around 8 pm and, true to his word, Bogi was there to greet me as I walked out of customs. I was also happy to see he had Kenny with him, who was another Taiwanese I had worked with back at the meatworks in Harvey.

I told Bogi I was feeling jetlagged after my trip from Canada, and he replied he had just the thing to help waiting in his car. I had never known beer to be a cure for jetlag, but I took Bogi's word for it and as we drove into the big city of Taipai, I was able to down a few cold ones. Seeing as Bogi was a local and I didn't know much about the country, I had left it up to him to organise my accommodation. However, after he started turning off into a few side streets and looking out the window like he was anticipating something, it started to feel like we were driving into the ghetto. I was beginning to regret my decision.

We finally pulled over in a dark side street and I went to check into the guesthouse Bogi had organised for me. The place was filthy, with water leaking from the ceiling right next to what looked like a live wire. Even worse, it appeared I was the only one staying there. Thanks, Bogi, but at least he tried so I was appreciative of that.

After a few beers with Kenny and Bogi in the guestroom at the otherwise deserted house, they told me they were off and would return in the morning to pick me up for some sightseeing. I was now alone, although after my long flight I was easily able to fall asleep to the sound of dripping water.

I rose early in the morning to go for a walk and explore the area. I had a coffee at Starbucks (which I seemed to be able to sniff out anywhere in the world) then made my way back to the guesthouse just before 11 am to meet up with the guys. Bogi arrived on foot, followed shortly after by Kenny on his scooter. I was impressed.

We went for lunch at a nice restaurant that served Taiwanese food, which I found to be an acquired taste – one which I had not yet acquired. I wanted to be polite though, so I told Bogi and Kenny it was delicious. That was a big mistake, as they then proceeded to put more and more food in front of me to try!

After lunch, we caught the subway to check out some ancient temples. At one, Bogi gave me a stick of burning incense and told me to pray, so I did. We also checked out the Taipei 101 building, which from 2004 to 2009 was classified as the world's tallest inhabited building, measuring 509.2 metres high. The record was overtaken in 2009 – the year I happened to visit – by the Burj Khalifa building in Dubai. I guess I have to plan a trip to Dubai next!

By dusk, I decided it was time to quench my thirst so turned to Bogi (my unofficial tour guide), and asked him to find a bar instead of another temple. As it turns out, he had been waiting all day for me to say that, so he was quick to oblige! Before I knew it, the three of us were happily relaxing in a bar enjoying a few cold beers and really getting into it. I discovered that Bogi and Kenny sure could party, as after a few hours, the night turned into a blur and I couldn't remember much until the three of us arrived back at the guesthouse, staggering drunk at around midnight.

Kenny took off down the road and stacked it just in view (thankfully he was ok) and Bogi and I passed out on my bed together. At some point, I awoke to find him snuggled up to me like we were a married couple. I decided not to disturb him and promptly fell back asleep myself, so I hope he didn't get any crazy ideas!

Back in Bangkok

The next day, Bogi dropped me off at the airport as I continued on to Bangkok for more fun and games. We were all feeling a little worse for wear, and the three-hour flight really took it out of me. I was starting to feel really exhausted. I had pushed myself to the limit this trip and to be honest, by this point it was almost a relief to be near the end.

I wasn't quite ready for the hustle and bustle of Khaosan Road, so I checked into a hotel not far from the airport to relax and rest up for a few days. The taxi driver offered me a brochure covered in hot chicks and told me if I doubled the fare, he would take me to them, but I just wasn't interested. All I wanted to do was get to my hotel and sleep, so I declined.

There was a beautiful view of the city skyline from the balcony of my hotel. I spent the next few days there, just resting and hanging out by the pool. Finally, on Wednesday morning, I decided it was time for one last boost up before heading home, so I caught a taxi into the city and checked into a guesthouse smack bang in the centre of Khaosan Road.

I spent the last days of my trip wandering this famous district, getting a massage here and there and a few big nights thrown in for good measure. Being back here brought up so many memories from when I visited with Adam almost three years prior, but unlike that trip where we ended up travelling all over Thailand and Laos, I stayed put.

On one of my nights out, I was sitting at a bar in Khaosan Road where I started talking to a local Thai woman. After checking her out for a while, I still wasn't sure if she was a ladyboy, but I decided to hang out with her for a while just to see how the night unfolded. She asked if I had ever been to Patpong, which is one of the world's most famous red-light districts. I hadn't, so I agreed to go with her.

We caught a taxi over to Patpong where my new friend and I entered a bar. I sat there shocked – I couldn't believe what I was seeing. Up there on stage was a group of naked ladies shooting ping pong balls out of their…. um….yes, there. All the while, they were being cheered on by drunken tourists. I certainly wasn't cheering. I personally found it degrading and appalling that these young ladies be subjected to that so the clubs could make money. I had mixed feelings about Thailand at that moment and I discovered that if you scratch the surface, you will find it corrupt to the core. Sitting there at the club, I felt so uneasy that I suggested to my lady friend that we leave, before I had even finished my first beer.

We ended up at a Westernised nightclub, where I felt much more comfortable so we stayed for a few hours, then spent the rest of the night together back at my guesthouse. In the morning, she got up and left, just like that – in and out of my life in one night. But, like a lot of other people I have met along the way, we shared a moment and she played a part in my story.

The following day was my last in Bangkok before finally heading home, so I ordered a beer and just relaxed in a bar, watching the people go by and doing a bit of reminiscing. I thought about how eleven weeks before I had been sitting in a park with Jono in London on the first day of my trip, not knowing what to expect. What followed had been the adventure of a lifetime. I had seen and done so much and I knew then while sitting in

Khaosan on my last day that the memories I had made along the way would stay with me for life.

The following day I headed to the airport in a cab for my eight-hour flight back to reality. My journey was over…for now.

Being back home, it felt as though something had changed in me. I was in the usual routine of working and catching up with friends, but I felt now more than ever how much I loved, and needed, travelling. I started thinking about the friends I had made on my trip, especially Marcia, who I had found to be such a friendly person during our time together on Contiki.

Seeing as she was now one of my friends on Facebook, a few days after arriving home I decided to take a chance and write her a message. I simply told her that it was great to meet her and hopefully we will get a chance to catch up again one day. I was over the moon when I received a reply a few days later to reciprocate my feelings and that if I ever find myself in Canada to let her know. With Adam still in Toronto and seeing as I had now made plenty of other good friends in the northern hemisphere, there was a very good chance I would get to see her in the coming years

Twenty-Four

Look Out, Sydney. Joel Is Back.

I didn't know it at the time, but heading towards the end of 2010 gave me the chance to travel again. My old friend Rhino was now living in Vancouver with his Canadian partner and had just proposed to her. The wedding was to be held in Bondi, a famous beach suburb of Sydney, right on the water's edge. It had been twelve years since that day PJ and I took off on our mystery flight to Sydney and seven years since he passed away. Heading back to Sydney was going to be emotional for me, but I was looking forward to reliving some of those memories and making some brand new ones celebrating Rhino's big day.

The wedding was the last weekend in November, but I decided to spend a week over there to make the most of it and have a bit of a holiday. My childhood friend Louisa was happy for me to stay with her while I was in Sydney and she also volunteered to pick me up from the airport. My friend Atho, who was a groomsman, was also spending a week in Sydney with his then-girlfriend, so we planned to meet up a few times before the wedding.

Louisa was there to pick me up, just as she promised, and it was fantastic to see her after all those years. We had a great chat on the drive, passing through King's Cross so I could check it out, but it felt strange to be there during the day! Louisa and her partner Adrian lived in a suburb called Ryde, which was a bit out of the city but seemed to be a nice neighbourhood.

The following morning, I rose early and Louisa dropped me off in the city on her way to work. I had breakfast at Circular Quay, then decided to go exploring. I started walking down William Street, the same place PJ and I visited all those years ago on that magical mystery trip and, as the harbour came into view, I started to feel quite emotional. I could feel PJ's presence, like he was somehow with me again. I continued to visit some of the spots we had been to and found it difficult, but at the same time comforting, to allow the memories to come flooding back.

At one point, I found myself standing on the steps to the opera house, just taking it all in. It was a rainy day down in the harbour and I have since discovered that this kind of weather really heightens my senses. After a while, I decided to head back to The Rocks to see if I could find the pub where PJ and I had met up with his uncle Mick for drinks. I remembered it was called The Orient and after a short stroll through the streets, I found it quite easily. I went in and ordered a beer, and now everything felt more surreal. While I was there, Atho called and we arranged for him and his girlfriend to come down to catch up for a beer.

We spent the afternoon checking out a few pubs around The Rocks and, by my standards, had a pretty quiet drinking session. We planned to meet up again around 11 am the next day to do the Sydney Harbour Bridge climb. So, the next day, Louisa again dropped me in the city on her way to work so I could meet Atho and his girlfriend. I was really looking forward to checking out the view from the summit of the bridge and it was another thing to tick off the bucket list.

We all found the tour and listened intently as the guide ran us through the rules and regulations. We also had to blow in a breathalyser to make sure we were sober for the climb. Thank goodness I didn't have breakfast beers that morning! Spanning Sydney Harbour across 48.8 metres of water, the bridge is an iconic Australian image, identifiable by it's intricate 'coat hanger-like' design. It is the world's tallest steel arch bridge at 134 metres from top to water level, and until 2012 was the widest long-span bridge in the world.

Climbing the bridge is a top tourist activity in Sydney – and I couldn't wait to join the masses of other travellers who had successfully walked to the top. We put on our harnesses and started the climb, which was set to take approximately three hours to reach the summit and back with a few photo opportunities (and chances to catch our breath) along the way. At first, I was amazed by the structure of the bridge and the size of the rivets and bolts used to construct it, but as we got higher, I found myself looking over Sydney Harbour and the awesome view it had to offer. It was breath-taking.

After what seemed a lifetime, we finally reached the summit, which made the sweat-inducing climb totally worthwhile. From up there, not only can you look out over the harbour, but there is a spectacular view of the Blue Mountains out in the distance. It really did feel like I was on top of the world. I looked over to the Opera House and thought of PJ again, taking photos of each other on the forecourt, and it brought a warm feeling to my heart. Finally, we started the journey back down, but I know I would take that view with me and remember it for the rest of my life.

That night, Rhino had organised a cruise on the harbour for everyone who was invited to the wedding as a build-up to the big day. So, instead of going back to Louisa's place, I headed out with Atho and his girlfriend to their accommodation in Bondi to spend a few hours with them before the cruise. At the designated time, we met up with the rest of the wedding crew at one of the piers and boarded the boat. I quickly found the bar and started mingling with the other guests. It was good to see Rhino again, and looking so happy. We talked about a few of the memories we shared when we visited Canada together five years previously.

I went up on deck and took in the sunset as it went down over the harbour. As the boat sailed underneath the bridge, I remember thinking that earlier in the day I was looking down from the top instead of up from the water! I was well behaved on the cruise and didn't get too drunk. I just mainly stayed up on deck and took it all in. Rhino, on the other hand, was quite tipsy and almost fell in the water a few times. I guess with the wedding imminent, he had the perfect excuse to let his hair down and make the most of the celebrations!

The night before the big day arrived, Rhino invited everyone out for dinner, but I wanted to spend a bit of time with Louisa and her partner Adrian, so I didn't go. Instead, I cracked open a bottle of Jacks and proceeded to get blind drunk while listening to Adrian bust out some tunes on his boombox. The first thing I did when I woke up in the morning was rush to the toilet and throw up, then I went and laid back down with a splitting headache, wondering if I had anything planned that day. Then it hit me. Shit. It was the wedding day.

I jumped up and changed into my finest attire, all the while I was dry retching. Due to my own self-inflicted illness, I was not in a good way, but it was my friend's wedding and I was going to be there with bells on – no matter what.

So, I caught the train and then a bus out to Bondi. While waiting for the bus, I ran into a guy I remembered from the cruise, and we decided to head to the wedding together. We arrived at the beach and made our way to the Bondi Icebergs Club, where the wedding ceremony and reception were being held. Being a little early, my new travel/drinking buddy and I found ourselves a nice bar overlooking the ocean, where we settled in and knocked back a few cheeky beers, which I found to be a terrific cure for my hangover.

The Icebergs is a classy place with a massive pool stretching out over the ocean. We had beautiful views out over the water from our vantage point, but could also see the wedding ceremony about to take place right below us. We wondered if we should just watch from there, but decided we should finish our drinks and head down. We got there just in time to see Rhino and Christine exchange vows. It was another magical moment, and I was so proud to be able to see another good friend get married – and in Bondi!

Straight after the ceremony, the wedding party went off to get photos done while the rest of the guests followed my new friend and I back up to the bar we had found earlier to start celebrating. It was just like a big reunion of all the people from the cruise a few nights before. Eventually, the wedding party returned and we all went into the function room for the reception. As was often the case at weddings, there was plenty of dancing, and I ended up getting blackout drunk and couldn't remember anything until I woke up in the morning on someone's couch.

As I started to gather my bearings, I saw that I wasn't alone, Atho and his girlfriend were there so I figured I had followed them back to their accommodation. I tried to make conversation, but the girlfriend was very icy towards me and I remember thinking, "oh, what did I do?" I decided the best course of action was to make a hasty retreat and head back to Louisa's place, still in my wedding finery but now covered in alcohol and dried spew.

I found out later that, as I hadn't planned any accommodation for that night, I was going around asking people if I could stay with them. I did have options, but in my drunken state I was determined to stay with Atho. He and his girlfriend had other plans and tried to politely get rid of me, even attempting to sneak out while I wasn't watching, but I found them and wouldn't take no for an answer. Long story short – I made it to their couch and proceeded to snore my head off all night, hence the unfriendly reception the next morning!

When I made it back to Louisa's, she took one look at me when I walked in and burst out laughing. "Looks like someone had a big night," she quipped. Unfortunately, I didn't have time to get changed before she had to drive me to the airport for my flight back to WA. It felt like one of the longest flights I have ever been on – trumping even my international travel – and I must have looked a right sight. But, I made it back home, safe and sound, and looking forward to a shower and some sleep in my own bed.

Twenty-Five

GATHER NO MOSS

At the start of 2011, even though I get on great with my parents, I decided it was time to move out again. My older brother Kelvin and I shared a house in Binningup and we had his daughter Alannah stay with us from New Zealand for a while. By the winter of 2011, it had been two years since my world trip, and I was starting to get the urge to travel again.

My cousin, Shane (Flemo) had met and fallen in love with a Canadian girl, Lyndsay, during his stay in the county and they were now planning to get married the following July in Toronto, so I decided that would be the perfect time to head overseas again.

I sent Marcia a message to let her know I was planning to head back to Canada and asked if she was going to be around Toronto at that time. I couldn't believe my luck when she replied a few days later to say that although she was at university in London now, she would be back in Toronto by July. I was so happy, I went outside and did a little dance in the rain!

So, it was time to start planning my next big adventure. Canada was set, now I just had to pick a few more destinations to discover along the way. I was still keeping in touch with Scottish Dave, so I decided to stop by Scotland again and spend a week with him. To finish this trip, I decided on another two-week Contiki tour through Europe as I had such a great time on the last one. It looked like world trip number two was in the making!

By this stage, Jono had met his partner and started a family up in Darwin, so we were now following different paths in life. This meant he couldn't join me this time. However, another friend from home, Brad (Crudder), heard me talking about my travel plans and wanted to join me on the Contiki tour – and I was over the moon that he could make it! Now, all I had to do was wait for summer in the Northern Hemisphere to hit and I would be taking off once again. You little beauty!

On a completely different note, but one certainly deserving of a mention, was PJ's 30th birthday at the end of 2011. His sister Sharon got in touch with myself and a number of his old friends to let us know the family were heading out to the Woky to celebrate his life and the milestone he was sadly missing. That night, December 2, the Woky was packed with PJ's family and friends. It was eight years since he passed, but it felt like he was still there with us all – I'm sure we would have made him proud with our celebration.

Near the end of 2011, after nearly a year of living with Kelvin, his circumstances changed and our lease at the house was up. My younger brother, Frog, reached out and asked if I wanted to move in with him and his girlfriend at the time, as they had a spare bedroom and figured I could help with the rent. They lived in a pretty big house on a hill overlooking Binningup with an amazing view of the Indian Ocean in the distance, so I jumped at the chance to live there.

So, 2011 ticked over into 2012 as I moved in with Frog and set myself up for another big year. I head from Marcia a few times, who told me she was so excited for my upcoming trip to Canada. I still couldn't believe I was getting the chance to see her again, three years after we first met on Contiki.

So much in my life felt great at that point; living with Frog in a beautiful house overlooking the ocean, planning my next amazing adventure and getting the chance to see the woman who I had become very fond of as a friend. But, all wasn't as perfect as I made it out to be. I began looking inward and learning a lot about more about myself now that I was well into my 30s.

I had first discovered alcohol as a teenager and don't get me wrong, I have had plenty of great times on the booze over the years, but I was starting to see a pattern emerge in my behaviour. For years, I had used alcohol as a social lubricant to help me navigate my way through the real world after leaving the comforts of the school crowd. As much as I tried to hide it, I was always self-conscious of my face, but after having a few drinks I was able to emerge from my shell and become the happy, fun drunk people came to expect.

When it came to drinking, I could easily go weeks without it, but when I did start, I would keep drinking until I woke up the next day (or a few days later) without much recollection of what happened. I had become a full-on binge drinker, and I began to get a little concerned about how this would affect my long-term health. With another world trip on the horizon, I didn't want my drinking to become any more of a problem in my life, so I booked in to see a counsellor to try to address it.

However, unfortunately, either I didn't have the tools or wasn't emotionally prepared at that stage of my life to fix the problem, even though I knew what was happening. I only made it to one counselling session. Sadly, this decision was to have dire consequences over the coming years, mostly regarding my friendship with Marcia, which I held so dear.

This is very painful for me to recall, but I have learnt some harsh lessons these past five years and by far the hardest one to learn was that if you fear something happening and dwell on it in your mind, eventually it will come true. My friendship with Marcia was one of the best things that had happened to me at that point in my life, and even at that early stage, I was so worried that one day I would get drunk and do something stupid that would ruin what we had. As I was to find out later on, that fear did come true.

In the meantime, we still had Canada in 2012 to make some great memories and a few more years of friendship before it all went pear-shaped and leave me heartbroken.

Twenty-Six

World Trip #2

Toronto

The time finally rolled around to once again head to the airport. I had organised with Crudder to meet in Paris in a month's time, as my old mate Matt drove me to the International terminal to head off on another trip of a lifetime.

Adam had married Nancy in Perth earlier in the year, and they were now back in Canada. I planned to stay with them at their apartment on King Street West for a week or so before heading out to Davisville to spend a bit of time with Boyd.

My flight had a stopover in Sydney and Vancouver, before finally landing in Toronto early in the afternoon on June 27. I caught a cab to Adam's apartment, and before long we were both enjoying a beer on the rooftop which offered a great view of the city skyline, including the CN Tower in the distance. It felt good to be back, three years on from my last visit.

I happened to be in town for Canada Day, July 1st, which is a national statutory holiday celebrating the coming together of three provinces – Nova Scotia, New Brunswick, and the Canada province, which then split into Ontario and Quebec – in 1867. This is accepted as the date Canada was officially created as it stands today. So, not ever needing an excuse, Adam, myself and our friend Newby (who had come over for my cousin Flemo's wedding) took off on a pub crawl which ended up lasting all day. I really was living the dream!

Adam had given me a phone to use while I was in Canada, so I sent Marcia a message via Facebook with the number and asked her to text me when she was free to catch up. That happened to be the day after our Canada Day pub crawl. We were sitting around nursing hangovers when the beep finally arrived. Marcia said she was on her way into the city and asked if I was free to catch up. Whatever plans I already had for that day completely went out the window as I hastily replied 'yes, would love to catch up'.

We planned to meet near the Hard Rock Café in an hour's time. While I waited, Adam, Newby and I went for lunch at a Korean restaurant. Instead of my usual beer, I ordered a lemonade. The boys couldn't believe it, and I guess I couldn't either! I was pretty nervous about seeing Marcia again, now that it was a reality. Usually when I was nervous, I would drink to calm the nerves, but this felt different, like it was an opportunity to put my best foot forward and not ruin the moment with booze.

After lunch, the boys headed off and I made my way to the Hard Rock Café. While standing there waiting, I felt like I was having a heart attack at one point – I was so nervous. It didn't help that Marcia had gotten off at the wrong station, so took her time getting there! My poor heart. Finally, through the sea of faces, I recognised hers from Contiki as she made her way towards me. It was like no time had passed at all since our European adventures, as we casually hugged hello and began chatting.

She asked what I felt like doing, and I suggested a nice walk down to the waterfront. My heart was racing, but it started to slow the more time we spent together and I began to feel more relaxed in her company. We made it down to the waterfront where I was able to take some great photos of the two of us. I was on cloud nine and still couldn't believe I had the chance to see Marcia in her home city of Toronto.

We found a nice little outdoor bar right on the waterfront, where we relaxed and enjoyed a beer together. I found out a bit more about her life and we talked at length about our memories from the trip three years prior. We both had a laugh about the night out in Florence when I passed out in the lobby instead of making it back to my room.

After a while, Marcia had to get the subway back to her place, so it was time to say goodbye. I was walking on air as I made my way back to Adam's place and, seeing as I still had over two weeks left in Canada, I was hoping I would get another chance to catch up with her before I left.

Over the coming days, while Adam was at work Newby and I just did the usual tourist things, including having lunch at the top of the CN Tower. That weekend, we hired a car and made the trip down to Niagara Falls, my fourth visit now and, as always, a huge highlight. We went on 'Maid of the Mist', then met up with some other friends for a night out. We checked out a few bars and casinos, and at the last one I ended up falling asleep at the Black Jack table. For once, this doze wasn't a case of being too drunk, just overtired after a big couple of days.

A few days later I caught up and stayed with Boyd, who I had met on my last visit. We had stayed in touch and it was great to be able to see him again too. He picked me up from downtown and took me back to his place in Davisville. As soon as I stepped inside, all of these great memories came flooding back. Boyd's brother Rob was living there now too, so that evening we all walked to the pub for tea and a few beers.

Over those few days in Davisville, while Boyd was at work I spent my time strolling around town or catching the subway into the city. On one outing I came across the barbershop where I had my hair cut the last time I was there, so I went inside and was surprised the same lady was still working there. I was even more surprised she recognised me straight away – but I guess I have one of these faces people don't forget in a hurry! We chatted for a while and she was amazed to see me back in Toronto, which is a world away from Australia.

It started to dawn on me that no matter where I travel in the world, I would always come across people who will never leave their familiar surroundings and travelling may not be something they get to experience. It was then that I decided with certainty that I would continue to travel and share my experiences, so in a way I was not only living out my dream, but inspiring them as well. I left that barbershop more confident than ever about what I wanted to do with the rest of my life.

The Canadian wedding

A few days later, it was finally the day of Flemo's wedding. I got myself dressed up and Adam and Nancy picked me up from Boyd's place. The wedding was to held in Barrie, a small ski resort town about an hour and a half north of Toronto. We picked up Rhino on the way, who was also in town for the big day but without his partner, who had stayed home in Vancouver. Anything could happen now – I was even sharing a room with the big guy!

We made our way up to Barrie and checked into our hotel rooms. True to form, I hadn't even had time to sit down and relax when Rhino cracked a beer. I didn't want to seem rude, so of course I joined in. Before long, a number of wedding guests had joined us in the room and were also indulging in a few cold ones to get primed for the big day ahead.

The bus picked us up shortly after and took us out to the Snow Valley Ski Resort for the event. It was a scenic place which was very popular with tourists, especially in winter when the ski slopes were at their peak.

The ceremony was touching, but as soon as it was over, off we went to find the bar and the celebrations really begun. It was one big reunion, right in the heart of the Canadian countryside, and I revelled in the chance to catch up with quite a few people from back home as well as those I had met on previous trips to the country. It was a massive night, as you'd expect, and at one point (apparently) I was sitting passed out on a chair in the middle of the dance floor, while people boogied their way around me. The night ended with a singalong on the bus as it drove us back to the hotel, where I fell asleep to the sound of Rhino snoring.

The following morning we made our way back to Toronto and said goodbye to Rhino (which my liver was quite happy about, as I don't think it could have handled much more alcohol!). My time in Toronto was quickly coming to an end, and I had done everything I planned to do – but there was one more quest, to catch up with Marcia again.

I knew she was busy with her own life, but I prayed she would take the time to catch up with me once more before I left Canada. I was hoping to take a trip out to the islands, as the last time I did that was back in 2004 and I was on my own, so it would have been nice to share the experience with someone like Marcia. But, as each day went by without hearing from her, I was starting to lose hope that I would see her again. In the meantime, I decided to make the most of the time I had left in Toronto.

A day to remember

Three days before I was due to leave Canada, my prayers were answered and Marcia sent me a message to say she was free the following day. I was so happy – what a great way to end my time in Canada! I already had butterflies in my stomach when I woke up in the morning, but I was quite excited about what the day would bring.

I met up with Adam at his work for an early lunch, then when the text came through from Marcia to say she was on her way into the city, I headed off to the Hard Rock Café to meet her, just like the first time. I arrived early, so decided to pop into the Café for a cheeky beer while I was waiting.

I didn't want to ruin what I knew was going to be a fantastic day, so I only had the one.

She arrived shortly after, as pretty as ever, and as we gave each other a hug I could feel my heart pounding. I suggested we do what we did last time, go for a nice walk down towards the harbour, but this time with the idea of catching the boat out to the islands. Again, chatting was easy with Marcia and the time just flew by. I felt we had a real connection. We made it down to the harbour and were happy to find the boat for the main island was about to depart, so I bought us tickets and we boarded.

We were lucky enough to get a spot on the upper deck, which gave us an impressive view of the city as we pulled away from the harbour. What a magical day it was shaping up to be, and it had only just begun! I took some great photos of the two of us on the boat and it reminded me of the first day on Contiki in 2009 when we crossed the English Channel, the first time we met.

The trip across to the main island took about twenty minutes, of which the majority was spent by Marcia telling me all about her trip to the east coast of Australia the previous year. I loved hearing about her adventures too. We hopped off the boat and walked out onto the island and it felt surreal that I was back, eight years on, but this time I wasn't alone. It felt amazing to be able to share a trip like this with someone as special as Marcia.

There were little bars and cafes everywhere and we stopped at one to relax and enjoy a quiet beer. It was a nice summer's day, and I knew this was going to be a day to remember forever. After we finished our beer, we went for a walk to the top end of the island where there was water as far as the eye could see, with no shoreline in sight. This showed just how huge the great lakes are, especially Lake Ontario. I remember throwing my arms up in the air in amazement while Marcia had a big smile on her face.

We then turned and walked the length of the island to the bottom edge, where I was able to take some more scenic photos of the Toronto skyline in the distance. All the while, we continued to chat and I felt we shared a deep connection that day. But, unfortunately, like all good things, the day had to come to an end. We caught the next boat back to the mainland and

I walked Marcia back up towards the subway, then it was time to go our separate ways.

We gave each other a hug and I thought to myself, what could I do to really touch her heart and finish a magical day on a great note? Then all of a sudden, I felt something come from deep within my soul and I looked at Marcia and started to give a big speech about overcoming adversity and hopefully by hearing a bit more about my life, that would inspire her to similarly overcome any challenges she faces in the future. After I finished, she looked up at me in amazement and said, "you are so inspiring". With that, we said goodbye and I turned and walked away, happy in the knowledge that the day could not have ended any better.

That night, I went out for tea with Adam, Robert and Boyd and try as they might, they couldn't get me to come down from cloud nine all night. I was walking on sunshine.

I spent my last night in Canada visiting a few bars with Adam and Flemo, enjoying some quiet beers. Between pubs, we ended up walking through a park in the middle of the city, where I had one last look up at the CN Tower and thought what a beautiful city Toronto was.

Scotland

The following morning, Flemo picked me up from Adam's to take me to the airport, but not before I enjoyed one last coffee at Starbucks just a few blocks from Adam's apartment. We stopped for breakfast on the way. It was a lovely drive and I took the opportunity to take in one last look at the Canadian scenery. I didn't know it then, but the following year I was to make one of the biggest mistakes of my life which has prevented me from visiting Canada since.

It was time to board my flight bound for Scotland, not knowing what crazy adventures lay in wait for me. While on the flight, I heard a song from the band Three Doors Down called *Heaven* that sang about 'getting lost out there in this world'. Like the Kid Rock song *I am* that I first heard on a flight eight years before, I found I could really relate to the lyrics.

I had a stopover at London's Heathrow airport and while I was waiting for my flight, I looked out the windows and thought about how the last time I was at Heathrow I was with Jono and we were about to start the greatest trip I ever went on in my life – Contiki 2009. Now I was on my own. Sitting at the airport that day, I found myself thinking about the good times we had on that trip and how I missed them. I felt a bit sad and wondered what all the people on that trip were doing with their lives, but I was grateful I had been able to see Marcia again.

I finally arrived in Scotland where Scottish Dave was due to pick me up from the airport. However, when I stepped into the terminal, I couldn't see him anywhere. I was starting to wonder what I was going to do, when all of a sudden I felt someone slap me on the bum and I knew straight away who it was.

We headed out to where Dave had parked his van and I saw he had two cases of beer waiting in the back and I remember thinking, "welcome to Scotland!". I had quite a few beers on the drive, so I was pretty tipsy by the time we arrived in Kelso. Along the way we had picked up Iain – that's when I knew the next few days were going to be pretty crazy! It was good to be back in Kelso, as I instantly recognised the cobblestone streets and it all felt wonderfully familiar, even though it had been three years since I last set foot there.

We made it to Dave's place where the party began and people came and went all night. After all, I had come all the way from Australia, so people seemed keen to have a drink with me! At one point I was hanging out the window having a smoke when I noticed an old abandoned castle across the road. "Only in Scotland", I thought. I also picked a good night to arrive as there was a street festival on in town, so all the locals were out and about and it was great to be able to experience a bit more of the Scottish culture.

After checking out the festival where I was amazed to see people drinking in the street (not allowed back home), we then hit the pubs of Kelso and, to be honest, I don't remember much of the next few days. I do vaguely remember waking up on the floor at Dave's with him telling me to get up, as we were about to head to the pub for lunch. I'm not sure what they mean by 'lunch' in Scotland, because I don't actually remember eating anything! I do remember Dave asking Iain if he remembered finding him crying in the cemetery in the middle of town the night before. I looked out the window of the pub, and sure enough, there was a cemetery. These Scottish lads are even crazier than us Aussies.

We didn't even have time to think about sobering up that day, as we hit pub after pub. Iain ended up being tied up by the barmaids at one place as a joke to try to stop him drinking.

I woke up the next morning with hardly any recollection of the previous few days, thinking that the next part of the movie *The Hangover* could very well be filmed right here in Scotland. Dave suggested we get out of Kelso for the day to go for a drive so he could show me a bit more of the countryside and a few beaches. We could even cross the border into England, which wasn't far from Kelso. I couldn't stand the thought of another day on the booze, so I figured it was a smart move as we both needed to dry out a bit.

So, we said goodbye to Dave's partner Laura (who was living with him at the time), jumped in the van and drove off into the vast Scottish countryside. We didn't want to come across any temptations that may lead to us getting back on the booze, so we decided not to pick Iain up on the way this time.

We stopped at the border where I posed for a photo of me sitting atop the English emblem made of stone. Dave then took me to a spot on the coast that had old trenches and ditches the English used to try to stop invasion from other countries during the wars. We then went for a drive to Bamburgh Castle, which sits on the coast of Northumberland in England. A castle overlooking the beach – I had never seen anything like it before.

Following that, we checked out the ruins of Aberdeen. Growing up in the area, Dave knew a bit of the history of the places we visited, so I was happy to not only have him as a friend to travel with that day, but as a tour guide as well!

The next day we decided to go for a drive into Edinburgh, seeing as I had shared so many great times with Jono there three years before. I had always wanted to visit again and I was sure it would bring back some good memories. Laura didn't have to work that day, so she was able to come with us. We arrived in Edinburgh mid-morning and straight away I could hear the sounds of the city I had loved so much last time. The melody of bagpipes echoed through the air.

The first thing we did was climb to the top of Scott Monument, which is a Victorian Gothic monument dedicated to Scottish author Sir Walker Scott. It is the largest such piece dedicated to a writer anywhere in the world. From the top, we were able to capture some awesome views of the city. I had also heard stories about the underground tombs of Edinburgh and that you could go on a tour, so after visiting Scott Monument, we headed off to check that out.

The tour guide led us on a short stroll through the old town before entering the tombs. I was shocked by how dark and eerie they were and I couldn't believe people actually lived down here at one point in history. The guide enthralled us with stories about hauntings, including the infamous headless 'Little Drummer Boy'. The day we were there was quite nice outside by Scottish standards, but I can only imagine what it must have been like during the harsh winter seasons.

After the tour, we thawed out with a drink at a bar on the Royal Mile, then started the drive back to Kelso. The following day we decided it was time to get back on the booze, so we drove to Iain's place in Galashiels. Dave left his car there while the three of us begun another massive pub crawl in a new town. At one place, we started chatting to an old lady with schizophrenia, who informed us she was also writing her life story, which made me wonder if someday I could complete mine too. I often think about that lady and whether she ever got her book published.

After the pub crawl, we ended up back at Iain's place where we drank and sang Scottish anthems until the sun came up.

I only had a few days left in Scotland after our all-nighter, so I took the opportunity to walk around Kelso and take in the sights. Dave had taken up kitesurfing, which apparently is quite popular in Scotland, so I went to the beach with him a few times to watch.

On my last night, Dave and Laura took me out for tea. I had the traditional Scottish haggis as we talked about the good times we had when I first visited Kelso three years ago with Jono. Dave told me that the place Iain was staying at back then was just across the road from where we were having dinner, so afterwards I took a walk to check it out. I found myself getting a bit emotional standing out the front, as a heap of memories came flooding back and a silent tear rolled down my cheek.

When we got back to Dave's, I sent Crudder a message to say I would be seeing him in Paris soon, then I promptly fell asleep.

The following morning, Dave drove me to the airport and it was time to say goodbye…again. No matter how many times I had to say goodbye to people on my journeys, I found it was something I never quite got used to as it always left me feeling a bit sad.

Paris

I boarded another flight bound for Paris and as I sat there listening to Lynyrd Skynyrd's *Free Bird*, I started to get pumped for my next adventure. The landing was smooth as I touched down in Paris. I went to the gate to collect Crudder, as our flights were due to arrive at roughly the same time, but he wasn't there. I began searching the airport – but no Crudder. I did try asking for help, but everyone who worked there spoke French (understandably). Paris is a lovely place to look at, but frustrating when you are trying to find your friend in a packed airport!

I finally gave up and decided to catch a taxi to the hotel. Even though Paris is a world away from small-town Harvey, I figured Crudder was a big boy so I just had to have faith he would be able to find his way to the hotel too.

I decided to wait it out for a bit once I had checked in, but got restless after a while, so I went for a walk down the hall. Just as I turned a corner, I almost collided with someone – and you wouldn't believe it. Crudder had made it! Before I knew it, we were both kicking back in the hotel beer garden enjoying a beverage. It felt quite surreal to be in a place like Paris with another bloke from Harvey. We ended up getting quite drunk and Crudder slept most of the next day (but we can blame jet lag there!). Welcome to the life of a traveller!

That evening we had a welcome dinner and meeting at the hotel as we met our fellow Contiki travellers. I remember chatting to a nice couple from the US, David and Rhianne. The next day was pretty much a free day to start the tour. After getting dropped off down by the Seine and given a certain time to meet back at the designated pickup spot, we were free to do a bit of sightseeing and explore the wonderful city.

Crudder and I paired up with the American duo as we set off into the gridlock that is Parisian streets. Seeing as I had visited here before, I lead the way. I was starting to become quite a seasoned traveller.

Our first stop was the Louvre where we checked out the usual sights, including the Mona Lisa. We then caught the subway out to Père Lachaise so I could show the others Jim Morrison's tomb and I also wanted to check out the tomb of Oscar Wilde, a famous poet also buried there. After grabbing a beer at a bar across the road from the cemetery, we made our way in the labyrinth that is Père Lachaise Cemetery. The place had a tranquil feeling to it, not at all what you would expect from such a place. We found Jim, then went in search of Oscar. Oscar Wilde's tomb had a big glass panel surrounding it and I was shocked to find it riddled with graffiti.

That night we all visited the Eiffel Tower, it was an amazing sight to behold at dusk, and we caught the lifts up to the top of the tower for some awesome views of Paris at night. It was then off to a cabaret show, where I was surprised to find it was pretty much the same show as we saw on our last night in Paris on Contiki three years before. There was another familiar surprise to come too – after the show, we all headed to a bar a few blocks down to have a few drinks and get to know each other and you wouldn't believe it. It was the very same bar we had farewell drinks at last time too! Very surreal.

Crudder said he was feeling tired, so he caught the bus back to the hotel instead of coming out to the bar. I headed in and ordered a beer, then perched myself in the back corner of the bar for some quiet reflection. I couldn't believe I was back at the very same bar and again I realised how much I missed all the people from the first Contiki tour. Although it was still early on in this tour, I already felt I didn't have the same connection with the people as I had in 2009. As had often been the case throughout my life, I was determined to make the most of this experience regardless.

The next day was the day Crudder and I had been waiting for, as we all caught the train to Amsterdam. We arrived at Central Station around midday and while our luggage was being taken to our hotel, and the rest of the day was free to explore the city and do as we pleased.

I wanted to check out the Anne Frank house before things got too messy, as I didn't get the chance to see it on my first visit with Jono. Unfortunately, the line was too long, so I gave up on that idea again and asked Crudder what he wanted to do instead. Before I knew it, we were sitting in a coffee shop each smoking a big fat Amsterdam joint of White Widow.

While sitting there with Crudder, at first I didn't feel anything, but then as soon as we stepped outside into the fresh air – bang. It hit me and I found myself feeling quite stoned. I suggested we go for a walk and explore the city, so off we went. It was one of the quietest strolls I have ever been on in my life, but when you are as cooked as we were, there isn't much scope for conversation.

We walked so far and saw so much, but in a way we didn't actually see anything at all. After a few hours, the paranoia started to kick in and I thought all the people on bicycles were trying to clean me up, so I darted into the nearest pub, ordered a beer and sat at the back in the darkness. Crudder knew me well enough to understand what was going on, so he just quietly ordered a drink and joined me in the dark.

We made it back to the hotel for dinner and a few more beers to calm the paranoia, which was still holding on. The tour guide had organised a night out, so it was soon back on the bus to head into the city. Crudder wasn't going to miss out on this one! He had a big grin on his face all night and seemed to be laughing a lot. I only found out afterwards that he had taken some magic mushrooms. Cheeky bugger, didn't share any with me!

It was another massive night spent mostly walking along the bridges on the canals, just enjoying the summer solstice in a drug-filled haze. As always, Amsterdam delivered the goods.

Berlin

The following day we were all a wreck as we made our way to Berlin. I took one look at Crudder and knew that Amsterdam had finished him, and for the rest of the tour he would just be going through the motions. We spent the next few days going on a few organised tours around the city, where our guide showed us a few of the places Hitler gave his massive speeches during the war. I found Berlin to be an interesting city, though not one that left a lasting impression on me.

As I mentioned before, even though there were all great people, I didn't seem to have the same connection as I had with the first group of Contiki travellers. By Berlin, instead of spending time with them, I found I preferred to just wander the streets of the city on my own.

Prague, Rome and bye-bye Contiki

Our next destination was Prague, which I was excited for as I had seen some great photos from when my friend Caliopi travelled there. Once we arrived, I headed straight off to explore and discovered that pretty much every photo I took looked just like a postcard – very scenic. I visited Old Town Square with the Prague Astronomical Clock.

I heard Prague had some of the best beer in the world, so I decided to sample the local products. I was impressed. So impressed, in fact, that I proceeded to get quite drunk. The following day, as part of the Contiki, we all went for a cruise on the Vltava River. I was able to talk Crudder into coming along as I wanted to show him there was much more to Europe than Amsterdam. The cruise was lovely, even more so because we got to sample some more local beer.

That night we all went out to party at a local nightclub, everyone, that is, except Crudder. He was happy to stay at the hotel. While waiting in line to get into the club again, I was overcome with the desire to wander off and do my own thing. I was never really a big fan of clubs anyway. You can never have a conversation because the music is so loud, and they are often full of try-hards on the dance floor pulling off silly moves to impress the ladies. Not really my scene.

So, instead of following the crew into the club, I disappeared into the shadows and spent the rest of the night wandering the streets of Prague, again, just me and my thoughts. While I am quite a sociable character, I was really enjoying some solo time checking out the incredible new places around me and just observing, taking it all in.

The next day, the Contiki bus took us to the airport where we were to catch a flight to Rome, our final destination on this tour. Another airport, another flight, I was becoming quite accustomed to it by this stage! I spent the last few days in Rome with Crudder, just relaxing and eating delicious food. Come to think of it, those few days in Rome I was able to taste some of the best food I have ever had the pleasure of eating on my travels.

To be honest, by the time we arrived in Rome, both Crudder and I were just going through the motions. It had been another long trip and it felt like a lifetime ago that I had first arrived at Adam's place in Toronto. I was very much looking forward to going home.

I still did a bit of exploring and took in the sights, as I had done three years earlier. The ruins of Rome were impressive and certainly worth another visit. So much history, so unlike anything we have at home.

One night, just on dusk, we went to check out the Palatina, which consisted of majestic ruins and memorable views. This place is where the city was founded in 753BC. We also checked out the Roman Forum, which looked magical just on sunset.

It finally came time to say goodbye to the Contiki group as I prepared to head home. Crudder had extended his holiday and was going to fly to Ireland to catch up with a friend for a week.

I had made some friends on this trip, despite my distance, and I hoped to stay in touch with them. Jay and Dan were part of a small group travelling together from San Diego and told me if I ever made it to their part of the world, to let them know and they'd show me a good time. I was sure I would take them up on their offer at some point!

We caught a cab to the airport in the early hours of the morning, then Crudder took off to his flight to Ireland and I boarded mine back to Australia. It was soon back to reality, but I had the mindset of a traveller; before I had even set foot on home soil, I was beginning to plan my next trip abroad.

Twenty-Seven

New Opportunities

Not long after I arrived home, I received a message from Marcia to say it was great to get the chance to catch up while I was in Canada and to get to know each other better. She told me I was a very special and inspiring person to know. Speaking to me had got her thinking about someday producing a documentary on people who have overcome adversity in their lives and gone on to achieve happiness and success, which was part of what she had learnt in university, 'prejudice reduction'.

This was one of the greatest messages I had ever received, and it really touched my heart to think I was able to inspire someone to do something like that. It gave my life and everything I had been through even more meaning, and I had a warm feeling in my heart for a long time after.

However, despite the many positives in my life, it was around this point that I became a little disillusioned with work. Even though I had become much more reliable and my work ethic had improved considerably, I was still pretty much doing the same thing as I was when I began there 14 years ago. It was time to see if I could do more. My father, Gordon, achieved so much in the industry, and now I needed to step up as well. I was beginning to feel the pressure of not living up to expectations and reaching my full career potential.

As luck would have it, at the same time as I found myself ready to take on a new personal challenge, Harvey Beef was offering long-term employees the chance to undertake a meat inspector's course. There were limited positions available, and by the time I heard about it and rushed to put my name down, I was the last on the list. I was ready and willing to grab this opportunity, as meat inspector positions were Government jobs and well respected in the industry. I wasn't sure if I would cut it in this role, but I was willing to give it my best shot.

I studied most nights and did everything required of me. I have always had a great memory, so when it came to the final exam, I aced it, 100 per cent! I was very proud of my achievement, now a fully qualified meat inspector, but that didn't guarantee me a job just yet. Now was the waiting game to see what opportunity came up next.

As it turned out, I didn't have to wait too long. Early the next year, 2013, a few of the inspectors took me aside and told me to expect a phone call in the near future with some good news. I had always gotten along well with these guys, so it was heart-warming to know they were gunning for me.

Not long later, I did receive the call and I was elated; it was time for new beginning and a career I could really make my own as I progressed through life. The only last stumbling block was that they would have to do a background check, which included bringing up my drink driving record as well as a few other minor charges from my younger days. This was a necessity as it was a Government job, and it made me quite nervous. I remembered dad had also done the course and aced it, but wasn't able to get a job as a meat inspector due to an old drink driving charge. I had heard they were a little more lenient now, but I would soon find out!

Thankfully, the rumours were true and I got the job – I was was over the moon! Finally, my days labouring at Harvey Beef were over and I was moving up the ladder in the industry.

Melbourne

Before leaving Harvey Beef to start my new job, I decided to book a trip to Melbourne. I sent Shaban a message to let him know I was coming over, and he agreed to make a plan to catch up. I hadn't seen him since our Contiki tour but was looking forward to seeing what he had been up to since the trip.

I also got in touch with one of dad's best friends, Robert, who said he would be thrilled to have me stay with him for a few days. He lived in an area of Victoria called Aurora, not far from Melbourne's CBD. Rob also offered to pick me up from the airport, and true to his word, there he was when my plane landed.

On the drive to Aurora, Rob told me a bit about all the good times he shared with dad in their younger years. It was great to spend those few days with him and experience life in country Victoria. We spent the mornings taking his dogs for a walk, and the afternoons enjoying a few quiet beers on his front porch.

This was Ned Kelly's stomping ground, where he and his gang were cutting loose in the 1800s. One morning Rob took me for a drive to show me a plaque erected in the centre of town commemorating the famous outlaw.

I spoke to Shaban on the phone and though he was busy working during the week, we organised to meet up in the city on the weekend and go to a Carlton game at the MCG, as he was a member. I couldn't wait, it would be an epic finish to my trip.

I jumped online and booked my accommodation in the city for the weekend, and on Thursday afternoon Rob dropped me off at the Aurora train station for the journey into Melbourne. I was a bit sad to say goodbye to Rob, but it was great to catch up and spend that time with him after so many years.

The day I took the train from Aurora to Melbourne happened to be ANZAC Day, so the carriage was packed with people in full uniforms travelling to and from various service in the area. I was looking forward to checking into my room, then going to find a good pub to enjoy a few beers and watch the traditional ANZAC Day AFL game between Collingwood and Essendon.

Once I arrived, I had a few hours to kill before bounce down, so I decided to go explore a bit of Melbourne. However, as is often the case, it didn't take long for me to get distracted. My Facebook post for the day is probably the best description of what happened;

"Just arrived in Melbourne and looking forward to exploring this great city. I have done quite a bit of travelling in my time and there is nothing like the excitement you get when you visit a new place. I see the trams are....oh WOW! Is that a pub? I LOVE exploring pubs. Oh well. Catch you all later. I'm off to have a beer."

So, I settled in to watch the game and got quite drunk in the process. The following day I chose the smart option of steering clear of the pubs to actually see what else Melbourne had to offer. I walked everywhere and took the opportunity to explore the old Melbourne Gaol, where Ned Kelly was held and subsequently hanged. I had lunch on Lygon Street and checked out Federation Square. I certainly worked up a pretty big thirst, so that night I spent another evening out on the town, checking out a few more of the local pubs. At some point during the night I made a phone call to my friend Ash, who was on holiday in Thailand, though I don't remember making the call until Ash told me about it a while later. We both had a good laugh about that.

The next morning I woke up excited as I knew this was going to be the highlight of my trip. Shaban sent me a text to say he was on his way into the city and to meet him at Crown Casino around 2 pm. I got myself organised and caught a taxi over to the casino. I was feeling a little anxious, so I decided to arrive a bit early to have a few beers and calm my nerves. I'm not sure why I felt that way, as Shaban was such an easy-going bloke, so perhaps it was the crowds and the expectation of the game ahead.

Shaban finally arrived and we picked up right where we left off on the Contiki, catching up over a few beers. We spoke of mutual Facebook friends from the tour and how everyone seemed to be going since. He asked how my catch up with Marcia went, and we both spoke highly of her and some of the other people we had met. After a good chat, we decided to walk to the MCG for the game. We wandered along the Yarra River and took in the scenic views of the Melbourne skyline and, as always, I had my camera clicking away at full speed.

We walked over the bridge and finally arrived at the home of football in Australia, the MCG, and ordered a beer to settled in and watch the game between Carlton and the Adelaide Crows. It didn't have the same atmosphere as the ANZAC Day game a few days before, but it was exciting to finally get a chance to watch a live game in Melbourne. Carlton won quite easily that night, poor Crows.

After the game, Shaban and I headed to a bar a few blocks from the MCG to continue drinking. The night turned into another blackout and I didn't remember anything until I woke up in my hotel room later the next afternoon.

I sent Shaban a text message to find out what happened and how the rest of the night went. He replied and told me that he had just arrived back home and was relaxing on the couch, where he planned to stay all afternoon. He said that later on in the night we were walking from one bar to another when I stacked it in the street, so he decided to play it safe and put me in a taxi to make sure I made it back to my hotel safe and sound. But, otherwise, he said it was a great night and was awesome to catch up with me again.

I was happy to hear that and felt relieved that I didn't do anything too silly, but I was getting a bit concerned again about where my binge drinking was heading. It was a bit of a wake-up call, as I finally began to think about the consequences of my frequent blackouts. One day, I may not wake up, or will do something I may regret for the rest of my life. It was a scary feeling, losing that control, but I didn't realise then how scary it would become.

I had a great time in Melbourne, but returning home (for once) I didn't have that same post-travel down feeling. I was eager to start my new job and thrilled to have the opportunity to really excel in my career. I finished up my last week at Harvey Beef, ready to take the next big step. After 14 years in the same place, it was high time I moved forward and knew it was going to be a challenge, but little did I know how much of a challenge it would be. It felt a bit surreal when I jumped in my car that first morning, and instead of driving to Harvey, I drove to Bunbury.

As is often the case, I got lost trying to find the vet's office. The vet's role was to oversee the inspectors and we had to answer to him when it came to the job. I found him to be hard but fair, and he was more than willing to give me a go if I had the right attitude.

I did find it to be a bit of a struggle at the start, as some of the inspectors were quite set in their ways and I was the new guy trying to fit in. I decided the best way to approach it was to observe, not say too much and not crowd their space. I made an effort to take in what they were saying and learn as I went along. Although I had done well in the course and understood the theory, now I was in the role, there was still so much to learn. I felt like a duck out of water, and that first winter on the job I came close to quitting and going back to my old job as a labourer, but something deep in my heart kept telling me to stick at it. So, I did, and I am glad.

Around this time, my brother Frog had broken up with his partner and he and I were living together at a house in Myalup. He was working fly-in, fly-out at that time and was away a lot, so if I had a bad day at work I would come home to an empty house and dwell on it. It was definitely a challenging time in my life, but I sought comfort in happy memories, especially the ones from my travels. I had stayed in touch with some friends from Contiki through Facebook, and social networking helped break the isolation I was feeling at the time.

One of the girls, Anastasia, seemed to have a similar outlook on life to me. I took a chance and sent her a message for her birthday; I am so glad I did as we have since stayed in touch and write regularly to hear about each other's lives.

Twenty-Eight

When It All Comes Crashing Down...

Looking back now, I am not sure if It was the stress I was under from the new job and living situation which led me to make one of the biggest mistakes I could imagine, or old habits catching up with me. But, blaming anything other than my own decision-making would simply mean not taking accountability. Another thing I have learnt over time is that we must take responsibility for our actions and admit when we have messed up. Yes, I was going through a difficult time in my life, but to blame what I did on that would just be making excuses, and I have never made excuses for anything. I own my mistakes, just as much as I own the triumphs I have achieved. These make us who we are, and I won't shy away from that.

As you would have already read in my younger years, I had a bad habit of drink driving and that is a part of my past that I am certainly not proud of. Looking back now with the wisdom I have gained over the years, it was unacceptable behaviour as my actions not only put my own life in danger, but other people's as well. I can honestly say in this book that from the time I got my licence back in my early twenties until more than ten years on, I had learnt my lesson. Whenever I was out drinking, I always planned ahead.

That was, until AFL Grand Final weekend in 2013.

Joel Whitwell

This is a very hard memory for me to write about, but I need to be honest in this book and this story is part of who I am. The Fremantle Dockers were in the Grand Final that year and I wasn't sure where I was going to watch it, but on the day I settled on heading out to the Woky. To this day, I still wonder about and regret that decision, because if I had gone someplace else to watch the game, the outcome would have been very different. But, no matter how many times I go over it in my head, I can't go back and change that decision.

I parked my car at the Woky with plans to either call a taxi later or organise for mum to pick me up and get my car the next morning. I went inside, caught up with everyone and, as I usually did back then, started drinking heavily. The day quickly became a blur. I don't remember anything from after the game until waking up in the back seat of my car around 8 pm to the sound of someone tapping on the window.

In my disoriented state, I first thought I must still be in the car park at the Woky, but as I got out of the car I discovered it was the police and I was in the middle of a paddock. They quickly informed me that by their reports, my car had left the road, jumped over a drain, smashed through a fence and came to a standstill in the paddock. They wanted to take me back to the station to breath test me for drink driving. I thought about the evidence stacked against me and knew straight away that I was in serious trouble. If ever there was a clear-cut case of drink driving, this was it.

So, they took me back to the station and, as I expected, I blew well over the legal limit and was charged with DUI. I didn't say much as I still couldn't believe what had happened, and all I could think of was, "what have I done?!" I could very well have messed up my whole life in one night. I called mum and dad and they came to pick me up from the station. Though they were disappointed, they were otherwise quite good about it, especially when I broke down crying. I had been foolish and I knew it.

The next day the reality of the situation kicked in, which put me in a very low place mentally for quite some time afterwards. To make things worse, I had also lost my ear. Dad drove me back to the paddock so I could grab some belongings out of my car. It was gloomy and overcast, which reflected my mood perfectly. I saw the damaged fence and the skid marks on the ground where my tyres had bottomed out before coming to a stop. I also noticed that the skid marks went right past a power pole. On further inspection of my car, I saw that the pole had taken my driver's side mirror clean off. I shuddered at how close I had been to never getting the chance to write this book.

I also realised that this wasn't just about me. My reckless behaviour had put other people in danger, which was an even more sobering thought. How could I make peace and live with myself if I had hit another car and injured or killed an innocent person? It was a costly mistake that could have had severe consequences.

When I looked inside my car, I saw that there were slices of pizza everywhere, so I figured I must have been hungry after leaving the Woky and driven into Harvey, picked up a pizza and was just on the outskirts of town when I ended up in the paddock. I was so disappointed. I had been doing so well before this, what made me commit this offence? That was just one of the many thoughts that were going through my mind as I stood beside my car that gloomy and drizzly day.

I found my ear underneath the driver's seat, which was a bit of a relief as I was dreading turning up to work on Monday with only one ear. It may not sound like much of a problem, but in my already fragile state, not feeling 'put together' had a huge impact.

Work. That was something else I had to consider. What would I say to my boss and would this situation impact my job? I might be back labouring at Harvey Beef quicker than I had planned due to my reckless, drunken behaviour. Luckily, my fears were calmed when I spoke to my boss, and he was ok with it as long as I was still able to make it to work every day and perform my duties. That was one less thing to worry about, but I had already let a tonne of extra stress into my life as I waited to feel the full impact of my punishment from the courts. At my age and with my experience, I should have known better, and I was prepared to accept whatever the outcome. However, it was a long wait for the final verdict.

This was definitely another dark time in my life and I spent many sleepless nights wondering how I put myself in that position to have done something so foolish. But, as I was to learn a few more times over the coming years, one of the hardest lessons I have had to take on board is that you can't go back and change things. I just had to find a way to move forward.

<hr>

It was during these long dark nights full of pondering that I remembered how much I loved travelling, so I decided I would use my next world trip as a launching pad, something to really aim for to lift myself back up and out of the ravine. With this new goal, I could finally see some light at the end of the tunnel, but before I could start planning the trip, there were a few things I had to do.

Firstly, I had to front up in court to face the judge and receive a verdict. I had previously been done for drink driving, but more than ten years had elapsed since then so I thought that would help my cause. Plus, seeing as I was just over the limit, it was a minor offence and at the lighter end of the scale. Unfortunately for me, the rules had just changed, which meant 20 years had to elapse before any previous convictions were dismissed. Not good news, but I only had myself to blame.

The one thing I had on my side was that I was quite a well-liked and respected person around the area, so I had managed to acquire a few glowing references from other high up people in the community. The judge took it all into consideration as he finally handed down a verdict. My license was to be suspended for 30 months (2.5 years), and I had to pay a pretty hefty fine. Steep, but it could have been much worse. I was determined to cop it on the chin, move forward and use this setback to try to become an even better person.

The second thing I felt I needed to do to move forward was to go and see the police officer who charged me with DUI and apologise for my indiscretion. So, a week later, I summoned up the courage to go into the police station where we sat down and had a good chat. He told me I had shown a bit of character by coming to see him. For someone who was as drunk as I was that night, I was very polite and cooperative towards him and his partner, which made their job so much easier. He then proceeded to tell me that he also heard some good things about me in the community, and from his perspective what he saw was someone who's heart was in the right place but had simply made a bad judgement call while impaired. The last thing he said was that he hoped I would learn from this also to go on to be a better person in the community. We shook hands, and as I left the police station on that warm spring day, even though I was still in a dark place, the light at the end of the tunnel suddenly seemed a little brighter.

I would like to take this moment to make a special mention to my dad here. We had always had a good relationship, but it was during this rough time in my life that I got a better appreciation of the type of person he was. He wouldn't admit it, but I know how proud he was when I secured a job as an inspector. When it sounded like my job was safe as long as I was still able to turn up every day and perform my duties, he stepped up to the plate and even though he had his own business to run, he still woke up early every morning to drive me to work and was there to pick me up when I finished. By doing that, he helped me to keep my job and my life together, and for that I will be forever grateful.

Thank you, dad.

Twenty-Nine

Global Impacts

Before my DUI conviction, the next travel plan was to catch up with friends in Canada and Scotland and to revisit the US to live out my childhood dream. However, both the USA and Canada had recently made it harder for anyone with a conviction to enter the country – including DUI. This meant my plans were suddenly all up in the air. I did a bit of research and though Scotland seemed ok, I found I had a bit of work to do if I wanted to visit Canada and the US on this trip. Seeing as the conviction was so recent, even in this very early stage of planning, it appeared the odds were certainly against me being allowed to enter either country.

But, as Mark Twain once said: "Twenty years from now you will regret the things you didn't do, rather than the things you did do". So, with that quote in mind, I decided to put my best foot forward and see what happened.

I found that with a conviction on my record, I would need to apply to the Canadian consulate in Sydney to gain access to the country. I was to post my application and all other documents by mail. On the other hand, to find out if I was eligible to enter the US, I was to visit the US Consulate in Perth where it looked like it was going to be a long, drawn-out process. It all sounded like a bit of work, and this put me off for a while. Was it worth putting in all this effort, only to be denied entry and end up disappointed at the end of it all? Should I just give up on chasing my childhood dream, and go back to Europe, a place I had also grown to love during my previous travels? It was a tough choice which I thought about it for a long time.

Being able to catch up with my friends in Canada, including Marcia, and to finally live out my dream to see America and icons such as the Golden Gate Bridge, was right there for the taking if I just put in the effort. So, I decided to follow my heart and do what was asked by the Consulates.

I gathered up a few references, prepared my application and sent it off to the Canadian Consulate in Sydney. I had done all I could, and now it was in their hands. I also paid a visit to the US Consulate in Perth as I figured I needed to allow as much time as possible to get this one sorted out. Not having a licence meant catching the train up to the city and taking days off work, which was not ideal and a little stressful.

On one occasion, they turned me away because I didn't have the right documents with me and wouldn't take the next step in my application until I had the correct papers. I was devastated as it meant more trips to Perth and more time. Seeing as the train didn't leave Perth for Bunbury until 6 pm, I had a bit of time to kill, so I spent the rest of the day wandering aimlessly through the streets of Perth in the rain. That day was the closest I came to chucking it all in and giving up once and for all, but something deep in my heart implored me to carry on.

Around this time, I received an email from the Canadian consulate asking me to provide further details on my previous visits to Canada. I took this as a great sign that they were seriously considering allowing me to travel there again. Sadly, this turned out to be false hope, as a week or so after I sent the information, I received another email informing me that after going over and considering my application, the recent conviction made me inadmissible to Canada. I was shattered; I had just been banned from entering a country I had grown to love and had made so many great memories during previous visits.

I had also waited my whole life to meet someone like Marcia, and now it seemed I had messed up any chance I had of meeting up with her again as well. The ripple effect from my reckless decision to drive that Grand Final night was really starting to make waves in my life. I was never going to stop travelling, though, so I started thinking of some other options of places I could visit instead.

I suddenly remembered the promise I made to my exchange student friend Julian when he left Harvey all those years ago that I would come to visit him in Argentina one day. It was time to follow through on that promise – so South America it was. While I was heading over that way, I factored in Peru and Machu Picchu, as I had always wanted to see that part of the world.

I was still waiting on the US Consulate to make their decision before I could plan my trip properly, but after what happened with Canada, I wasn't all that confident it would go my way. In March I received my passport back in the mail and was also expecting to receive a document letting me know of my travel status. My heart sunk again as no accompanying decision had been made. I thought for sure my dream was over and I wasn't going to be seeing the Golden Gate Bridge any time soon.

Then, as I flicked through my passport, I came across a page that had been stamped with a Visa to enter the US! I jumped for joy as my spirits soared and the dream was back on! You little beauty – I was finally going back to America!

A lightbulb went on as I remembered Niagara Falls is only an hour and a half south of Toronto and right on the border, so I figured if I could get to the Falls for a weekend, Marcia might be able to head down and meet up with me there. We could still get a chance to catch up on this trip after all. Now I was really starting to get excited!

Before I got in touch with Marcia about my plan, I had to organise the rest of the trip. I booked a Contiki tour of the West Coast of the US and a four-day tour of Cusco and Machu Picchu in Peru. Around this time I was talking to my friend Luke over the phone, telling him about my travel plans, when he suddenly decided that instead of always hearing about my trips, he would finally become part of one. He said he would join me in the US and would book the same Contiki tour. How awesome – the third tour I got to spend with a good mate from home!

Thirty

World Trip #3

My trip was all set now. I would spend a week in Ushuaia (right down the bottom of Argentina) with Julian where he was living. Then it was on to four days in Peru, then two weeks on Contiki covering the West Coast of the US. After that, I would travel up to Niagara Falls for a weekend where I hoped to catch up with Marcia, before another week in New York where I was going to meet up with Luke again, then finish up with a week in Scotland. Wow – what a great trip I had in front of me!

A week or so before I was meant to fly, I sent Marcia a message to let her know that I will be in Niagara Falls in the first weekend of August and it would be great if we could catch up. But, when it finally came time for me to board the plane, I still hadn't heard back from her, but I had hope in my heart as I settled back in my seat. I was ready for another amazing journey!

The first leg included stopovers in Auckland, Santiago and a night in Buenos Aires, before heading off on the final flight down to Ushuaia (otherwise known as 'The End of the World'). I landed in Auckland and had an hour to kill at the airport before heading to South America, so I found the internet and decided to check Facebook. I had a message from Marcia informing me that she would love to catch up with me at Niagara Falls. I couldn't believe my luck, and I was practically dancing my way down the aisle as I boarded my next flight. Everything was starting to fall into place nicely.

As we started the descent into Chile, I remember looking out the window at the Andes Mountains and thinking how spectacular they looked from above. I had a feeling that South America was going to be an awesome experience. After spending a few hours at the airport in Santiago, I then flew onto Buenos Aires in Argentina for an overnight stay. After catching the shuttle bus to my hotel and checking into my room, I fell into a deep and exhausted sleep, but not before organising a wake-up call through the hotel as I had an early flight to Ushuaia in the morning.

Ushuaia

I had sent Julian my flight number and arrival time as he was going to pick me up from the airport. I was boosted and couldn't wait to see him again. Unfortunately, the flight ended up being delayed by a few hours and I had no way to get in touch with Julian. There wasn't much I could do at that stage.

As expected, Julian wasn't at the airport when I arrived at the other end, so I had to make a choice – wait there in case he came back looking for me, or catch a taxi into the city to look for an internet café so I could message him. I chose the latter and on the cab ride into the city, I couldn't believe how beautiful the place was. The taxi driver dropped me off at an internet café where I quickly sent Julian a message. He replied not long after saying he was at the airport (oops, should have taken option one!) but for me to stay where I was and he would come to meet me. About ten minutes later, all those years on from when we said goodbye to one another back in Harvey, we were now embracing outside an internet café at the end of the world.

We jumped into Julian's car, and after giving me a quick tour of Ushuaia, we drove up to his cabin located at the bottom of the mountains overlooking the city. His place was small but cosy. He had one room and a bathroom with a small staircase leading up to a loft area in the roof where Julian slept. I was to sleep on the couch in the downstairs room, so I put my things down and made myself at home.

Later on, we drove back into the city to find a nice restaurant for dinner. It was great to relax and enjoy a few beers with my old friend. We spoke about the times we shared while he was an exchange student back in Harvey, and caught up on what had happened in our lives since. Julian was originally from Buenos Aires, but he had secured a job in Ushuaia and had recently made the move down. Thanks to social media, Julian knew I had done a bit of travelling, but he was surprised about how much when I started listing it all out!

We headed back to the cabin after dinner for an early night. Julian had to go to work during the day, but he left me his tablet so I could keep in touch. So, over the next few days, I followed pretty much the same routine; get up, shower, wander down the mountain towards the city while gazing up at the snow-capped mountains. It was awe-inspiring. Once I reached the city, I would just wander the streets, taking it all in. It was always windy, but I loved it anyway. If the weather got a bit much, I just popped into a warm bar to enjoy a quiet beer.

One day while wandering through the city, I decided to head down to the waterfront and check out the harbour. I have been lucky enough to see some incredible harbours all over the world, but Ushuaia was by far the most spectacular of the lot. There was a strong wind blowing off the ocean, which chilled my face as I leaned against the railing overlooking the water. It was the gateway to Antarctica, and as I stood there that day, I wondered what the ice-covered continent was like too. I hadn't seen much snow on my travels to date, but Julian assured me I would soon get a chance to see plenty of it – and he was right.

I awoke one morning to Julian urging me to look out the window. I couldn't believe what I saw, snow was falling hard and everything was white for as far as the eye could see. Growing up in Western Australia, snow was not the norm for me, and boy, was I excited! I poured out the door in a flash and walked through the snow, feeling like a kid again. This was what travelling was all about! I could feel and hear the bottom of my shoes crackling in the snow. As I approached the city, I noticed a lot of lights on in houses and on the streets, because the snow made the daytime sky darker. I headed back down to the waterfront where I was able to get a great photo of Ushuaia harbour on a snowy day.

The next weekend, Julian took me for a drive through the mountains around the city. There was snow everywhere, and I was amazed at Julian's ability to drive in those conditions. We stopped for lunch at a ski resort and, at one point, stopped by the side of the road for a great view of the snowy glaciers in the distance. I was standing next to a cliff face and noticed that people had signed their names and left messages from all over the world. My eyes found the initials, PJ. I knew it wasn't the PJ I had known, but it was a nice thought that my friend was watching over me and travelling alongside.

After that, we went and checked out a few national parks and the train station to 'the end of the world'. To finish off a great day, we went around to a friend of Julian's to watch Argentina play in the Soccer World Cup. They ended up winning and after watching all of the people dancing in the street in celebration, I figured any excuse for a party is a good one, even though I wasn't a huge soccer fan.

I only had a few days left in Ushuaia, so the following day while Julian was at work I walked back down to the harbour where I booked myself a ticket out to the islands to see the sea lions. These majestic creatures are scattered all along the South American coast and resemble a seal. The males have a very large head with a well-developed mane, making them the most lionesque of the eared seals. The males also weigh more than twice as much as the females, averaging around 300kg!

I boarded the tour boat, wrapped up in as much clothing as I could. I knew it was going to be cold, but the wind whipping off the ice was next level! I huddled up in the cabin as the boat pulled away from the harbour, but I didn't want to miss too much. There was a nice guy from Buenos Aires in the small group, and we decided to brave the cold up on deck together to get the best view of the wildlife and scenery. I got some amazing photos of the Ushuaia skyline in the distance and felt like a modern-day Mark Twain. Right there and then, I truly understood his inspirational quote. The wind and rain were lashing our faces, but we were determined to stay out as long as possible to make the most of this experience and capture memories for the future.

While gazing out over the water, we suddenly heard some strange barking sounds. We turned, and to our amazement found we were not far off the main island the sea lions called home. With great manoeuvring by our skipper, he was able to get the boat close enough so we could all hop off and explore the rocky outcrop. Our guide took us for a brief walk around the island and told us all about the history of the South American sea lions. By this stage, the wind and rain had picked up and a storm was rapidly approaching, so it was time to head back to the boat.

During my travels over the years, I have really come to respect pilots for the awesome job they do keeping us safe in the air, but now I also had to have faith that our skipper would get us back to the mainland. We all buckled down in the cabin and got ready for a wild ride as we pulled away from the island into the stormy sea. I watched as the waves smashed against the window where I was sitting and the boat bobbed up and down on the rough ocean. I must admit I was tempted to head back out on deck to take some more photos, as the ocean looked incredible with its raw power, but I figured it would be a suicide mission so I had better stay in the safety of the cabin.

We could see the lights of Ushuaia gradually getting closer, and after what felt like an eternity, we finally pulled into the harbour. My faith in our skipper was well-placed as we breathed a collective sigh of relief. I was glad I lived to travel another day! After saying goodbye to my Argentinian friend and the other's on the tour that day, I made my way back to Julian's cabin where I had the best shower I had ever enjoyed in my life.

After catching Julian up on my day's adventures, he suggested that for my last day in Ushuaia, I catch the bus out to one of the best ski resorts to do a bit of skiing. I thought that sounded like a great idea, so we jumped online and he booked me a ticket. He unfortunately couldn't join me as he had too much to do, but I was excited at the chance to learn a new skill.

The days are a lot shorter in this part of the world during winter, so it was still dark and snowing as I walked down to the end of Julian's street to meet the bus. I had donned my hooded jacket, which made me look like something crossed between an Eskimo and a snowman. The bus finally arrived and I was off to the resort. After seeing how steep the slopes were and the amount of snow falling, I decided to leave the skiing to the professionals. Instead, I wandered around the slopes for a while, then accidentally walked into a bar where I settled in for a nice meal and a few quiet beers!

Sitting there sipping my beer while looking out at the snow made me realise how far I had come since boosting it up in my home town of Harvey all those years ago. From small-town Harvey to the magic of Ushuaia – what a fulfilling journey it had been! It ended up being a pretty long day before I caught the bus back to Ushuaia and arrived at Julian's cabin just before dusk, but I enjoyed the change of scene and experiencing snow unlike anything I had seen before.

That night Julian's friend came over, and the three of us sat around in the cabin chatting as we did on the first night I arrived. It was a great night, very chilled out, but I was starting to get the feeling I get while travelling when I knew a stage of my journey was coming to an end – and another goodbye was on the way.

I booked a taxi to pick me up from the front of Julian's cabin to head to the airport very early in the morning, so that night was really our last chance to spend a bit of time together and we both wanted to make the most of it. After his friend left, we stayed up chatting long into the night, but finally couldn't put off the inevitable any longer. I hope he didn't detect a tear in my eye as we said goodbye. As I laid down on the couch, I started thinking about the next stage of my journey – Peru and the magic of Machu Picchu.

The next morning as I caught the taxi to the airport, I took in the beautiful scenery one last time, and as the sun was rising over the city, I hoped I would get the chance to come back some day. As a traveller, I have been in so many airports all over the world, and this is the part of the gig I don't enjoy so much. A lot of things can go wrong in airports! I also find the routine of going through customs quite repetitive and boring. I was starting to become what you would call a 'weary traveller' in some respects, but I still wouldn't change it for a second. To me, travelling is a great way to really experience life, and like any experience, you have to take it as a whole – airports and all.

Machu Picchu

I was about to see one of the most significant historic places on the planet, and I couldn't wait to get there – and the excitement really started to kick in as I settled into my seat on the plane. As I had done on my way to Ushuaia, I had a stopover for one night in Buenos Aires before flying into Cusco to start the pre-booked tour.

As I hopped off the plane in Buenos Aires and walked into the arrivals hall, I could see there was a large group of people holding signs as I frantically began looking for my driver. Near the back of the group I saw a man holding a sign that read 'Chimu Adventures', which was the name of the tour operator I was with. I assumed this was the right driver, so I went up and introduced myself. He carried my luggage and put it into the boot of his car and we took off into the city. He seemed quiet and it was at this point my imagination started to go wild, because even though I was now a seasoned traveller, I had always caught a taxi or bus from the airport. This was the first time I had a driver booked.

Maybe I had read too much about some of the bad things that can happen in South America, but all I could think was that he was going to drive me out to a back road somewhere and rob and kill me, or perhaps kidnap me for ransom! I thought the best action was to play mind games with him, so I looked at him and smiled to show no fear. He smiled back, which wasn't the reaction I was expecting from a serial killer. I was really getting frightened now and kept looking out the window to make sure there were still buildings and people around and we weren't heading out to some back alley. Wait…was he speeding up? He was, but only to get through a traffic light, thank goodness. The driver seemed relaxed, which didn't help how I felt.

We finally arrived at my hotel and suddenly my fear seemed irrational. The driver was polite, he got me to my destination safely, and I was still breathing. I made a promise to myself to not let my imagination get the better of me again!

I put my luggage in my room, then jumped on the internet at the hotel to check my messages. I was happy to see I had received a message from Anastasia. It had now been just under a year since we had been in touch and reconnected for the first time since we met on the Contiki tour back in 2009. True to form, it was a long message from her and seeing as I was about to visit Machu Picchu, she wanted to share her experiences from a similar trip. She also told me to build a snowman if I got the chance. Dammit, I should have done that in Ushuaia! It was great to hear from Anastasia anyway, as I was starting to feel a little disconnected and lonely as this was one of the first times I was travelling solo while on my journeys. I really appreciated hearing from friends I had met along the way and learning more about their experiences and trips to help me make the most of my adventures.

I left the hotel for a little bit of exploring, but seeing as I was only there for one day and it was starting to get late already, I decided not to wander too far from the hotel. Even though the danger signs were there and I was slowly starting to recognise them at that point in my life, I still hadn't addressed or properly come to terms with how bad my binge drinking problem was. So, while in Buenos Aires that night, I took the opportunity to settle into a bar and have a few beers while waiting for my meal. One thing lead to another and, as was often the case, the night became a blur. The only thing I remembered was when I was leaving the bar to head back to my hotel, someone from the bar chased me down and handed me my wallet, I had left it on the table. So, instead of my fear of getting mugged coming true, instead, I was having my money handed back to me by a kind-hearted stranger! However, I was still on my own in South America and getting blind drunk – not a clever move.

Thankfully, I must have had the sense to organise a wake-up call with reception, as my head was still spinning when the phone rang the next morning. Great, I thought. Not only do I not remember the night before, but I now have a long day of airports, customs and flying ahead of me with a raging hangover. "Why do I do it to myself?" I wondered as I stumbled out of bed and went down to reception to wait for my driver. It was still dark as we drove back to the airport and I thought about all the early morning flights I had to catch over the years. The normal routine of going through customs was more torturous than normal due to the state of my head, but thankfully the flight to Cusco was quite short. It was only a few hours, and I think I slept for most of it.

Back on the ground, I had a stressful moment when I couldn't find my luggage on the baggage carousel and all Il could think about was, "great, I'm hungover as hell and looks like I'm going to be spending the next few hours shopping for clothes here in Cusco". But, finally, my luggage appeared, so I picked it up and went through the exit doors and stepped out into the hot sun. Man, the heat and humidity hit me straight away and I almost collapsed.

Cusco was the historic capital of the Inca Empire from the 13th to the 16th Century Spanish Conquest, and in 1983 was declared a World Heritage Site by UNESCO. It was a fascinating place and I couldn't wait to explore more, but first I needed a cool place to recover. I found my driver and this time I didn't let my paranoia get the better of me as I relaxed and settled in for the trip to my hotel. Cusco felt entirely different from any of the other cities I had visited on my travels. I felt like my childhood hero Indiana Jones, travelling through South America in search of a lost treasure….maybe my imagination was running away with me again…or maybe I was still drunk.

Cusco is nestled in the Peruvian Andes, and even though I could see mountains in the distance, to me it felt like the entire city was surrounded by desert. Also, I couldn't believe that just over a day ago I was freezing cold in Argentina, and now I was sweating like a pig in Peru! I noticed there weren't many bitumen roads here, just mainly dusty cobblestone streets.

The driver turned the car down a side street (which was more like an alleyway) and parked out the front of my hotel. Was this really where I was staying? It looked pretty ordinary and nothing like the hotels I can become used to. The driver told me to check in, then meet him in the foyer to go over the details of my tour over the coming days. After checking in at reception, I walked into the foyer – and wow, it was amazing inside! The room was massive and the ceiling was mostly glass, with the sun beaming straight down into the foyer. I should know not to judge a book by its cover, and this was a brilliant reminder. I remember thinking about how this reflected on my own life. What made it more amazing was that this place was situated down a dusty side road, certainly not somewhere you would expect to find a luxury five-star hotel.

After going over the tour plan with the driver, I headed up to my room to settle in. Now I was feeling even more like Indiana Jones, so much so that I was tempted to go out and buy a whip and hat! But, I decided that instead of dreaming about following someone else's path, I would continue to forge my own. In a few days I was going to be visiting the sacred icon of Machu Picchu, while just nine months before I had been hanging out on the outskirts of Harvey, standing in the rain looking down at my wrecked car thinking about what a mess I had made of my life. Through strength of character, I had proven to myself that I could bounce back from the biggest mistake of my life to finally reach the summit. That thought gave me a warm feeling as I fell into a deep sleep in a beautiful hotel on the other side of the world.

The following day was free of planned tour activities, so I decided to go for a bit of a wander to explore Cusco. It was an amazing place, with interesting cobblestone roads and ancient artefacts. Around midday, I decided to relax, enjoy a coffee and just watch the world go by. After a while, a local sat down next to me and started trying to sell me a painting of Machu Picchu. I must admit, it was a decent painting, but seeing as it was my first full day in the place, I wasn't interested in purchasing anything. Plus, the thought of lugging around a painting for the rest of the trip didn't sound appealing either. I politely told him so, but he was very persistent. Eventually, I got a bit fed up and didn't want to be rude, so I started looking around for a place I could escape. I spied a bar just down from where we were sitting and figured it wouldn't be good for business if he followed me in there. This was perfect. I waited for the right moment, then made a dash for it.

Unfortunately, he was wise to my plan and followed me to the bar, but stopped at the door while I scurried inside, took a seat at the bar and ordered a beer. A wave of relief washed over me, until I looked out the window and saw he was still hanging around near the door and it looked like he was planning to stay there until I came out so he could continue his sales pitch. Oh no, what should I do? Then I remembered where I was and smiled. I was in a bar, a place I discovered I could go into anywhere in the world and feel at home. Even better, I had a free day – no time schedule to keep. The painting seller would be in for a long wait if he planned to battle it out!

I ended up staying at the bar all afternoon, and just on dusk as I was starting to feel quite drunk, I peeked out of the window and discovered the painting seller was gone. You beauty. I decided to make a dash for it back to my hotel. As I hurried outside, I caught a glimpse of him at the far end of the courtyard, no doubt trying to offload his painting to some other unsuspecting tourist. I didn't even look back as I made my way safely to the hotel.

The following morning I rose nice and early to meet up with our tour guide in the lobby. This was a smaller tour group, mixed with people of all ages. We spent the next few days exploring Cusco and surrounding areas, including Plaza de Armas, Sacred Valley, Sacsayhuaman and a cathedral in the city. I was also to discover that more than any other place I had travelled to in the world, in Peru the culture seemed to value what was in the heart and soul of a person, not the looks. Maybe it was part of my destiny to travel there.

I found myself looking up at the sky a lot, and even that appeared different, more alive – it is hard to explain, but the only word I can think of is 'magical'. As always, I met some good people on the tour, which made the experience even more rewarding. For the first two nights of the tour, I stayed at my hotel in the city, but on the third, the night before our trip to Machu Picchu, they booked me into a hotel in a valley in the middle of nowhere, just outside a small town.

For some reason, Cusco reminded me of Florence in Italy. On the second night of the tour we were at a gift shop in the mountains overlooking the city, and as I stood there looking down at the bright lights with a full moon in the distance, it all felt so surreal. Late in the afternoon on the third day of the tour, we were heading back towards Cusco when our tour guide told me to "get ready" as we were just about to pass through the small town where I was to jump off the bus and meet up with my driver, who would take me to my hotel on the outskirts of town. I wondered if anyone else from the tour was also staying at the same hotel, but that question was answered pretty soon – I was on my own. Looking across the dusty road, I saw a man sitting in a car wave at me. I took him to be the driver and put my bag in the back, jumped in the passenger seat and off we went.

The guy drove like a maniac – and I loved it. This was travelling at the most extreme and I felt like I was really living it. This feeling was a stark contrast to how I felt with my first driver on leaving the airport in Buenos Aires! I guess I was finally starting to relish the excitement of solo travel. The driver was not only speeding along the road, but he was talking a hundred miles an hour too and I couldn't seem to get a word in, which suited me fine. To be honest, I didn't really understand what he was on about anyway. He was still rambling on when he stopped suddenly, dropped me off and told me I would be picked up again first thing in the morning to go to the train station (luckily I understood that bit). Then, he was off in a cloud of dust. I looked around and was pleasantly surprised by the hotel. I checked in at reception and found my room. After a warm shower, I took a walk around the hotel grounds, taking in the serenity. It was just on dusk and it felt so tranquil out there. I heard a howl way off in the distance that sounded like a coyote, and I wondered if they have coyotes in Peru.

The next morning, it was time for my much-anticipated journey to the sacred grounds of Machu Picchu. I was up early and made my way to reception to meet my driver, who was already there waiting. We took off like the wind on another crazy drive into town, where he dropped me off at the station, then whoosh – he was off again.

The train trip was unique, to say the least. I was sitting across from a young hippy looking guy and there was some kind of Spanish music playing as we made the journey up the mountains. It still didn't seem real that I was about to visit Machu Picchu. The hippy guy just bobbed his head along to the music without really saying much. We arrived at the station and I quickly took off in search of the bus station, as I remembered my friend Anastasia telling me in one of her messages to try to get up there early to avoid the massive lunchtime crowd. I checked my map and found the bus station easily enough, and was able to board one of the early buses for the second leg of the journey. This was a quick trip and when the bus came to a stop, it finally dawned on me the journey was complete – I was there.

As luck would have it, I came across some of my tour group standing outside a gift shop near the entrance, so I joined them. We then found ourselves a guide, and I must say, he was brilliant. He knew the history of Machu Picchu and spoke in a way that really built up the anticipation. As we walked along the tracks through the forest that led up the mountain, I thought about a poem written by Robert Frost that we all received after we graduated from year 12 back at Harvey High School. One passage has always stuck with me: "Two paths diverge in the woods. I took the path less travelled and that has made all the difference".

Joel Whitwell

The guide told us to look out to our right, so I kept watch but all I saw were trees. Then we made it to a clearing and I looked around again, and there it was. The most amazingly beautiful sight I had ever seen in my life. We were standing on the edge of a slope, and laying below us was the ancient ruins of Machu Picchu. It was an awe-inspiring sight, and I stood there for a minute or so just taking it all in and snapping a few photos to add to my ever-growing collection of travel memoirs. Thanks to my new friend Rob from the US, I was also able to get some photos of me standing in front of the ruins, which I hope to show future generations of my family one day.

Our guide then took us on a tour through the ruins as we heard more about the history of the Inka people. We walked up some of the steepest steps I had ever encountered in my life, and for a while there, I thought we were going to fall. I had heard a lot of people choose to hike the Inka trail up to Machu Picchu, but I like to think I did it the smart way and caught the bus most of the way!

That day was one of the most magical of my life. Just like the day I spent on the islands in Toronto with Marcia, and my time at Sydney harbour with PJ, this moment would also stay with me forever.

After a few hours, the other people on our tour decided to meet at the gift shop for lunch, but I wanted to try to make it back to Cusco by nightfall. I said my goodbyes and started the long journey back down the mountains the same way I came up. As luck would have it, I found myself sitting opposite the exact same hippy guy as I did on the way up. I remembered seeing him up on the mountain too, just wandering around, listening to his iPod like he didn't have a care in the world. As I watched him again bobbing his head along to the music, I imagined it was just a natural thing for him – wandering the world, plugged into his tunes and exploring places around him. He looked so laid back and relaxed, like he had just come back from a day spa, not visiting one of the most iconic and incredibly awe-inspiring places on the planet.

The journey back took longer than I expected and it was after nightfall when the train pulled into Cusco station. Luckily I had most of my things packed, as it was quite late when I arrived back at my hotel room. I was exhausted too. My head hit the pillow thinking about my next adventure, on to North America.

LA, baby!

The next day was the same old process of airports and customs, but as they called for passengers to line up for the flight to Los Angeles, the customs officers seemed a lot stricter and were searching passengers thoroughly. I was very nervous, but also relieved I had gone through the correct process with the US consulate back in Perth. I got through and settled into my seat on the plane, but I knew customs at one end was only half the battle – I still needed to get through at LAX on the other side. I arrived in Los Angeles around sunset, and after a few anxious moments, I cleared customs there too. I couldn't believe it. After my DUI conviction, I thought I had blown any chance of getting into America – but here I was! I was elated when I stepped out into the warm LA night in search of a taxi.

I could not contain my excitement all the way to the hotel. I had successfully cleared every hurdle and was now in America! Better still, it was almost certain I would be catching up with Marcia at Niagara Falls in a few weeks, or so I thought. As I checked into my hotel, I wondered how Luke was going on his arrival into the country, as we had booked into different hotels but had planned to meet up at mine the next day.

In the morning, I was down at reception enquiring about something when I felt a slight punch on my arm. Lo and behold, it was Luke! I was happy to see that he had also arrived into the US safe and sound. We had a free day before the Contiki tour was due to start and he had always wanted to visit Six Flags at Magic Mountain to ride the rollercoasters, so I decided to go along with that idea. We walked to the station to check when the trains were leaving for Magic Mountain.

We were both wearing backpacks, but at some point, Luke misplaced his. We tried not to stress as we retraced our steps and finally saw it sitting on the ground in the middle of the station. However, the backpack was not alone – it was surrounded by security guards. It didn't take us long to realise they saw it as a bomb threat, but it took forever to convince them that we were just tourists from Australia who had accidentally left their backpack behind. Seeing as this was post 9/11 and the country was still hyperaware of terrorism threats, they made us empty the entire contents to prove there was nothing sinister inside. Great start to our time in the US!

Once the bomb threat was dealt with, we caught the train to Magic Mountain where I quickly discovered Luke was right about this idea – it was awesome. I had never really been on a rollercoaster before, but these ones were monsters. Most of the time I had my eyes closed, but I could still feel the adrenaline rush. By mid-afternoon, we decided to call it a day and caught the train back to my hotel where we were due to meet up with the Contiki group at about 6 pm.

Even though we were living it up, one thing I did notice as I walked around LA was how big the homelessness problem was, which made me appreciate the comfortable life I had back home even more. This was certainly a big eye-opener on my travels.

Back at the hotel, we met up with the group on time and, as I looked around the room at all the new faces, I couldn't believe I was doing this for the third time. Luke and I got chatting to another couple of Aussie guys from New South Wales, Brodie and Chris, who would go on to be great travel companions. After the meeting, the four of us went to a Chinese restaurant down the road from the hotel. We wisely called it a night early, eager to begin the trip the next morning.

Thirty-One

CONTIKI #3

I was up early the next morning, eager to start my third and final Contiki tour. I met up with Luke and the rest of the group down in the lobby. Once we all boarded the bus, our guide Matt (Contiki Matt) went over the rules and what was required of us while on the tour. After all my drunken antics on the first two Contiki's, I still managed to finish both alive, so I was quietly confident that, again, I would be fine.

Contiki Matt then introduced us to Jojo, a large purple stuffed panther, and informed us that whoever was late for the bus in the morning after a big night out had to hang out with Jojo for the day. They would also have to get up in front of everyone and do a dance. Now I was a bit worried, not at the thought of hanging out with the panther for the day to help nurse my hangover, but getting up in front of everyone sounded quite daunting! Oh well, I would just have to see what happened!

San Diego

Next minute, we were off, bound for our first destination – San Diego. We arrived in the coastal city around midday, and after a quick tour, we were straight into the first day's activities – speedboat riding in San Diego harbour. What an action-packed first day this was going to be! The boats were small and only designed to hold a few people, and seeing as I had never driven a boat before, I let Luke take the reins. We were off, cruising through the harbour. Luke decided to be a bit of a daredevil as he upped the speed and started doing zig zags as I held on for dear life. At one point, we even stalled the boat right in the middle of the harbour, but it wasn't long before we were off again.

After a bit of fun on the water, it was back on the bus to check into our hotel and get ready for our first night out together. Seeing as San Diego is right near the border, the area we went first for dinner had a real Mexican feel. We had a bit of free time before we were all due to meet up for dinner, so Luke and I hooked up with Brodie and Chris to find a bar for a few pre-dinner drinks. Even though we were still in the US, I could have sworn we were in Mexico. Everything just felt so naturally Mexican, so of course, we had to drink Mexican beer. After a few drinks, we crossed the road to meet up with the others. The dinner table looked quite full by the time we got there, so the four of us took a seat at the bar instead – and forgot about dinner altogether. I was certainly discovering on my travels how effective beer was as an icebreaker.

After the others from the group finished dinner, one by one they started joining us at the bar, and in no time at all, I knew each of them pretty well. After a while, the bus took us down the main street, which was filled with bars and overflowing with patrons as another crazy Contiki tour was well and truly underway.

Luke and I had booked separate rooms for the tour due to my capacity to snore, but I finished the night curled up in the foetal position on the edge of Luke's bed before staggering back to my room as the sun was coming up over San Diego boulevard. The next day was a free day, thankfully, so while everyone else went to the beach for the day, Luke and I slept off our hangovers before wandering down the road in search of a fast food outlet.

For our second night in San Diego, I already had a bit of an idea what we were going to do. A few years back while I was travelling through Europe with Crudder on my second Contiki tour, I had met a group of people from San Diego and we got along great. As I do, I promised that if I were ever in San Diego, I would be sure to catch up with them again for a few drinks. Here I was, so I messaged one of the guys. Quick as a flash, Jay replied and told me to meet up at Stone Brewery in Liberty station around 7:30 pm.

While the rest of the tour group was gathering at the designated meeting place for their second night out in the city, I sent the tour leader a message to let him know where we were going and that we planned to meet up with them later on. We then went our separate ways as Luke and I caught a taxi out to the brewery. Once we got there, I couldn't believe how big the place was.

Us (being the typical tourists) got lost pretty much straight away and, somehow, we ended up in the takeaway/bottleshop section of the brewery. Jay must have sensed we were there and came looking for us. As we were asking the guy behind the counter for directions, I heard someone say from behind us, "make sure you ask them for ID!". There was no mistaking that voice. I turned around, greeted Jay and introduced him to Luke. We followed Jay out to the beer garden, filled with bars, people and even a series of ponds adorned with koi. I was impressed! We found Dan, Sandy and Jay's partner Kristie who I had also met on the previous tour. It was great to see them all again and have a reunion here in San Diego as the beer started flowing and the reminiscing poured out.

Dan and Sandy had recently become parents and had their young son with them, so after many laughs and stories, they needed to get him home. Jay, on the other hand, was not ready to call it a night and wanted the reunion to continue, so he got one of his friends to drive the three of us to the bar where we were planning to meet up with the rest of the Contiki crew. We walked in to a big cheer and the party continued for another few hours.

Jay headed home after an awesome night and I told him I hoped to catch up with him again in San Diego one day. Luke and I headed back to the hotel with the rest of the Contiki tour, where some of us continued on at the after-party in Maddie and Scott's room (a couple from Melbourne). The next morning, as expected, we all boarded the bus with massive hangovers, bound for our next destination – the Arizona desert.

Arizona

After another long day on the bus, we finally arrived in Scottsdale, Arizona. The hotel we were staying at had a massive pool area, so after checking into our rooms, we all gathered for a pool party as we left our hangovers back in San Diego. After we had all reached our required levels of intoxication, we gathered in groups to catch cabs into town to hit the bars. Here, the taxi's weren't like those you see in other cities in the world – these reminded me more of the tuk tuk's Adam and I used in Thailand all those years before. Passengers sit on the back in the open air in these vehicles, not shut up closed in a cab.

We all met up at the first bar and I got chatting to a few of the locals. They were all cowboys over there, but friendly enough. We all kicked on and eventually found ourselves at a nightclub. By this stage in my life, I was completely over the nightclub scene as I couldn't think of anything worse than standing in a darkened room so jam-packed with people that you can't get to the bar or talk to anyone. Luckily, Luke, Brodie, Chris and another tour participant from New Zealand, Adrian, all felt the same, so we left and found a bar just down the road. The music was better and it was a lot less crowded, so we were able to sit at a table and – even better – we could actually get to the bar to order drinks. This place was definitely more my scene.

We were sitting around the table chatting when all of a sudden one of the guys burst out laughing. We looked towards the dance floor to see our new friend Adrian getting amongst it and busting out a few choice dance moves. I had never seen anything like it, not that he was a bad dancer (he was actually quite good), but he was hilarious and obviously quite drunk. He had us in stitches as he returned periodically to grab a sip of his drink, then head back out to the dance floor to rip it up some more!

The night finished with us all back in Luke's room with Adrian passed out underneath a table. We managed to wake him up and get him to his room eventually, and I made it back to my bed for a quick half-hour nap before we were all due to catch the bus for the Grand Canyon.

I sat on the bus next to Luke and straight away figured he hadn't been to sleep yet. That assumption proved to be correct as he told me that once we all left his room, he couldn't sleep so decided to go for a walk around the hotel grounds. He had met another bloke who was in a similar state to him and extended an invitation back to his room to continue the intoxication. The guy kept telling Luke how good a rapper he was and even had his own YouTube video. By the end of their session, Luke felt as though he was hanging out with an A-grade celebrity.

On the way to the canyon, we stopped for a few hours in Sedona, which was a small resort town nestled in the Arizona desert. While walking around Sedona, I remember thinking we were definitely in the Wild West, just like in the movies! Just at the moment, a big cowboy-looking guy walked by, and I couldn't believe it. He was wearing a holster and carrying a real gun. My paranoia started kicking in at seeing the weapon, but luckily he just winked and continued on his merry way, while I just breathed a massive sigh of relief.

After a few hours, we left the cowboy town for the big hole in the ground – the Grand Canyon. We were all booked to stay in the cabins at the campsite, but just before checking in, the bus took us to one of the lookouts so we could get our first peek of the canyon. I stood up on a massive rock, looked out over the spectacle that is the incredible landmark, and in a very laid-back tone said, "not bad!". Everyone on the tour seemed to hear me, and I'm not sure why, but they thought it was the funniest thing they had heard in a while. Perhaps the desert air was getting to them?! From then on, whenever we saw an impressive sight, we would say, "not bad!"

We heard there was a bar called The Piano Bar situated not far from where we were staying, right on the rim of the canyon. After checking into our cabins, Luke, Brodie, Chris, Adrian and I went for a walk to check it out. While walking near the edge and looking out over the vast openness of the canyon, we pretty much all took turns in saying, " not bad!"

Joel Whitwell

We sank a few beers at the bar and listened to someone play the piano (as the name suggested) then decided to walk back the way we came. By this stage the sky was pitch black and we couldn't see anything except the camp lights in the distance, but we all knew that just to our right in the blackness was a massive hole ready to swallow us if we took a few careless steps in that direction. Hence, we limited our beer intake as this walk was hard enough sober, and none of us, especially me, trusted ourselves to do it drunk. Heck, if we were all drunk, Adrian probably would have been dancing his way along the edge of the canyon!

The following morning, some of us on the tour went for a bike ride around the canyon. We followed some well-worn tracks and it was a bit of an adrenaline rush, especially when we stopped so Luke could take a photo of me standing on a rock that jutted out over the edge. We were pumped after our ride and took that feeling all the way to dinner and beyond that night. A group of us ended up back in Luke's room again and it was another awesome night, finishing with me curled up in the foetal position on the end of Luke's bed (again) before wandering back to my cabin to sleep it off before we hit the bright lights of Vegas.

Vegas

Later that morning, after packing up our things and waving goodbye to the big hole in the ground, we started to make our way through the desert towards Sin City. Vegas, baby – you beauty! After our drunken escapades in the Grand Canyon, I was starting to think Luke and I were like the characters out of the movie, *Fear and Loathing in Las Vegas*, but as I was soon to discover, we were more like the characters in *The Hangover*.

We passed the famous Hoover Dam as we made our way into Las Vegas. Besides that, it was just desert as far as the eye could see. We rolled into Sin City around mid-afternoon and checked into our hotel. It was a high-rise and my room had an impressive view overlooking the city. On the way out to dinner later on, the bus stopped at the Las Vegas sign for a group photo.

Our first night in Las Vegas was spectacular, to say the least. After dinner, we went for a cruise along the strip, witnessed a mock wedding between a couple on the tour, and rode a limousine to a strip club. This place was quite entertaining, and I ended up scoring a little extra on a lap dance. My belt buckle got caught on the dancer's tights and, try as we might, we couldn't get it to come undone! After trying for a while, we decided we needed a bit of help. So, still stuck together, we started walking around the club asking patrons if they could remove my belt buckle from her outfit. It was a bit of an embarrassing scene, but what else could we do?! Finally, some kind soul was able to free us and we went our separate ways – each with a story to tell, no doubt! We finished our first night in Las Vegas having drinks at a bar not far from the hotel until almost sunrise.

The following day, Luke convinced me to ride the New York-New York rollercoaster with him, which I did while nursing yet another hangover. That thing was intense and way scarier than the ones we experienced on Magic Mountain – but what a rush! Afterwards, we decided to head back to our rooms to relax for a few hours, as we probably had another big night ahead of us. Little did I know just how big that night was going to get!

While kicking back in my room, I dug out a book Luke had given me called *Hard Time*, written by Shaun Attwood. I read on the cover that after growing up in England, Shaun had left to travel to America, chasing his dream. By his twenties, he had become a millionaire stockbroker and was doing very well for himself, but then got involved in the drug scene. This led him down a path which eventually led to the SWAT team kicking in his door, and the writer having to serve time in one of America's deadliest prisons in Arizona.

I was immediately intrigued by Shaun's story and I couldn't wait to read more. Little did I know that day when I first opened his book, that in a few years I would actually get a chance to meet him and become friends.

Before long it was time to get ready for our second night out in Las Vegas. Now, earlier in this book I touched on my binge drinking and how

I was prone to blackouts, but other than a couple of trips to a counsellor, I hadn't really taken steps to overcome it. So, here I was in Las Vegas at what was apparent to be the height of my drinking problem. I had already rolled the dice once and was lucky to have made it through that first night here without any major dramas, but I was about to roll the dice a second time. One thing I learned about this city was that it may give you one chance, but if you try your luck a second time – more often than not, it will eat you alive.

Looking back now, I should have known that my second night out in Vegas was never going to end well.

It started fine, as we all went to see an amazing live show. It included high flying trapeze stunts which were very impressive. Afterwards, we hit the bars and clubs where I started to drink heavily, and that is when the night really went pear-shaped. As was often the case, the blackout came on suddenly, though after talking to people on the tour over the coming days, there were rumoured sightings of me around Vegas until almost sunrise.

The first thing I remembered when I started to come to the next day was the knocking at the door, and even that felt hazy. I answered the door in my underwear to see Luke and Contiki Matt standing there. Oh no. I knew straight away what that meant. I was late for the bus and they had to come looking for me. Bloody Vegas.

As I put on some clothes and quickly grabbed my things, and remember thinking I was going to have to spend the day with Jojo and at some point dance in front of everyone. This hangover was going to be a beauty, but things were only going to get worse. As expected, not long after I took my seat on the bus, Contiki Matt made a big announcement that I was to be Jojo's friend for the day and he handed me the purple panther. I placed the stuffed toy on my lap and promptly passed out. Around midday, we stopped for lunch and some shopping, so I stumbled off the bus too. I must have looked a right sight walking around the shopping centre carrying a big purple panther. The thing had a permanent grin, and I couldn't help thinking, "you wanker, Jojo. I feel like death, and all you can do is keep grinning at me."

I went to an ATM to get some money out for lunch, and to my horror it came up with 'insufficient funds'. Alarm bells started to go off in my head as I knew yesterday I still had over $3k in my account, which was pegged to get me through the last few weeks of the trip. Surely I didn't blow it all on one night in Vegas? I tried to convince myself that everything was okay and it was probably just a faulty machine, but deep down I knew I had stuffed up and was going to have a Vegas story to tell in the years to come. I decided to wait until we reached our next destination, Bass Lake, to look more into it.

Bass Lake

We arrived at this scenic place in the evening and headed to our Contiki cabins. Each housed four people, so naturally Luke and I teamed up with Brodie and Chris. To help us get around, the people who worked at the camp drove golf-type buggies. We were due to meet up at Contiki Matt's cabin for dinner and drinks around seven, so on the way a few of us went for a walk to check out the lake. On the way to Contiki Matt's cabin we passed by the general store, where I decided to get it over with and try to find out more about what happened to my money in Las Vegas. I tried the ATM in the stores, and as suspected, the error 'insufficient funds' came up again. I now wanted to get on top of it so I could relax and enjoy the rest of the tour.

So, before heading to dinner, Brodie and I went back to our cabin so I could use my phone to look up my previous 24-hours transactions. To my shock, I discovered I had indeed made two withdrawals, each totalling over $1500. By the address on the transactions, it looked like I was at a strip club. I shook my head in disbelief. How could I have been so foolish? How could I have ruined my whole holiday for one big night out?

Luckily for me I have such a supportive family, so straight away I rang home and dad answered. I explained the situation, but didn't want to admit I had spent it all on strippers, so I ended up telling a few white lies. Regardless of how I lost the cash, dad knew I was very good at paying back my debts, so he was more than happy to lend me some money. He just had to wait until the bank opened on Monday so he could go in and make a deposit.

I felt a wave of relief wash over me. Thanks to my dear old dad, it looked like I was now going to be able to finish another trip. My brother also owed me a little bit of money, so dad said he would get in touch and see if he could come through with that as well. So, Vegas had almost destroyed me, but thanks to my family, it didn't beat me.

By the time we got back to Contiki Matt's cabin, I was in a better frame of mind knowing what happened, though I wasn't out of the woods just yet. $3k was a lot of money to just throw away, particularly on a night I can't even remember, so I was still stressing over it. I have found in my life that during times of stress, I often turn into a clown to make other people laugh and by this time, everyone on the tour had heard about my big night out. So, after a few drinks I loosened up and had everyone cracking up by making jokes about it all.

The next day, Luke, Brodie, Chris and the newly married couple, Aaron and Rachel, hired a boat and spent the morning out on the lake. Sadly, I was still dwelling on what had happened in Las Vegas and just wanted to be left alone with my thoughts, so I stayed back and slept on the couch. Just after midday, the boys arrived back at the cabin and started playing a drinking game. That got me off the couch and shook me from my hole. We were out of control on that tour. Come to think of it, I was out of control on all of the Contiki tours I had been on, but I survived to tell the tales, and these trips certainly gave me a lot of stories to write about!

We had just started the drinking game when there was a knock at the door. It was our Kiwi friend Adrian, who always seemed to know when we were doing fun things like drinking and wanted to be a part of it – and we were happy to have him there. So, the five of us just sat in that cabin all afternoon playing drinking games and getting tipsier and tipsier. It was a fun time and another great memory from my travels.

That evening we were due to meet up with the rest of the tour, then go for a boat cruise on the lake. I remember thinking what fine form we would be in by the time dinner rolled around. At just the right time, we all stumbled to the restaurant on the water's edge. At one point, I am pretty sure Luke actually fell in the lake and got his passport wet. Why he had it on him, I do not know. At dinner, I sat with the two Melbourne girls, Jess and Melissa, and we had a great chat. After dinner it was time to board the boat for the cruise, where I had the chance to get to know one of the other girls, Genevieve. It turned out to be a lovely night out under the stars with the group.

San Fran

The following morning, I rose early with an excited feeling in my stomach – we were headed for our next destination, San Francisco. This meant I was on the verge of living out another childhood dream. Ever since I first saw the Golden Gate Bridge on *Full House* as a kid, it had been on my bucket list to see it in person one day. This vision was now in my grasp and to say I was excited is perhaps a bit of an understatement.

Even better, I received a message from Marcia that morning to say she couldn't wait to catch up with me at Niagara Falls in a few days. You little beauty! After the horror of Las Vagas, the trip was starting to get better by the day. The excitement continued to build as I boarded the bus and we started our journey to the bay area. On the way, we stopped at a supermarket where I watched a couple of the guys check out a heap of guns. Even though I had heard about it, I was actually quite shocked to see firsthand how easy it was to buy guns in America.

We continued the journey towards the Golden Gate Bridge and my dream. The desert was now behind us, and we were instead surrounded by lush green hills. During my life, I had made my way to so many cities all over the world, but this was definitely one of the most thrilling.

After the usual routine of a quick city tour, we headed straight to the Fisherman's Wharf and Pier 39. San Francisco is a vibrant city, very much alive with a diverse range of people adorning the streets. It goes without saying by now that a quick beer was in order at Fisherman's Wharf before we headed to our hotel rooms to get ready for a night out in the city. A few hours later, the bus dropped us back at Pier 39 so we could experience a boat cruise out on the bay. To be honest, this was the part of the trip I was looking forward to the most, along with my upcoming catch up with Marcia at Niagara Falls.

The water was choppy, but it was beautiful out on the bay, especially as it was evening and we got to see the sun setting beyond the iconic Golden Gate Bridge. We could also see Alcatraz off in the distance. Life was bliss. Like I had experienced in Ushuaia harbour, there was a strong wind blowing, but I was too fixated on the bridge to take much notice. With the sun setting beyond the arches, it felt as if the entire universe had conspired to make my dream seem as beautiful as it could. I stood there in awe as a tear rolled down my cheek, and it was certainly one of those moments that I was truly happy to be alive. I had finally lived out one of my long-held dreams, and no one would ever be able to take that away. I sometimes wish moments like that could last forever, but I had to come out of my trance eventually.

We docked back at Pier 39 and went for dinner at Bubba Gump Shrimp Co. on Fisherman's Wharf. After a big feed of their specialty, it was time to party. We walked along the wharf area and found ourselves a bar to settle in at for a few hours of drinking Contiki-style. I ended up walking hand-in-hand back to the hotel with one of the girls and thought I may actually score some action, but as always I couldn't quite seal the deal and ended up heading back to my hotel room alone…again.

I sometimes wonder why I've never been able to score with the ladies, but the more I experience life, the more I realise that my purpose here on Earth is far greater than being hooked up with a partner. I guess I just have to have faith in the whole process. I have made some strong and heartfelt friendships with women over the years, and these I hold extremely important. In the long run, I believe friendships mean so much more than a casual fling here and there.

Luke was quite surprised I made it down to the lobby to meet up with him in the morning, because after my big night, he didn't expect to see me at all that day. But, we were booked in to do a bike ride over the Golden Gate Bridge, and I knew I would regret it for the rest of my life if I piked on that one. I hadn't done much bike riding in my time and Luke could tell I was struggling big time as we started the ride through the streets of San Fran and down towards the bay. The bridge was just in front of me, and I was determined not to give up on my goal. Ride on!

On the way, we stopped to check out the Palace of Fine Arts Theatre, which gave me the chance to not only see another piece of impressive architecture (which, incidentally, was featured in the movie *The Rock*) but also to catch my breath. The mist coming off the bay and under the bridge was amazing to see. Every time I stopped to rest, I found myself taking in the impressive views of this amazing city.

By this stage, my legs were killing me, but I had to keep going. My goal was in sight. After what felt like forever, I finally rode up a small embankment and out onto the Golden Gate Bridge. I was so happy, I jumped off my bike and did a small victory dance. It was like I had waited my whole life for this moment, akin to the feeling of reaching the summit at Machu Picchu. I had reached my dream – and on a pushbike nonetheless! I was also quite hungover and almost threw up over the side of the railing, but I wouldn't have it any other way.

It was such an emotional moment in my life, and I ended up so mentally drained that I didn't even head out with the tour group that night, instead opting for an early one. It was a bit of a shame, as that was our last big night out together as a group – which I normally would not miss. I remembered telling Marcia on the day we explored the Canadian Islands together a few years earlier that it was my dream to see the Golden Gate Bridge. As I fell into an exhausted sleep that night in San Francisco, I had a triumphant smile on my face. I couldn't wait to tell her all about it.

The next day was free of planned activities, so Luke and I went for a walk to find a laundromat. We found one, but it was in a dodgy part of town. We found ourselves surrounded by beggars and homelessness. As soon as we walked into the laundromat, we were confronted by a scene of a man and woman in the midst of a heated argument, then the man walked up knocked the woman to the ground with one punch. She then got up, and they both casually walked out while an onlooker threatened to call the cops. We only wanted to do a bit of washing, and yet there was all this chaos around us! I didn't think a trip to the laundromat could be so scary.

We finally got our washing done and made it back to our hotel in one piece to spend our last night in San Francisco having a few quiet beers and wandering the streets of this beautiful city. It was also time to say goodbye to more new friends, as half the group were finishing the tour in San Fran instead of coming back with us to LA. Brodie and Chris were leaving; it was sad to see them go as I had a lot of fun with them on the tour. I knew in my heart that this was going to be my last ever Contiki tour, and as I started saying my goodbyes, it began to sink in that this was it.

On the journey back towards LA along the Californian coast, I found myself looking out the window at the ocean and thinking that a chapter in my life was coming to an end. The Contiki chapter was closing, but it was time to move on. It had begun while sitting in a park with Jono in London five years earlier, just about to start my first tour and not knowing what to expect. What followed was three awesome tours over the five years, where I was lucky enough to have met so many great people and created countless incredible memories.

The tour bus stopped in Santa Monica for a few hours for lunch and a bit of a look around. I took a walk with one of the girls towards the water's edge, but I was feeling pretty burnt out. I reflected on the past few years and the difference in myself, from that park in London to there in Santa Monica. I once didn't think I would ever leave Harvey and my comfort zone, but I had been able to use travel to grow as a person and gain confidence in myself. "Life begins at the edge of your comfort zone". More than ever, I can relate to that quote.

I was going to miss these trips, and sadly, something was going to happen at Niagara Falls that would make me miss them even more – but I didn't know that yet.

After walking around the pier and beach for a while, we went for lunch at Bubba Gump Shrimp Co. Then it was on to Los Angeles and, for the third time in five years, it was time to say goodbye to a lot of great people as we all went our separate ways. Luke and I went back to the same Chinese restaurant where we had dinner the first night and spoke of our plans for the next few days. I was planning to head up to Niagara Falls to catch up with Marcia, but Luke didn't want to be the third wheel, so he decided to head to Chicago to live it up before we planned to meet back up in New York for a few days.

Thirty-Two

BRIDGE OVER TROUBLED WATERS

The next morning I started my journey up to Niagara Falls. At the airport, I bought a copy of Jack Kerouac's book, *On the Road* and I was off. I had butterflies in my stomach as the excitement of seeing Marcia again was starting to build. After spending the night at a rundown hotel not far from JFK Airport in NYC, I arrived up at Niagara late on a Thursday afternoon. I didn't know it at the time, but at roughly the same time I stepped off the tarmac, there was an accident on the Skyway Bridge involving a drunk truck driver that resulted in the closure of the bridge for the duration of my stay at Niagara Falls.

Seeing as that is the main bridge that connects Toronto with Niagara Falls, this was not only to have dire consequences for my upcoming catch up with Marcia, but it also set the wheels in motion for me to go on and completely ruin the friendship, for which I still have not forgiven myself. Once I arrived, I caught a cab to my hostel and couldn't believe I was about to see my friend again after having to jump through so many hoops to get here. I really couldn't believe my luck!

As the taxi drove into town, I looked out at the river and imagined Marcia and I walking along the water's edge chatting about life, just like on the day we spent together out on the Islands in Toronto a few years earlier.

However, after trying to check into the wrong hotel and being turned away, I spent the next hour wandering aimlessly around the streets of Niagara cursing my luck and wondering where I was going to stay. It was only then I realised my mistake and found the right hotel – my head was obviously all over the place!

The hotel, although the correct one this time, was a dive. It reminded me of those rundown hotels off the beaten track I used to see on American B-grade movies. I swear the lone guy in reception could have passed for the Norman Bates' character in the movie *Psycho*, but just a darker version. He didn't say much as he glared at me with his beady eyes. "OK", I thought, "time to get to my room". I headed down the hall and locked the door behind me once I was safely inside my designated room. No Norman Bates lookalike is going to get in here tonight. I certainly slept with one eye open… although I always do because my glass eye is never properly closed anyway.

Seeing as I wasn't due to catch up with Marcia until the Saturday, on Friday I decided to explore the American side of the falls, seeing as I had seen the Canadian side four times before. They may have only been separated by a river, but the two sides were worlds apart. While the Canadian side was buzzing and bursting with tourists, I found the US side to be a little derelict-looking. Abandoned shops and businesses seemed to be on every block. It was a bit of a depressing feel, sadly. However, my spirits were still high as I was here for one reason – to see Marcia again.

Later that day I received a message from Maddie and Scott from the last Contiki group I was with to let me know they were staying in Buffalo, which isn't far from Niagara, and they could come to catch up with me for a few hours. I liked that idea, so they met up with me out the front of my creepy hotel and the three of us went for a walk down to the falls before dinner at Hard Rock Café. It was great to see them again, and it showed what genuine people they were.

After Maddie and Scott left to go back to Buffalo, I thought it was too early to head back to my room, so I decided to go for a quiet drink at a bar just down the road. I was feeling on top of the world and didn't want the day to end so quickly. At the bar, I met a guy called Jason, and one drink led to another as we got chatting. So much for a few quiet drinks – it turned into a pretty big night with my new friend, and I don't remember much until waking up in my hotel room sometime the following day.

As I gathered my bearings, it suddenly dawned on me that today was the day I was to meet Marcia. I quickly checked Facebook on my phone and saw I had a message from her. She seemed very distressed and upset as she told me that due to an accident on the Skyway Bridge, they had to close it for a few days. As this was the main route between Toronto and Niagara, she couldn't make it down to see me.

I was dazed and confused as I slumped back on my bed. Did I just read correctly? How the hell did this happen? I was going to miss out on seeing her again due to something as random as the closure of a bridge. You wouldn't read about it…oh, wait…you are. But I felt as though the universe was having a lend of me. After all the excitement I had as I headed up here, my soul was now crushed.

I spent the next few days just wandering aimlessly around the town like a lost soul, wondering why this happened and what could have been. I looked out over the railing across to the Canadian side of the falls and remembered all the fun times I had over there, and now I felt all alone. There was a slight drizzle, which washed away the tears.

That night I laid awake in my room thinking about the situation. I thought about the foolish things I have done in my life, including my drink driving indiscretions. Was this karma, that now someone else's drink driving had impacted me as well? Was the universe teaching me a lesson? People would say it is just bad luck and bad timing, but surely there had to be more to it. I sent my good friend Caliopi a message, who at that time was working as a chef on a boat somewhere in the waters off the Greek Islands, a long way from Niagara Falls where I lay on my dingy bed, alone and sad.

I finally drifted off into an exhausted sleep. When I woke in the early hours of the morning, Caliopi had replied. What she wrote was nice, but one passage in particular really touched my heart. She wrote; "Sorry to hear you didn't get to see your friend, but just think of all the cool and amazing things you have seen on your travels and surely you will have a smile." Thank you for that nice message, Caliopi. I could always rely on the friends I grew up with from back home.

I looked online about the bridge closure and still couldn't get my head around the timing of it all. I went back over Marcia's message and could sense that she was also upset she couldn't make it down to see me. There was a deep sadness in my heart as I packed up my things on Tuesday morning and caught a taxi to the airport. It was a gloomy and rainy day, which mirrored the way I was feeling.

I looked out over the same river I had while coming into town a few days earlier, but this time in the opposite direction. That was when it all really started to hit home, and more tears rolled down my face.

Luke was waiting for me in New York, so I had to pull myself together, stay strong and try to finish off this trip in the best possible way. I was an emotional wreck, but having a good friend from home waiting to meet me in NYC was definitely going to help.

On the taxi ride into the Big Apple, the skyline loomed large just as it had on my visit five years prior, and I was just as amazed by the sheer size of it all. That lifted my spirits a little, but I still had a long way to go. As expected, Luke was waiting for me out the front of the apartment he had booked for us and we had a warm embrace as I stepped out of the taxi.

After settling in, I told Luke what had happened up at Niagara Falls and he could see I was feeling a bit down, so he suggested we go for a walk to explore New York. The week to follow was a lot of fun, and Luke helped me keep my mind off the negative things.

One day we went for lunch in Times Square, had a few beers and the next thing we knew we were arriving back to our apartment at 4 am the next day, nice and drunk. But, through it all, the spectre of Niagara still hung by me. I had sent Marcia a message before I left Niagara and one morning while I was in New York, she replied. She was quite positive, which really helped lift me back up again. At least our friendship was still intact.

With me now suddenly in a better mood, Luke and I decided to visit Central Park. Being inside the park and seeing the skyscrapers all around us was like a different world. On one of our last days in the city, we met up with Leigh from Contiki 2009 for a few drinks at a bar on the Hudson River. It was fantastic to see her again and take a trip down memory lane as we spoke about the adventures we had on that tour.

That week in NYC was just what I needed, and although Luke lost his passport on one of our drunken nights out, he had a great time too. Around 4 am on Monday morning, I wished Luke farewell (and good luck getting home with his emergency passport replacement!) and caught a taxi to the airport for my flight to Scotland.

I spent my first few days in Edinburgh wandering around the city. It was overcast and rainy during the day, "just another typical Scottish summer", I thought to myself. Walking through the city brought back so many memories, especially from when I first visited with Jono five years earlier. I felt a little sadness in my heart as I remembered that great time in my life. Edinburgh had always been one of my favourite cities in the world, and I especially admired the architecture and culture of the place.

It was on one of those first nights in Edinburgh while relaxing in my hotel room I heard the news that Robin Williams had passed away. Like the rest of the world, I was shocked. I had grown up watching him on the big screen, and *Dead Poet's Society* was one of my all-time favourite films. The quote from the movie, "carpe diem", or "seize the day" really spoke volumes to me.

The next weekend, Scottish Dave picked me up so I could spend a few days with him. He had moved away from Kelso and was living in another small town called Boswells. Iain had also moved, and came over to Dave's to meet up for a few drinks. It was a fantastic reunion, albeit minus Jono. Dave had become a dad since our last adventure here, so was a lot tamer than he had been on our trip five years ago – and even Iain was well-behaved this time! It was quite therapeutic to spend the last days of this trip with Dave. I was in awe with how well he had adjusted to this next stage of his life with his growing family.

In stark contrast to last time we were all together, this weekend was not all about drinking. We had some good chats and heart-to-hearts. We spent a bit of time down at the beach while Dave kite-surfed (it was way too cold for me!) and generally took it easy. Eventually, the time came for Dave to take me to the airport as another epic adventure was coming to an end. On that last day, I saw something I had never seen before in Scotland, the sun peeking through the clouds. It was a sight to behold!

After saying goodbye to Scottish Dave, I boarded my flight for home. As always, I did a lot of thinking on the long journey back to WA. On this trip, as you would expect, my thoughts kept drifting to Niagara and what could have been. As crazy as it sounds now, I couldn't shake the thought that there was something more to what happened than plain bad luck, like I was somehow, cosmically, responsible. In times like these, I find music helps me see things more clearly, so I put on my headset and almost straight away the song *Bridge Over Troubled Waters* by Simon and Garfunkel came on. How appropriate! It really did relate to how I felt about what happened at Niagara Falls, and now whenever I think of Marcia, I also think of that song.

As we descended back into Perth, I was uplifted to remember that our friendship was still strong and seeing how much I travel, there would be another chance sometime in the near future for us to meet up. Little did I know that I was heading home to make another one of the biggest mistakes of my life.

Thirty-Three

My Biggest Regret

Life resumed back home as normal, and I sent Marcia a few messages just to make sure everything was still good between us. For some reason, she wasn't getting back to me. I tried not to stress though, and as another year finished and we headed into 2015, I was still confident that things would turn out alright. Then one weekend in early March, everything came to a head as I completely ruined any chance of continuing this friendship that meant so much to me.

Saturday started like any other weekend did back then. My mate Ash and I decided to head to the Collie Bridge Tavern for a few beers, which was about half an hour down the road from where we lived. As was often the case, a few beers led to a few more, and before we knew it, we were both quite drunk as we kicked on at the tavern all afternoon. Things were very blurred by the time a taxi dropped me off at home that night, and I don't remember much about what happened next, but I do get flashbacks of me laying in bed thinking, "you could have made it", so I must have been thinking about Marcia, and managed to work myself up into a frenzy.

With the way technology is these days and how easy it is to contact people all over the world, this desperate, lonely (drunk) feeling I was experiencing was destined to end badly. Even though to this day I don't remember what I wrote, or writing anything at all, at some point I must have jumped out of bed, opened up my laptop (which was in the loungeroom) and during a drunken outburst posted something on Marcia's Facebook wall. I can only guess that I went to town on her for not making it down to catch up with me at Niagara Falls, then passed out in my drunken stupor.

I woke up with a start in the early hours and knew straight away I had done something silly. I checked Facebook on both my phone and laptop, but couldn't find Marcia's profile anywhere. What I feared happening in my mind had come to be true. She had blocked me. But, I still hadn't finished making a mess of things.

I was still half-drunk and not in the right frame of mind, so I put up a post on my Facebook wall saying that something had affected me quite deeply and I was going to kill myself, so I will "see you all in the next life". With that, I fell back to sleep. It was daylight the next time I woke up, and unlike my post to Marcia the night before, I did remember what I wrote on my wall. I checked, and sure enough, I had many messages and comments on my post from concerned friends who were obviously worried about me.

What had I done?

What had started as a great day down at the pub with my friend had turned into a nightmare, and it was all my own doing. I deleted my post straight away, but the damage had been done and I felt very sheepish that morning, a lot like how I felt after my DUI. I had now messed up in epic proportions while on the booze, and suddenly getting blackout drunk didn't seem so exciting and funny anymore.

Things had become quite serious, and it finally dawned on me that I may have a problem. Ash saw my post that morning and, being the good friend he is, dropped around and spent time with me that day. I will always be grateful for that as it wasn't wise for me to be on my own.

Even though I had messed up, life had to go on, so I had to keep turning up for work and move forward from this as best I could. To be honest, in those early stages, I expected that seeing as I had done everything perfect in my friendship with Marcia until my drunken mistake, I hoped she would see it as out of character and eventually make contact so we could work it out. Sadly, she never has.

It was also around this time that, after three world trips and plenty of wear and tear, it was time to get myself a new ear. My old one would take its place on the mantlepiece for surviving this far! That helped to keep my mind off things, and I felt a little better with a new ear adorning the side of my head.

Not long after all of this turmoil, my brother Frog and his partner Michayla wanted a change of scenery and moved over to Melbourne to try to make a go of it. I decided to head over to catch up with them and spend a few days over east, and my travel partner from the year before, Luke, came with me. A couple of days in Melbourne was just what I needed. We explored the city, went to a footy game at Etihad Stadium, and spent an afternoon out at St Kilda beach. Bliss. We even went and caught up with my friend Rachel to celebrate her birthday in Richmond.

I flew back home alone as Luke had taken a liking to Melbourne and decided to change his ticket and hang around a bit longer. As it turns out, he permanently relocated to the city not long after and is now happily settled in Geelong with his own little family.

Thirty Four

Moving Forward In Hard Times

By this stage in my life, I had started to discover that whatever you put out into the world eventually comes back to you in one way or another. A few days after I returned home from Melbourne, the universe finally decided to reward me for keeping a positive attitude. Justin Rake was a young bloke who also grew up in Harvey and had started working for the Bunbury Mail newspaper. He had been following my life on Facebook and had come to the conclusion that I certainly had a story worth writing about in the paper, so he reached out to ask if I would be happy for him to do it. Of course, I was over the moon!

We did the interview and when it came out in the paper, I thought he did a great job at capturing my message. The local community was really starting to notice and be inspired by my story, and I believe that was the start of a snowball effect of opportunity. I was finally able to get my story out into the world, and I was excited by what could be.

Later that year I finally gave public speaking a go as I was invited to share my life and travels with a local youth camp in Binningup and the Lions Club in Harvey. Both were great experiences, though I found public speaking to be the most daunting thing I have ever done in my life! Looking back now, I'm not sure if it was just coincidence or part of the plan that all this started to happen after Marcia cut me out of her life. Either way, after spending that day on the Islands with her, I felt that she really believed in me, so it was such as shame for her not to be in touch when these opportunities came up.

As we headed into 2016, I felt the best way to really move forward was to start planning my next overseas adventure. As much as I love Canada, that country was currently out of the equation, so I decided to focus on Europe. I remembered reading Shawn Attwood's book *Hard Time* in Vegas, and he seemed like an interesting bloke with an exciting life story. I wondered if I could somehow get in touch with him and arrange to meet at some point.

One night I checked Facebook and found he had his own personal page, so I figured I had nothing to lose if I took the chance and sent him a message to introduce myself. I didn't think anything would come of it, so you can imagine my surprise when he replied a few days later. After a string of messages, he said he would love to meet if I was ever in London, which was where he was based at the time. I couldn't believe it! I had already planned to head back to London, seven years on from Contiki 2009, and now I had even more reason to add the city to my travel itinerary. While I was up that way, I decided I would also check out a new place I had never been to before. I settled on Iceland as it looked like an intriguing place. I also settled on Scandinavia for my third destination, and my plans were falling into place.

The big difference between this trip and my previous ones was that I was travelling entirely alone. This prospect scared me a little, but I felt I was ready for it. I knew this trip could make or break me, but I was heading off regardless. I did manage to get in touch with a guy I knew back in Harvey, Jaxon, who was living in Denmark. He said he'd love to catch up when I was in Scandinavia, so although I was travelling alone, the thought of seeing a familiar face was reassuring.

Not long before I was due to fly out, something happened that gave my upcoming trip even more meaning. My old school friend Lisa's daughter Zara tragically passed away at a young age, and seeing as it was her dream to see the world, Lisa asked if I wouldn't mind taking a picture of Zara with me on my trip. In a way, she would be experiencing her dream in spirit. I felt honoured she asked me to do that, and it brought a tear to my eye. It meant I could do something to help my friend who was experiencing so much pain, and perhaps bring a little smile to her face knowing her daughter was, in a way, travelling as she had always dreamed of. Lisa and I met up at a café in town and she gave me the photo, which I safely tucked into my luggage when I got home.

London

I took my usual route overseas with a stopover in Hong Kong. Stepping off the plane and into the airport, I always look over at the mist covering the tops of the mountains, and this is the signal I have come to love that I am, indeed, travelling again. I made it to Heathrow and headed to a hostel in the heart of Russell Square, not far from the hotel where we had started and finished Contiki '09. On the tube ride, I ended up taking the exact same route I rode with Jono and it made me a little sad that time was over. Back then, I was with a friend and about to embark on the greatest journey I ever went on in my life, and now I was on my own. That feeling became more intense as I walked out of the subway at Russell Square and went in search of my hostel.

I checked in and then sent Shaun, the author, a message to plan a catch up. To my great surprise and excitement, he messaged back straight away with his address out in Guildford. He told me to catch the train out there that evening and he would meet me. Despite my feelings of excitement, I was also pretty anxious about it. My first day back in London for seven years and I was about to meet the person I had hoped to meet since I first started reading his book in Vegas two years prior. I guess life really does work in mysterious ways. I wasn't sure what to expect, but I knew it would all turn out alright.

Later that evening I boarded the train to Guildford then went looking for Shaun's place. He lived not far from the train line, so I found it quite easily. Standing out the front of his house, I could feel my nerves start to rise, similar to how I felt when I was about to see Marcia in Canada and Shaban in Melbourne. The only difference this time was that I hadn't actually met Shaun before, I only knew about him from his book.

It was now or never, so I forged ahead and knocked at his front door. Almost straight away, a bald man answered (who I took to be Shaun) and invited me in. He offered me a cider that his housemate had brewed, which I was more than happy to sample. Shaun didn't drink these days. We started chatting and he was very friendly and easy-going, so I quickly relaxed in his company. He then suddenly said he had something for me and disappeared upstairs. He came down with signed copies of his other books – I was over the moon! Such a generous gesture, I couldn't wait to start reading them.

As it was getting late, Shaun asked if I was keen to head out for dinner as he knew a good place over in Woking that served great Mexican food. That sounded fantastic, so we headed out. Just as we were leaving, a friend of Shaun's, Richard, turned up. He joined us for dinner too. Richard was also a lovely guy, and the three of us got along famously. He also had some of his work published, so I was in very good company! At one point in the evening I was able to get a photo with Shaun while holding a copy of his book. It was a magical evening, but eventually I had to get back to the hostel. Shaun and Richard dropped me off at the station and I headed back to my hostel with a huge smile on my face.

I had a few days in London before heading to Iceland, so I thought it was a great opportunity to head back to some of the places I had visited with Jono just to reminisce. The hotel where we had started and finished the Contiki tour was a short walk from where I was staying, so I started there. I found the bar where Jono and I had spent a significant amount of time and ordered a beer (for old times' sake!). As soon as I sat down, the memories came flooding back. It certainly felt surreal being back there, and I became quite emotional. Looking out the window at the crowded London street, it all seemed eerily familiar. This made me feel sad and excited at the same time; to be back in the same place that I had first created some incredible memories.

I finished my beer and went for a walk around the hotel and out to the forecourt where I had first met Marcia and the others on the Contiki tour. I remembered the conversation we had, and I felt my heart break a little more over what I had done. Life's lessons can be harsh sometimes, but I made the mistake and now I needed to live with the aftermath. Another Contiki tour appeared to be gathering while I was there, and seeing them reminded me of how excited I was seven years ago as I similarly gathered with our eager group of young travellers.

My day finished with a walk and some relaxing in the park where Jono and I spent time that first day we arrived. My plans for London – meeting Shaun and reminiscing – were complete, and I was ready to move onto the next part of this journey, Iceland.

Iceland

By this stage of my life, I had travelled pretty much all over the world, but had never been as far as Iceland. I wasn't sure what to expect, but I knew it was going to be an incredible experience. I flew out of Gatwick airport and started my journey. I knew very little about Iceland, other than its reputation as Viking country. But, as they say, "travel is often the best teacher", and I was ready to learn more about this intriguing part of the world.

I had no one to meet up with for a while, so I was about to find out what solo travelling was really about. I was staying up in Reykjavik, located on the coast as the capital of Iceland. The plane touched down, and as I stepped onto the tarmac, the first thing I noticed was the mist in the air. It was a bit chilly, but nowhere near as cold as I expected. I caught a shuttle bus and as I waited in line at the arrival gates, I noticed a quote on the wall that read; "A weight greater than wisdom, a traveller cannot carry (A Viking Quote)". Not sure why I noticed this, but I have always loved quotes, not only about life, but especially about travel. I was hoping to gain more wisdom from my life journey here in Iceland.

I checked through customs and caught a bus into the city. The thought crossed my mind – years ago I was drinking with my mates down at the Harvey pub, and now here I was heading into the capital city of Iceland on yet another amazing trip! It is surreal how things change over time.

After the shuttle bus dropped everyone else off, the driver told me he wasn't sure where my hotel was. I tried not to panic, as I had read somewhere that Iceland was one of the safest places on the planet, so I was sure I would be fine. We did finally find the hotel, the Arctic Comfort, and as I stepped off the bus, a cold chill hit me. I was in Iceland, alright!

There was only one lady behind the counter as I checked in, and I noticed she had green hair. Her name was Asa. After a brief chat, I headed back outside into the cold to find my room which was located in the complex next door. As was often the case during the summer in the northern hemisphere, it didn't get dark until after 10 pm, even though the sky was gloomy. After a nice warm shower, I decided to call it a night.

It was windy and drizzly when I woke in the morning, so I wondered how I was going to spend my first day in Iceland. Should I do the sensible thing and go for some sightseeing? Or, go on a pub crawl as a way to meet some locals? I figured the wind was probably going to blow me into a pub anyway, so I decided to do a bit of both.

Harbours have always fascinated me for some reason, so that was the first place I headed. I grabbed a map and set off in search of Reykjavik Harbour. I felt free to be travelling again, being able to make my own plans and forge my own path as I wandered the globe on each new adventure.

Once at the harbour, I saw numerous ships docked and wondered where they, too, would be headed next.

From my vantage point at the water's edge, I could see some majestic cliffs way off in the distance, and (like in Ushuaia,) a chilly breeze flew off the water. After a few hours of exploring, I had worked up quite a thirst, so it was time to hit the bars. I asked around and learnt that there were plenty of cool places to drink at on Laugavegur, the main shopping street in Reykjavik. Out came my map again as I took off in search of my first stop. I finally found the street, and to my great delight, the info was spot on. There were bars everywhere as well as so many great places to eat. I was in heaven!

After a big feed of pizza, I was ready to begin my pub crawl and start drinking like a Viking! At the first bar, I found myself out in the back garden chatting to a bunch of locals, who started passing around a big fat joint. I felt obliged to join them. This was not a wise idea; one toke lead to an hour of me then wandering the streets of Reykjavik in a haze, until the fog finally lifted and I was able to continue on my mission. At some point later on, I was with a group who had a similar green offering, but this time I politely declined.

Around midnight I was invited to a college party at an apartment in a highrise overlooking the city. There were people in the loungeroom drinking, while others were out on the balcony smoking their choice of leaf. I moved between the two, chatting and getting to know the people, then after a few hours decided it was time to call it a night.

I got myself into a taxi, but halfway back to the hotel I had another idea, so I asked the driver to drop me off at a strip club. I knew deep down this was a bad idea and I should have opted for sleep instead. Hadn't I learnt my lesson from Vegas a few years earlier? I was beginning to realise the stark difference between the sober me and the drunk me. Sober Joel was full of wisdom and often made the right choices, no matter what, whereas drunk Joel was just out to have fun at any expense. That night in the taxi was the full-on drunk version, so the strip club won the battle of good and evil.

I gave my bank card to the guy at the front of the club and spent who-knows how long having a good time with the strippers. Eventually, I decided it was time to make my way back to the hotel, but as the sun was starting to come up. I couldn't find a taxi, so using my map as a guide, I made the walk back in the early morning sun, all the while cursing myself as I was beginning to sober up.

I slept most of the day and when I did finally rise, I was apprehensive to check my bank account. I had no idea how much cash I had dropped at the club the night before. Thankfully, it was nowhere near as bad as I feared (and not a drop on Vegas!) but it still left a dent in my finances. I decided the best way to rectify the situation and ensure I still had enough money left to spend on the rest of the trip was to have a few days off the booze. Instead, I would spend the next few days exploring the beauty of Iceland.

The next day I booked a day trip out to the Blue Lagoon, a geothermal spa in southwestern Iceland. It was mid-morning when the bus picked me up from my hotel. As we journeyed out of the city, I was amazed by the landscape. It felt like I was in a whole new galaxy, with all the rock formations and these weird streaks in the sky. We finally arrived at the lagoon and even from the sign it looked extra-terrestrial. I looked around at the lava fields off in the distance as far as the eye could see, as I walked through the entrance of the building.

The lagoon was spectacular – a milky blue colour and 39 degrees Celsius, like one giant spa. I chose not to get in that day, but instead wandered around the edge while tourists from all over the world frolicked in the steamy blue water. It was just on nightfall as I caught the bus back into the city and the whole way I was looking out the window hoping to catch a glimpse of the Northern Lights (but to no avail).

The next day, seeing as my time in Iceland was coming to an end with only a few days left, I decided to book another tour. This time I went on another day trip to check out the tectonic plate that separates the American and Eurasian continents. It was another early pick up, so I booked myself a wakeup call through the hotel. I sat around my hotel room for a while, wondering what to do. They say idle time is the Devil's time, and I guess that is true. I figured that seeing as I hadn't been on the booze for a few days and this could be my last chance to have a night out on the town in Iceland, surely one drink couldn't hurt, could it?

So, I made my way back to Laugavegur Street, where I went that first night out, and found myself a bar. As had become a regular pattern in my life, one drink led to a few more as I started to feel pretty relaxed chatting to some local girls with green hair (what is it with Icelandic women and green hair?). Then all of a sudden, as had also become a regular pattern, the next thing I remember is waking up in my hotel room with the phone ringing right by my head.

Oh shit – it was my wakeup call. I quickly jumped out of bed, grabbed my wallet and phone and hopped on the bus. I sat down and thought about what had happened. Suddenly it hit me. I had had another blackout after drinking too much. It felt quite scary as it started to dawn on me that this habit was something I was really struggling to overcome.

It was a bleak and overcast day, which reflected my mood. I was still wearing the same clothes from the night before and my thoughts were scattered all over the place. However, I had to pull myself together as I was about to see something I may never get the chance to again, so I was determined to make the most of the day.

Our first stop was to see some thermal baths, which are known to have some volcanic activity. We also saw a few geysers, which had plenty of steam arising from them. We then went to check out the tectonic plate, located at the bottom of a stream with rugged cliffs on both sides. If you hadn't heard about it, you wouldn't even know this place was so significant, but it is definitely worth checking out if you ever get the chance. Even with my hangover, it turned out to be a great way to spend my last day in Iceland.

The following morning I awoke with that familiar feeling I had come to recognise while travelling. Even though I didn't have anyone to say goodbye, I was saying goodbye to a beautiful part of the world, and I wondered if I would ever get the chance to visit again one day. It was time to move onto my next place – Copenhagen.

Copenhagen

As I boarded the plane, I wondered what experiences and adventures awaited in Denmark. I was staying at a Wakeup hotel, a high rise with a big Wakeup sign on the roof. "At least I won't get lost this time", I thought to myself, because you could see this sign from all over the city! I decided to start exploring Copenhagen straight away, but sent Jaxon a quick message first to let him know I had arrived safely and would see him soon. I had planned to head to his hometown in about a week. He replied telling me about a festival that was happening in Copenhagen, which was all I really needed to hear, so I was straight out the door.

I walked past the Tivoli Gardens, an amusement park and gardens not far from my hotel. I finally found the festival and headed into a bar for a beer to begin enjoying the festive atmosphere. While I was there I got chatting to a couple from Finland, and as is often the case in my life, we became fast friends. Before long we started consuming shots of liquor, and the next thing I remember was walking into my hotel a few hours later, feeling dismayed that my room key wouldn't work. I went back downstairs and fell asleep on a couch in the lobby.

I was woken not long after by an employee of the hotel. I explained that my room key didn't work and, after showing him my key, he explained there were two Wakeup hotels in Copenhagen. I was in the wrong one! As you could imagine, I felt pretty sheepish as he gave me directions to the right place. As I walked back out onto the street, I shook my head and wondered how I kept getting myself caught up in these misadventures, especially after I'd had a few drinks.

The next afternoon, I finally decided it was time to get out of bed and go for a walk to clear my mind after the big night before. Around the corner from my hotel was a big river where locals and tourists alike sunbathed on the sandy banks. I was feeling down and, as I looked out over the river, I realised I was also feeling quite lonely. This was my first time travelling solo, and I was finding it hard to adjust. I missed Jono, I missed Lukey, I missed the friends I met on Contiki – including Marcia. I knew the drinking wasn't helping the way I was feeling, but after all the fun times I have had over the years, I was finding it hard to turn away from that lifestyle.

Later on that evening I was relaxing at my hotel when I received a message from Jani, the guy from Finland I was drinking with the night before. He asked if I was keen to meet up again for a few cold beers down at the Nyhavn. I certainly was!

Nyhavn (New Harbour) is a 17th Century waterfront, canal and entertainment district that stretched from Kongens Nytorv to the harbour front. My first impression of the place was how colourful it was, with bars, cafes and restaurants lined up along the street. With the cobblestone laneways and canals stretching through the city, Copenhagen reminded me a lot of Amsterdam. It was a brilliantly lively place.

After a few beers with Jani, he suggested another bar he knew. It was in a different area of the city, so we jumped on a bicycle taxi and, with music blaring, we cruised the streets in style. Jani was a champion, always with a grin on his face. That night I did take it a bit easier though and tried to appreciate the moment more, rather than once again ending up written off and passed out.

Eventually, our night out had to end and I said goodbye to my new friend. This time, I made it back to the right hotel! The next day I woke up feeling relatively fresh, so I sent Jani a message to see how he pulled up. He replied saying he had woken up at the airport without his glasses, wallet or phone. Wow, I didn't realise he was that drunk! I must admit, it was reassuring that there were other kindred spirits out there with the tendency to end up in awkward situations late at night!

I only had a few days left in Copenhagen as I was planning on catching the train up to Stockholm to check out the area before heading to Jaxon's hometown, Aalborg. I messaged Jaxon to see what he could recommend I do for my final days in Copenhagen, and he told me I should definitely check out Christiania.

This place is a commune, also known as Freetown Christiania, located in the Christianshavn area. The community have its own rules and regulations, completely independent of the Danish government. There were stalls along an area known as 'The Green Light District' and there was often live music playing. It sounded like my type of place!

I grabbed my map and headed out the door in a flash, walking alongside the canals and through the cobblestone laneways until I found it. A friendly Canadian lady also gave me directions at one point, for which I am very grateful. I walked across a bridge into a wooded area and couldn't believe a place like this existed in a major city. I saw some other tourists walking along a path, so I decided to follow.

The wooded area gave way to a crowd of people – it seemed this once-hidden treasure had been discovered by the world (including myself!). A stage was set up which, as I was soon to find out, was to host live music. Some of the stalls were also set up as bars where they were selling beer in tall plastic cups. Naturally, I had to try one or two.

The band started, and I took a spot near the back of the crowd to take it all in. I got chatting to a few people who were a bit….different….but friendly enough. Then I thought, maybe it was me that was different?! After watching the band for a while, I decided to go for a walk to check out the stalls and found one that was selling marijuana cookies.

As I have always been open to trying whatever is on offer at the places I am fortunate enough to visit, and this case was no exception. So, I bought a cookie and gobbled it up, then went back to my spot in the crowd to continue watching the band.

Almost straight away, the alarm bells started going off in my head. I had tried mull cookies twice before in my younger years with friends back home. Both times I had gotten so body stoned and had such intense head spins that I passed out in the foetal position on the lawn for about four hours, unable to move. The difference was back then I was with friends who could look after me. Here I was on my own in a foreign city a long way from home, surrounded by strangers. I had rolled the dice again.

The head spins were starting to kick in, so I had to make a decision quickly – do I make a dash for it and try to get back to the relative safety of my hotel before I passed out, or ride it out and hope for the best? I decided the first option was the best. Not far from the commune I came across a busy intersection, and as luck would have it, a taxi was coming down the road. I hailed him down and told him I was staying at the Wakeup and prayed he took me to the right one.

The head spins were so strong by this stage, I couldn't make out what the taxi driver was rambling on about and I was in no state to hold a conversation. Every now and then I forced myself a little nod and grunt. It was starting to get dire.

Thankfully, he finally dropped me off at the right hotel, so I hurried up to my room and passed out on my bed where I stayed for the next twelve hours, mostly in the foetal position. I was still feeling lightheaded when I rose out of that spot in the morning, and I cursed myself for being so foolish. That was a very close call.

Sweden

I had my fun in Copenhagen; now, it was time to start planning the next stage of my journey – Sweden. I jumped online and booked myself a train ticket for Stockholm the following day. While searching for accommodation, I discovered there were rooms available to stay on a boat moored in Stockholm harbour. A floating hotel – that looked interesting! I booked four nights on the boat and got ready to depart for Sweden the next day.

The journey took just over five hours as I relaxed on the train and watched the beautiful scenery whizz by. There was plenty of forests as we crossed the various bridges, and I loved seeing the spectacular landscape. I wasn't sure what experiences lay waiting for me in Sweden, but seeing as I was now a seasoned traveller, I wanted to explore and see as much as I could on each trip.

We finally pulled into Stockholm station mid-afternoon, and I caught a taxi to the main harbour where the floating hotel was moored. Construction seemed to be everywhere at the harbour as I walked past a sea of workers, over the footbridge and onto the boat. I made my way to the reception area, checked in, and the guy behind the counter handed me my key as he said, "welcome aboard!" Nice touch.

Once inside my room, I found I couldn't see much through the porthole window, but I knew I would be able to get some great views up on deck. That evening I went for a stroll around Old Town and had dinner. The place reminded me a bit of Venice. Later I was able to take in some spectacular views of the harbour at sunset from the hotel deck. I had basically killed two birds with one stone; for once I didn't have to travel from my hotel to check out another beautiful harbour in a foreign city!

Over the coming days I followed the same routine: wake up mid-morning, walk over the bridge that led me into the New Town, have coffee at Starbucks, then go for a stroll into Old Town where I would begin a pub crawl along the bars and cafes. This eventually led me back to my boat. On one occasion, I came across an old man playing chimes that echoed throughout the alleys and laneways of Old Town. I was really enjoying my time in Stockholm, but as I listened to the music, something was brewing inside of me.

As I have mentioned, this was the first time I had travelled completely solo, and I had already experienced some intense moments of loneliness. That feeling was now starting to overwhelm me. Stockholm is such a beautiful city and I was trying to tap into that appreciation to lift my spirits, but I was finding it hard. I felt very alone.

Seven years earlier, my first world trip had been a significant high point to my travels, but that memory now felt so long ago. This brings me to one major issue I have found with alcohol. I have found that when I drink, my moods and feelings become intensified. Often when I drink I am surrounded by friends and having a great time, but as I sat drinking my beer at the bars in Stockholm, I felt very lonely. I chatted to a few random strangers to try to lift my mood, but nothing seemed to be working. I was falling into a dark hole in one of the most beautiful cities in the world, and I was worried I might not be able to find my way back.

One night after another of my many pub crawls, I found myself standing on the deck of the hotel wondering whether or not to jump overboard. Did I really want to take my own life by drowning in the waters of beautiful Stockholm Harbour? It would just look like an accident…My mind wandered to what happened between Marcia and myself and how I had ruined a good friendship due to my drunken behaviour, now over a year in the past. As I stood there, old wounds came to the surface as I looked into the black water. Eventually, common sense prevailed and I escaped into the comforts of my hotel room to sleep it off. I hoped I felt better in the morning, as they say, "new day, new hope".

I woke up just after lunch the next day to find myself still feeling a bit low. I started my usual routine of heading into New Town for my coffee fix, but decided to give the pub crawl a miss this time. It was definitely a wise decision seeing as it was my last day in Stockholm, and I wanted to try to make some sense of why I was feeling the way I was – without adding alcohol to the mix.

I had done a lot of soul-searching on this trip, and after a few weeks travelling solo, I missed seeing a familiar face. After bouts of loneliness throughout this adventure, it all came to a head there in Stockholm. I was very much looking forward to catching up with Jaxon in a couple of days. Even though I hadn't seen him since he left Harvey almost 20 years ago, I still remembered him well and couldn't wait to reconnect and reminisce about old days back home.

Copenhagen

Thinking about that lifted my spirits, and the next morning I was feeling a lot better as I checked out of my floating hotel. I headed to the train station and made the journey back to Copenhagen. Seeing as I was only staying the one night, I had booked into an old hostel not far from the station. They had sent me an email to inform me that to get in, I had to pick up the key from the old man behind the counter at the newsagency next door. I had never had a check-in like that and wasn't sure what to think!

All went fine with the key pickup and I headed up to my room on the second floor. It was a large old-styled room with three king-sized beds. The first thing I noticed as I put my bags down was how quiet it was, and not just in the room, but the whole building. I walked back out into the hallway to notice closed doors to the other rooms. You can usually hear other guests moving around or talking, but not here. It began to dawn on me that it was likely I had the entire building to myself, and I wondered what I had got myself into this time.

The only noise I could hear was the voice in my head telling me to get out of there, but against my better judgment, I chose to stay and ride it out. I poured myself a hot bath and, as I lay in the tub, I listened through the closed door and out into the hallway for any signs of life. It was still eerily quiet. My mind shifted to all the horror movies I had seen over the years, and I imagined an entity appearing out of nowhere and attacking me. I shuddered at the thought and tried to shake the image out of my brain.

Back in my room, I looked out the window and down onto the hustle and bustle of the street below. How could a city like this have such an eerie hostel right in the heart, which I had somehow managed to find? As dark descended upon the city, I decided to watch a bit of television to help me sleep. There was only one channel and you will never guess what movie was on – *Hostel* – a horror movie. Just my luck! I got about ten minutes into the movie and thought I heard a noise out in the hallway. That was it, television was off and I spent the rest of the night hiding under the covers.

I managed to fall asleep at some point, and when I woke up, I prayed it was morning. I peeked out from under the covers, saw sunlight flooding through the window and thought, "you beauty, I made it through the night!" What an experience that was!

I sent Jaxon a message to let him know my arrival time, and he said he would be at the station to pick me up. I took the key back to the old man at the newsagency before heading to the train station. It was a five-hour journey, and again I spent most of the time gazing out at the beautiful scenery as it whizzed by. We passed over so many bridges and I had flashes of the many bridges I had seen on my travels; the Sydney Harbour Bridge, Golden Gate Bridge, Brooklyn Bridge, the Bridge of Sighs and the bridge over the River Kwai. It was also a bridge that derailed my meeting with Marcia and created the domino effect of our friendship falling apart. Just like my fascination with harbours, bridges also seemed to pop up in my life at significant moments too.

Aalborg

As the train pulled into Aalborg Station, I looked out to the sea of faces waiting to greet friends and family as they disembarked the train. I recognised

Jaxon straight away standing in the crowd – he had hardly changed a bit in the 20 years since we hung out in Harvey. I had opted to stay at a hotel for most of the visit, even though Jaxon had offered his place for me to stay, but decided to accept his offer for the first night. He had a young family and his mum was also visiting from Australia, so I didn't want to intrude too much.

As we made our way to his place, we took a walk down Jomfru Ane Gade, one of Denmark's best-known streets and renowned for its nightlife and tourism. He pointed out the hotel I had booked into the following day as we chatted like old times. We wandered over the bridge that led to the area Jaxon lived and dropped my things off, before heading back to the main part of town to enjoy a few beers. It was awesome to see each other again.

The next day I checked into the hotel, and over the coming days I would either walk over the bridge to Jaxon's place, or he would pick me up from the hotel and show me around Aalborg. We went up a tower that provided great views of the town, and I tried Danish food for lunch down by the harbour. We went for a drive to check out the surrounding areas with an abundance of incredible churches and museums, and headed out to the coastal town of Skagen for a day trip. Jaxon's mum joined us a few times, and it was lovely to get to know her as well.

Skagen is beautiful, situated on the beach at the top of Denmark where two oceans meet and is rich with classic Danish architecture. We began our tour of the town at a brewery for lunch and a quiet drink while listening to a local band play melodiously in the background. Skagen seemed to be a very welcoming place with a relaxed atmosphere, and I fell in love with the place straight away. I was in my element, and Jaxon even came up with a nickname for my travel-persona – "Worldwide Whitty".

After lunch, we took a drive to the beach to check out the place where the Baltic Sea and the North Sea meet. After my visit to Ushuaia Harbour – the gateway to the Antarctic – and now being at the highest point in Denmark where the two oceans collide, I can now say I have experienced the top of the world and the bottom! I haven't quite made it to the Arctic, but perhaps I will one day. On the way back to Aalborg, we stopped by Skagen Harbour – as I like to do at each new place.

For my final night in Aalborg, Jaxon and I met a friend of his from the US, Blair, and we headed out to a concert on the waterfront before hitting the bars. My last full day in the town was thus spent nursing a hangover, but it was worth it. The night before I left, Jaxon and his family hosted me for dinner. It was the perfect way to top off my visit to this amazing part of the world and reconnect with an old friend. I knew another emotional goodbye was imminent, but it had been a great week. The following morning, Jaxon dropped me off at the airport and I headed off to board my flight to one of my favourite cities in the world – Amsterdam.

Amsterdam

It was drizzling as the plane landed and I caught a taxi to my hotel. I didn't notice when I booked online, but as I stepped out of the cab and walked into the hotel, it dawned on me that it was the same hotel Crudder and I stayed in on our Contiki tour four years earlier!

Over the coming days, just like in Stockholm, the routine didn't change too much. I would walk to the end of the street and catch a streetcar which would take me into Dam Square. Here I would sometimes do a spot of window shopping, chat to some of the locals and then catch a taxi back to my hotel.

One day, I decided to do something a bit different and try some magic mushrooms; I was in Amsterdam, after all! I wasn't sure what the experience was going to be like, and seeing as I was on my own, I chose to play it safe and waited until I got back to my hotel before trying one. I almost threw up from the taste, but once down, it wasn't so bad. I headed down to the lobby and kicked back while I went on a journey to another galaxy in my twisted mind. At one point, I tried to go for a walk down the street, but ended up freaking out and scurrying back to the safe confines of the hotel. I got through the night, and can now say I have tasted Amsterdam's finest fungi.

One Eye, One Ear – No Worries

It was drizzling during my last few days in Amsterdam, which I chose to spend just wandering around the canals in the rain thinking about the journey I had been on. I had found this trip to be much more challenging than the others, being my first time travelling solo. The two highlights and big positives were catching up and spending time with Jaxon again after so long, and meeting Shaun Attwood and Richard. But, another trip was coming to an end, and I did my usual bout of soul-searching as I walked. The next morning was the familiar ritual of packing up and heading to another airport, destined for home soil.

Thirty-Five

BITTER REFLECTION

Once back home, it was business as usual. My boss had me travelling around a bit with my work as an inspector, which kept me busy, plus it was a fantastic opportunity to check out more of my home state. Ironically, I had now travelled the world three times, but there was so much of home I was yet to appreciate.

While staying at Narrogin, I was put up at the Albert Facey Motel, named after the author of the book, *A Fortunate Life*. I had recently read the book too, which made it all the more interesting at the time. At the Kojonup pub, I enjoyed one of the best steaks with pepper sauce I have ever eaten. City people are great, but I must be honest, some of the greatest characters I have ever met in my life were at a good old country pub.

Amongst this new routine of work and travel, I couldn't help but be haunted by what had happened with Marcia, even though some time had now passed. I was struggling emotionally, and I just could not make peace with the thought that there was someone out there in the world who I had hurt so badly through my drunken misjudgement.

In early 2017 I took the advice of friends and went back to see a counsellor, who helped me unravel my thoughts and try to make sense of the horrible feeling that would not budge. I had first met Marcia in 2009 on

Contiki, and I still remember chatting to her that first day in London like it was yesterday. I also vividly recall sitting next to her on the bus on the way to Austria and our amazing day on the gondola in Venice. She was such a kind-hearted and open person who touched my soul immediately. As you know from my story, once I returned home to Australia, we kept in touch and I was thrilled to see her again three years later in Toronto. It was here we spent the day out on the Islands, chatting and relaxed in each other's company.

I felt we had shared a deep connection and had settled into a friendship I thought would last a lifetime, despite the geographical difference. She also said she had been inspired by me and had ideas of producing a documentary on people who had overcome adversity to achieve success and happiness in life. This was part of what she described as 'prejudice reduction', a term she learnt about in her psychology studies at university. Even now, this connection was the greatest story to come out of my travels. It wasn't just the friendship, but the fact that I had met someone who was inspired by my life and wanted to do something positive for the world one day. Circumstances like that don't just happen every day.

Why do I believe things turned out the way they did? This is my perspective. Marcia and I came from different worlds and very different backgrounds. From what I knew, she grew up in the bright lights of Toronto and went on to do some amazing things in her life, including spending a year abroad studying at a prestigious university in London. I grew up in a small town which had a bit of a binge culture, which I have discovered many small towns seem to. As the saying goes, "you can take the boy out of the town, but you can't take the town out of the boy".

I may have had the courage to live out my dream of travelling the world, but as I have touched on a few times in this book, binge drinking is a problem I often struggled with. In saying that, I was always a funny and happy drunk, hence why I got away with it for so long. After building such a beautiful bond with Marcia, I began to fear that drinking may lead to me saying or writing something that would cause irreversible damage. This fear manifested to such a degree that I feel I gave it too much power, and eventually, that fear became a reality.

To this day, I still don't know what I posted on her Facebook page that night after a drinking session at the Collie Bridge Tavern in 2015. Every time I go back over it in my mind, I keep coming back to the conclusion that I must have had a go at her for not making it down to see me at Niagara Falls the year before. Whatever it was that I wrote, it clearly upset her, and there is no excuse for that kind of behaviour. Even though it was very out of character, I must accept the consequences, regardless of how harsh they are. The fact is, I hurt a friend I cared about, and this is something that will haunt me for many years to come.

I must also stress that at no point have I ever blamed Marcia for the way our friendship ended, I take full responsibility for my actions. I am deeply sorry for the pain and hurt I caused, and I hope one day it will make sense. As Adele sang in her song, *Someone Like You*, "sometimes it's a lesson learned, but sometimes it hurts instead".

Another quote I find comforting whenever I dwell on this topic is this; "Whatever is meant to be will always find its way back". That gives me a bit of hope that our story may not be over and she may one day find it in her heart to forgive me. In the meantime, I can only control my own actions moving forward and try each day to become a better man.

I ended up seeing a few different counsellors during this time to help me out of the darkness, and one I spoke to was so inspired by my life story, she asked if I had ever heard of TEDx. I had seen it on YouTube and knew it was quite popular, especially overseas. The reason she asked was that TEDx was being held in Bunbury next and she recommended I apply to give a speech to tell my story.

Straight away, I loved this idea. I felt it was the perfect opportunity to move forward after my big mistake with Marcia and open new, positive possibilities in my life and that of others. I submitted my application, and not long later I received the great news that it had been accepted. I was to share my story from a TEDx stage! The organisers said they were intrigued by my story and the message behind it, so all was set.

The counsellor was also very supportive. She assured me that even though I was suffering from a setback, if I kept doing what I was doing, kept pushing my message and meeting new people, I would continue to nurture many more friendships. She also said that travelling was the key to my long-term happiness, as that was what made my heart soar more than anything else.

So, before I was to stand on the TEDx stage, I had to book another trip. I decided on London again and hoped to catch up with Shaun while I was back, but I also liked to add a new destination to each itinerary. This time, it was Spain. I planned a Topdeck Tour starting in Valencia and finishing in Madrid. I booked to return home to Australia on the 19th July, with the TEDX appearance scheduled for the 22nd. I knew I was cutting it fine, but I was up for the challenge. Besides, what better way to be inspired for an upcoming speech than doing what I love – travelling?

Thirty-Six

It's A Small World

At the time, terrorism threats were big news. Unfortunately, there had been a spate of unrest in London just before I was due to leave, including an attack on London Bridge that put the city on alert and very much on edge. It also got me thinking, and I very nearly turned my trip on its head, as London didn't feel like a safe place to visit. I was also very aware not to mess up my opportunity with TEDx.

I started to overthink the situation, which lead to fear, but then I realised that is what the terrorists want – for us to live in fear. London is a big place, but I could easily end up in the wrong place at the wrong time. I had to make a decision, and that was causing me quite a bit of anxiety.

It is not often you get the chance to meet someone like Shaun Attwood, and I was really looking forward to catching up with him again in London. But, after a phone call with a friend, I decided to play it safe and rebook to stay in Switzerland instead. My head was going around in circles.

Before clicking on the booking confirmation, I thought I would sleep on the decision, and I am glad I did. The next morning I came around in my thinking and was determined not to let the terrorists succeed in pushing fear on this traveller. I followed my heart and stuck with my plans to visit London for the third time.

I was off on my next adventure, pumped to be heading to the UK again and getting to experience Spain. I took my usual route overseas, stopping in Hong Kong then landing at Heathrow. As I started walking towards the tube from the airport to head to my hotel, I thought I recognised the lady walking towards me, but I wasn't sure. All of a sudden, she said, "Whitty?" Surely not…I was on the other side of the world from home! It was a lady I knew from growing up in Harvey, Alicia, who was then living in London. What a small world it is! You never know who you will bump into when you travel.

Alicia and I had a good chat and hoped to tee up a proper catch up while I was in the bright lights of London. I continued on to my hotel, all the while shaking my head in bewilderment at the chance encounter with a fellow Harvey-dweller.

The hotel was in Islington, roughly half an hour's walk to the banks of the River Thames. For the first few days of the trip, I would walk down to the river, cross one of the many bridges and spend my day at the many pubs on the riverbank. I could see Saint Paul's Cathedral in the distance as I sipped on my beer. One morning I was walking along London Bridge when I came across a pub I recognised from the news reports about the terror attacks that had occurred here a month or so earlier. I decided to pop in as a sign of remembrance to the victims, and even though it was only a small act of defiance, I really savoured that beer. Once again, I vowed not to live or travel in fear – they will not win.

This trip, I decided to take a ride on the London Eye, which offered amazing views of the city skyline. Later that day, I went for a walk through the park next to Westminster Abbey, which again brought back fond memories of my visit there with Jono eight years earlier. While London Bridge itself I found to be rather unremarkable, Tower Bridge was spectacular as it loomed large over the River Thames.

After a few days exploring, it was time to catch up with a few friends. Even though social media has its downfalls, Facebook does have a lot of positives about it, and one big one was the opportunity to reconnect with so many people I hadn't seen in years. Claire was one of those people.

Claire and I went to primary and early high school together back in Harvey, but she left before upper school, first for study and then to travel the big wide world, before eventually settling in the UK. We had reconnected over Facebook a few years earlier and kept in touch. Claire had been out of town last time I was in London, so we were hoping to be able to catch up this trip.

Our plans fell together nicely. We arranged to meet up for dinner in Soho the following evening, which happened to be one of my favourite parts of London. So, the following evening I arrived a little early to the restaurant we had planned to meet at and, as I waited for Claire out the front, I thought about how surreal it was that we were about to catch up again after more than twenty years – and in Soho, London, of all places. She finally arrived, and we had a great evening chatting about the previous 20 years and more.

The best thing about travelling is the moments you get to share along the way, and it is funny how life works sometimes. We were just kids in a small town the last time we saw each other, and now here we were, on the other side of the world, all grown up!

I had also hoped to see Shaun Attwood again on this trip, although I was aware of how busy he was. However, he was equally keen to catch up with me and kindly carved out some time that suited. He was doing Body Combat training once a week, so he invited me out for a meal with his gym friends in Guildford the next Tuesday evening. I couldn't knock back an invitation like that!

So, off to Guildford on the train it was. I arrived Tuesday morning and spent the day checking out a few of the pubs while Shaun was busy.

A river runs through the centre of town, and I found some beautiful pubs overlooking the water. Eventually, Shaun sent me a message to meet him at his place at 6 pm. When I arrived, he offered me a glass of his housemate's cider, which I happily indulged in. Wow. I don't usually drink cider, and I certainly felt the effects after this one. My head was spinning as Shaun filled me in on the latest big things he had been doing. "How's the cider?" Shaun asked, as graciously as ever. "Going down fine, mate", I managed to slur.

We headed to the Guildford Recreation Centre, where I went to wait at the bar area while Shaun did his training, then he and his buddies joined me. By this stage, I was still quite drunk from the cider and trying my hardest to keep it together. Shaun is such an easy-going and laid back person that I knew he wouldn't have cared if I was drunk, but I noticed we were also joined at the table by some beautiful English girls. I thought I really should behave. Shaun's housemate also joined us.

Shaun was pretty big around the UK as an author and public speaker by then, and it was an honour to be invited out in his company. I needn't have worries about the cider effects, as it ended up being a great night, and Shaun even invited me to one of his speeches the following night in London. What a privilege that was!

After dinner, Shaun dropped me off at the train station in Guildford and told me he would pick me up from my hotel around 11 am the next day. We could then hang out a bit before the speech. How awesome – not only had he invited me out again, but he also wanted to hang out, and all because I started reading one of his books way back in Vegas!

Shaun was a man of his word, so the following morning he arrived at my hotel to pick me up at 11 am sharp. We decided to head to Soho for lunch, as there are plenty of good places to eat. On the way over, Shaun gave me tips on how to become a better writer and public speaker. The biggest thing he taught me was the ability to tell a story – your story. Shaun is a highly intelligent man who I was eager to learn from, so I lapped it all up. I asked him so many questions as we ate our lunch then went for a walk through Soho's gardens.

Before long, it was time to head to the speech venue, which turned out to be at the back of a pub. I watched as Shaun set up the projector and screen so he could display his photos, and I was a keen student as I took note of how he arranged his space and prepared. The room started to fill, and in no time it was packed. I took my seat and watched in awe as he delivered an incredible speech about his life that really touched everyone there. I was thrilled to not only see his presentation for myself, but to be there as Shaun's guest was amazing. I pictured myself up there in the spotlight one day.

Shaun's speech marked the end of this visit to London, and it couldn't have been a better way to end this part of my trip. Next stop was Spain, as I prepared for the usual routine of packing up and heading to the airport for my flight.

Valencia

After a pretty stress-free run with airports and flights of late, my luck was about to turn. To begin, my flight to Madrid, where I was stopping for a transfer before flying on to Valencia, was delayed. Also, little did I know that I had to collect and check my luggage through again at Madrid. The transfer was only 40 minutes, which after the delayed flight left me less than five minutes to get from one end of the airport to the other. No worries, I thought as I took off sprinting through the terminal. I felt like Jim Carrey from the movie *Dumb and Dumber*.

I quickly ran out of puff, so I stopped to ask for directions to my gate and was told that I had to go outside and catch a shuttle bus to a different terminal. I conceded defeat. After all my years of travelling, this was the first flight I had ever missed, and I was not happy about it – but it was out of my control.

I rescheduled my flight to Valencia, which wasn't leaving until just before midnight. I had six hours to wait. My transfer had just gone from 40 minutes to six hours, "welcome to Spain". Once I realised I had to check my luggage through again at Madrid (and therefore it wasn't heading to Valencia without me), off I went in search of my bags. After asking at all the help desks, I finally found it later on that night. I then realised that if I had made it to the original flight, then my bags would still be here in Madrid waiting to be checked through. Either way, this was destined to be a test.

I finally boarded my flight at around midnight and arrived at my final destination at 1 am, roughly 14 hours after departing London. I shrugged it off. I was here, in Spain! I caught a taxi to my hotel, all while looking out the window wondering who I was going to meet on my upcoming Topdeck Tour. After checking in, I fell into one of the most exhausted sleeps in my life. When I finally woke up, I headed out to spend my first day in Spain, strolling around to explore the local area.

It was drizzling with rain as I walked the streets of Valencia in a Melbourne Demons football jumper. I tried some typical Spanish food, including tapas and croquettes, and I had a good feeling about the place. In the evening, I met up with the Topdeck Tour group in the lobby of the hotel. This was going to be the first time I had done a tour solo, so I was a bit anxious and nervous as I didn't know what to expect. Vincenzo was the tour guide, and he was very engaging and made me feel welcome straight away.

That first night we went out for dinner in the heart of Valencia, and I found myself sitting next to Tonia. We got chatting and I found out that she was also a solo traveller and had just joined the group. Tonia was from Sydney and was travelling through Europe after graduating from university. Although we had only just started the tour, we were already forming a good friendship. Little did I know that two years later we would catch up again in Sydney, twenty years on from when I first visited the city with PJ.

I told Tonia about my upcoming TEDx talk and she was genuinely excited for me. During dinner, the sangria came out and the atmosphere lifted, and that's when I really felt like I was on tour. Vincenzo then took us on a sightseeing expedition around the port city. Like most of Europe, Valencia had buildings dating back hundreds of years, including the Serranos Towers and The Silk Exchange.

After admiring a bit of history, it was time to hit the bars to experience the modern nightlife. I got to know a few more people from the tour, including Riley, James, Eric and Kirra. I must have drunk a bit too much sangria though, because as I often seem to do when I join a tour, I lost the group after the second or third bar and went off on my own little walkabout.

I did manage to make it back to my hotel at some point and woke up the next morning with a bit of a headache, but I loved the Spanish experience so far. On today's itinerary was a boat ride to Ibiza and I was very excited. The group met at the designated time and caught the bus down to the port, where we boarded the ferry.

There were a pool and bar area up on deck, and as the ferry pulled away from the port, I was already relaxing at the bar and enjoying a beer. There was Spanish music playing and the atmosphere was amazing. I made eye contact with the barman, and he gave me the thumb's up and a big "cheers", and I returned the gesture. We seemed to be both loving life right then, and how could you not? We were sailing on a boat to Ibiza!

It was a pretty big day, and by the time we arrived at the hotel later on that night, I was pretty tired and ready to hit the sack. However, some people from the tour were keen to go nightclubbing, and James somehow managed to talk me into joining them. Well, it wasn't every day that I got the opportunity to experience a place like this, right?! We ended up at Eden Nightclub where I started to drink bourbon. Before long, I was back in the mood. I met an English girl named Emily who was in Ibiza celebrating her 21st birthday. We exchanged contact details, and as it turns out, I was able to catch up with her in the UK the following year.

I quickly fell into my nightclubbing groove and ended up kicking on until 5 am, when I finally caught a taxi back to the hotel. I still felt drunk when I woke up later that day and made my way to the pool and bar area to order another beer. After a few hours, I stumbled back to my hotel room and was just about to pass out when there was a knock at my door. It was

Vincenzo looking for me, as we were all about to head to Ushuaia Beach Hotel for an afternoon rave.

Ushuaia Ibiza was another incredible experience. I took a spot at the bar to watch the ravers and it felt like one big holiday where everyone was really living it up. Reality was left at their respective homes – it was party time!

While I was there I got to know Mat and Alex, two friends from Melbourne who were also on the tour. After the rave, a big group of people from our group decided to kick on at Amnesia Nightclub and they wanted me to join them, but I had hit a wall, so I opted to give it a miss and head back to the hotel for some much-needed sleep.

Barcelona

The following day we were due to catch a flight to Barcelona. I was still feeling a bit under the weather as I listened to my tour friends tell me about Amnesia. "I wish I was in my early twenties again," I thought. Once we got to Barcelona, I decided to spend a few days drying out and doing a bit of sightseeing.

On the bus ride to the city, we stopped at a lookout that provided scenic views over the buildings. Vincenzo told us about Barcelona's history, including how big hosting the 1992 Olympic Games was for the area.

Once checked into our hotel, I planned to meet up with some of the other tour participants in the hotel lobby so we could head out for some dinner. We ended up at a long table outside where we ordered a few bowls of paella to share amongst us. Paella is a rice dish that originated in Valencia and is usually full of fresh seafood and local vegetables. It was absolutely delicious! After dinner, a few of us went for a walk through the streets of Barcelona, taking in the sights and sounds of the city.

The next day I went off on my own to explore and ended up down at La Rambla at lunchtime, which is a tree-lined pedestrian street with a great variety of cafes. Unfortunately, it's popularity with tourists made it a target for terrorists about a month after I was there. Someone drove a van into pedestrians on La Rambla, killing 13 people. This shook me up a bit when I heard, as I still had the concerns rattling around in my head about London Bridge and how I had been in the same spot as an attack there as well. I kept reminding myself not to fear, not to let them win, and I would continue to travel no matter what.

The night after my tour through La Rambla, the group went to a Spanish stage show, then a few of us kicked on at a nightclub. I guess my plans to dry out had come to an end! We were due to leave very early in the morning as we had a long bus trip to San Sebastian. So, just to be on the safe side, I had booked a wakeup call to my room through the hotel reception before heading out. Lucky I did, because, as I am prone to do, I got caught up in the moment, lost track of time and only made it back to my room in time to answer the call. In fact, the phone was ringing as I walked in.

The party's over

The bus trip was long and filled with interrupted sleep, but I was willing to take any opportunity for some shuteye I could. I only had myself to blame, but I was wondering if I was getting too old for all this partying! We finally arrived in the resort town of San Sebastian. That evening Vincenzo took us all for a walk along the picturesque bayfront promenade overlooking the beautiful beaches of San Sebastian.

I spent my last full day on tour casually checking out the surrounds. Some of the tour group had decided to take the train back to Pamplona to see the Running of the Bulls, and although I was tempted to go with them, I had a good vibe about San Sebastian and wanted to see more of the city. That night was our last night on tour together, so we planned a big night out.

After dinner, we headed to a local bar to celebrate another successful tour and to give a toast to new friends. Tonia and I took a spot at the bar and had a great chat. We had connected on the tour, and I knew we would remain friends after our trip was over. She asked me how the planning for my upcoming TEDx talk was going and, to be honest, I hadn't really thought much about it. I was pretty confident that this trip would inspire me enough to nail it, but I was aware of how great an opportunity I had been handed. I had booked a few extra days in Madrid after the tour before I headed home, so I planned to take some time then to plan and practice my presentation.

While we were chatting, Tonia told me a bit more about her life and it sounded like she had a lot of exciting things going on for her back home in Sydney. We continued our conversation back at the hotel, by then were joined by James as well, all chatting until almost sunrise.

I pretty much slept on the bus the next day to Madrid, then it was time for more goodbyes. Tonia had another plane to catch to continue her travels through Europe, so she had to leave as soon as we arrived. James was preparing to get his next flight to Croatia. The group split, and it was time I turned my attention to my talk.

Back in my room, my mind started ticking over; how would I inspire the audience? What aspects of my story should I focus on? I was still a long way from home, but my brain had already shifted from holiday mode to reality, as I had to be prepared to step onto the TEDx stage as soon as I returned to Australia. I spent the next few days sacrificing sightseeing in favour of standing in front of the mirror in my room, practicing what I was going to say. I had the chance to leave a bit of a legacy, and I really wanted to make the most of this amazing opportunity.

I thought back to the movie that had inspired me back in school, *Dead Poets Society*, and the popular quote, "carpe diem". I was ready to "seize the

Joel Whitwell

day"! The time came to head to the airport, bound for home and one of the biggest days of my life. I had planned and practiced my speech in Madrid, but could I deliver it to perfection on stage in front of a live audience? My mind was racing on the long flight back home, but I was determined to give it my best shot.

Thirty-Seven

Speak From The Heart

I arrived back in Perth late on Wednesday night, and the TEDx event was booked for Saturday. This left me a small window to settle back into home life – and settle my nerves. I spent some time seeing my counsellor and catching up with the TEDx Bunbury organiser, Suzie. She filled me in on what to expect on the day, and I asked the question I had been dreading knowing the answer to; how big was the audience going to be?

Suzie told me there was going to be over 200 people in attendance, which was way more than I thought. My heart started racing as my anxiety went through the roof. It was too late to pull out, so I knew I had to find the courage to go through with the plan. I woke up on Saturday morning feeling a sense of destiny and excitement, mixed with equal parts nervousness and anxiety. It was time to "seize the day".

TEDx was being held at the Bunbury Regional Entertainment Centre (BREC). I arrived early with mum and nanna, who had come along for support. We went for a coffee at a café around the corner, and I could hardly hold my cup, I was that shaky. There were a few other people giving speeches that day, and I was booked as second on stage. I met a few of the other speakers and they seemed full of confidence. They were friendly and engaging, and I felt a little out of my element.

As I sat backstage going over my palm cards, I could hear the crowd gathering and I felt on the verge of a panic attack. Then I thought of my old friend PJ and that brought me a sense of calm. Was he watching over me? I like to think so. Finally, a TEDx helper appeared and led me to the spot where I was to wait until I heard my name called to walk out on stage. This was it. It was now or never.

After what felt like an eternity standing there in the wings, I was introduced and walked out to a massive ovation. I was under the spotlight, about to share my story. It felt like my whole life had come down to this moment. The audience was in the dark, so I couldn't really see them, which helped me to relax a little. "Speak from the heart, and you can't go wrong," I told myself. I looked down at my first palm card, then back up towards the audience, and started to speak. I felt calm again, and over the next ten or so minutes, I delivered my speech with great heart and emotion, especially when I mentioned PJ and how his passing had inspired me to travel.

The audience seemed captivated, and they all stood up to cheer as soon as I finished. While I was basking in the applause, something stirred deep inside of me as a tear rolled down my cheek. For all the mistakes and stuff-ups I had made over the years, I had never given up and had finally found the courage to overcome my fears. That moment will stay with me for life.

I hadn't even made it backstage when people were already coming up to congratulate me on my speech. After a while, I felt I needed to gather my thoughts, so I went to the bar area and ordered a quiet beer and just sat there contemplating. Before long, the area was packed as the other speeches had finished too, and I found heaps of people wanted to come up to shake my hand and have a chat. I must admit, I didn't mind at all. In fact, I seemed to relish the attention. My story was being heard.

After the TEDx experience, I ended up giving a media interview and a couple of the local papers included an article about the Harvey boy who became a TEDx speaker. It was around this time that the snowball effect started to play a part in my life. The snowball, as it starts rolling down the hill, gradually increases in size as it gains momentum – and that is what was happening after the success of my TEDx talk.

My friend Cassie came up with an idea to piggyback on the speech success. Later on that year, the movie *Wonder* was due to come out in cinemas. It was based on the New York Times bestseller of the same name, which tells the heart-warming story of August Pullman. Like me, August was born with a facial difference, and the story begins as he starts at a mainstream elementary school for the first time.

Cassie had seen the preview for the movie and came up with a great idea. She wanted to hold a fundraiser at the premiere of the movie at Grand Cinemas in Bunbury and have me deliver my speech before we all sat down to watch the movie. I loved that idea and was all in from the start. I was confident that Cassie and I knew enough people to draw a decent crowd, plus we would do as much promotion as we could on top of that. She asked me where I would nominate the proceeds to go, and I didn't hesitate as I told her Princess Margaret Hospital. That was where I'd had the surgeries on my face as a young child, so it was only natural to now give back.

The movie premiere was about a month away, on 3rd December. Interest quickly grew, and we ended up seeling about 70 tickets. On the day, I arrived early with Ash, who has always been a great mate and constant support in my life. Cassie was already there handing out tickets and getting organised – she was amazing, and I hope she knows how much her efforts meant to me.

Once everyone had gathered, Cassie introduced me, and I stood up in front of the crowd. I used the same sort of speech format I had with TEDx, but this time I was relaxed from the start. It was incredible to see so many familiar faces in the audience, including mum and dad, Kelvin, Frog, Nanna, Adam, Ash, Josh, Normie, Mark – and this list went on.

The movie was also very inspirational, and the whole day was an incredible success. After the movie I went for a quiet beer with Ash, Josh and Josh's partner Aenga. We had shared so many great memories together over the years, and this was definitely another as we took a trip down memory lane. The fundraiser was able to raise $700 for the Princess Margaret Hospital Foundation, which they were overjoyed with.

I wanted to hand over the donation personally, so I got in touch with the Foundation and arranged a suitable time for me to drive to Perth. It ended up being the following March. Unfortunately, Cassie was unable to come, so I went up to Subiaco on my own and met Anne from PMH to give her the cheque. The money turned out to be great timing, as a new children's hospital had just been built and PMH was about to shut down for good. I was saddened to hear this, as the hospital played a big part in my childhood.

There was some good news though. It was still open that day in March I visited, so Anne asked if I would like a tour while I was there. Walking through the corridors and wards of the old hospital certainly brought back plenty of old memories, especially ward 5A where I spent some time as a ten-year-old back in 1989.

I thought of my friends from the hospital, Clinton and Simon, and wondered what became of them. I was very thankful to Anne who took the time that day to show me around and allow me to revisit a big part of my life before they closed the doors forever. It was a pleasure and privilege to be able to give back and help make a difference to children who, like myself, face adversity in life. I hope I can continue to do my bit to make the world a better place.

What a journey I have had, from first arriving into the world at Harvey Hospital all those years ago, to where I found myself in early 2018, standing in the corridors of the hospital that had once been a second home.

Thirty-Eight

Lessons Learned

While my story is far from over, there are so many things I have learnt and grown from that I want to share with you before concluding this book. The first is the subject of drink driving. So many people still risk it, despite the illegal and potentially life-threatening consequences.

As you are aware after reading my story, I was guilty of drink driving on more than one occasion in my younger years. While growing up I had a bit of a blasé attitude towards my own safety and that of those around me, and I feel shame to admit that it took a lot longer for me to learn this lesson than it should have.

Drink driving is unacceptable – it causes so much heartbreak in the community. My life would have turned out so differently had I hit someone while impaired, and I am lucky to have escaped that torment.

I believe life does have a way of evening things out for the bad choices we make – in other words, what we often call karma. After my DUI in 2013, I believe my punishment was being made inadmissible to Canada the year after and not getting the chance to see Marcia at Niagara. That DUI was by far the biggest mistake I had ever made, and I am sorry for all the stress it caused my family.

It took me a long time to come back from that emotionally, and I still shudder at the thought of all the other possible outcomes that could have occurred by my decision to drive that night. I remember looking at the car the next day and seeing the driver's side mirror swiped clean off, and realising I had been handed a second chance at life that night. For that chance, I am eternally grateful. I hope my story can stop more young people from making the same mistake.

I am determined to make the most of my second chance now and continue to share my story of triumph, overcoming adversity and a lot of incredible travel. I have learnt some harsh lessons through my actions over the years, including what ultimately happened with Marcia. I have to be honest with myself; she did nothing wrong, it was a combination of my binge drinking and tendency to overthink things that ruined our friendship. That is on my shoulders.

I still hope one day she can find it in her heart to forgive me, but only time will tell. I believe anyone who comes into your life can leave a special memory, and that day we spent together out on the Islands in Toronto will always be a highlight in my life.

In the months after she cut me out of her life, I was feeling a bit lost and needed to try to make some sense of it all, so I wrote a little poem about that day together which I called *Memories of Toronto*.

I will always remember, it was late afternoon when we boarded the ferry back to the mainland.

The Toronto skyline stretched out before us like God had crafted it with his own hands.

The sky was blue that awesome summer's day, and for a while there, I just wished everything golden in my life will stay.

The birds chirping in the distance made a melodic sound, and before or since, no greater memory have I ever found.

Another lesson I have learnt along the way is that you can always change and improve your circumstances as I did with my career in the Meatworks. From where I started as a labourer to working my way up to becoming a Government Meat Inspector shows what can be achieved by being resilient and not giving up"

And finally, for the first time since my early twenties I am taking the steps I need to get on top of my binge drinking problem. Better late than never, but it's a start. I mainly stick to light beers these days and I am more aware of the triggers and knowing when to stop. Hopefully I have now put the dice away for good as life can only give so many chances and I feel now more than ever that I have a purpose and so much to live for"

I have now come to the conclusion of this book. My life has certainly been a rollercoaster! I like to think that my achievements in life speak for themselves, but I felt it important to take note of my mistakes. It is how you deal with these errors and adversities that really shape who you are. For me, I believe the best is yet to come, and I strive to keep my positive attitude and pushing to make my mark in this world.

To conclude, I would like to share a line from Robert Frost's *The Road Not Taken*, which our year 12 graduating class was given back in 1996.

"Two roads diverged in a wood, and I— I took the one less travelled by, and that has made all the difference."

www.ingramcontent.com/pod-product-compliance
Lightning Source LLC
Chambersburg PA
CBHW062025290426
44108CB00025B/2786